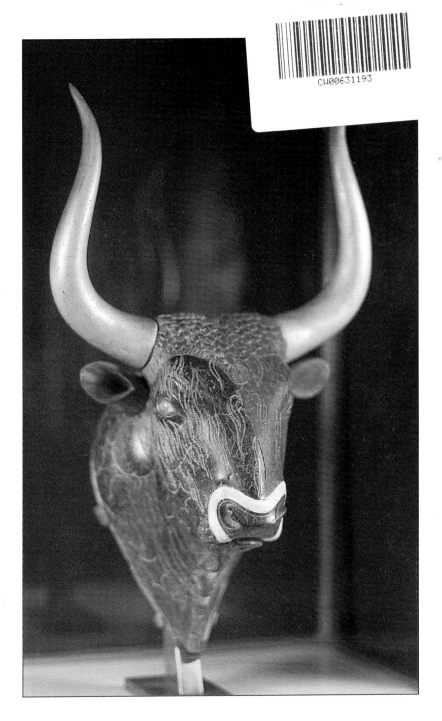

CRETE

First Edition
1990

TABLE OF CONTENTS

FEATURES

GUIDELINES

LIST OF MAPS

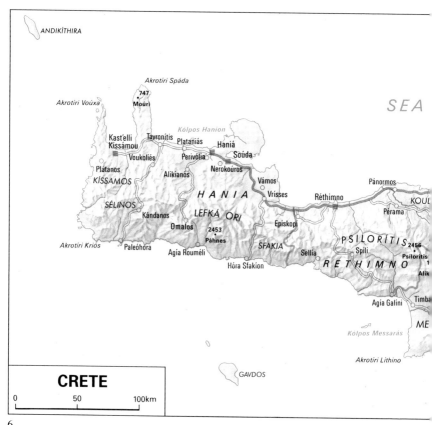

Please note: in some cases the spelling of the place names on the maps is not the same as in the text, because the spelling on the maps is according to UN guidelines, whereas the usual English spelling is used in the text.

AN INVITATION TO CRETE

"Found most beautiful green stone. Come immediately"

- Zorba -

This guide tells the story of Crete, the "Great Island". It tells of the sea kings of Knossos and the famous labyrinth guarded by the Minotaur; it traces the history of this ancient civilization through its myths and legends and the archaeological discoveries of the last century. In it you will learn of the rise and fall of kingdoms and empires, of revolt and revolution, and of the stubborn heroism that is the legacy of the Cretan people.

My first memories of Crete are of picking grapes in the blazing August sun on my father's farm, playing hide and seek at Minos Beach and seeing the dolphin fresco at Knossos. I returned to Crete again and again in later years to swim, explore and photograph what I saw. Walking the chilly sidewalks of New England in winter, I would remember the warmth and vitality of Crete and the Cretans.

I hope that you will feel the same magic that I have felt when you see Crete, breathe its aromatic air and read about its legends and its history.

- Michele Macrakis -

Preceding pages: A soapstone statue of the bull Rhyton from the Little Palace in Knossos. Typical old Cretan. Left: A picture postcard landscape in Iraklion.

THE ISLAND

Geography

Crete's 8259 sq km make it the single largest of the Greek islands and the fifth largest island in the Mediterranean after Sicily, Sardinia, Corsica and Cyprus. It is located between the thirty-fourth and thirty-fifth parallels, i.e., on the same latitude as several African cities. At its longest the island is 260 km; its width ranges from 12-61 km. Crete is also Europe's southernmost point which probably explains why Zeus, in the guise of a bull, used it as a bridge while carrying his beautiful "Europa" on his back, thus giving a continent its name. Whatever his ulterior motives in this piracy, the great Eastern civilizations also offered imports. Under the rule of the Minoans Crete, lying 200 km from the coast of Asia Minor, 300 km from the beaches of North Africa and 96 km from the Peloponnese became a center of the maritime power of Thalassocratia.

Over 960 km of coast encircle the island. Much of the landscape is mountainous and it is therefore hardly surprising that the mountains drop steeply into the sea at many places on the coast. The three principal ranges of Crete are the White Mountains or Lefka Ori to the west with a maximum altitude of 2452 m (Pahnes), Mount Psiloritis or Ida in the center, with an altitude of 2456 m, and Mount Dikti to the east at 2148 m. Besides these there is a series of smaller ranges such as the Asteroussia Mountains in the south of the island and the Thripti range in the east.

Preceding pages: Sea and sun. The port of Iraklion. Left: Inland mountain landscape.

Hardly any other Mediterranean island has as many gorges as Crete. The most famous is the 18-km-long gorge of Samaria that drops steeply toward the southern coast. A number of further gorges run parallel to this from the White Mountains to the southern coast, such as the Eligias Gorge, the Aradena Gorge, the Imbros Gorge and the Kallikratiano Gorge near Frangokastello. Scenically the "Palm Gorge" near Preveli and the gorge known as the "Valley of the Dead" near Zakros are of particular beauty.

A special aspect of Crete's landscape is the many undrained almost circular plateaus. The most famous is the Lassithi Plateau with its host of white windmills that once served to pump up the water to irrigate the plains. Progress made no exception here and most of the mills have been replaced by diesel-run pumps.

Vegetables, potatoes and grain grow 815 m up, on an area covering almost 39 sq km. The other plateaus allow only for limited agriculture. The Omalos Plateau is 1050 m high and the Nidha Plateau 1355 m.

Economy, Traffic, Administration

Agriculture in this mostly mountainous country is concentrated in the fertile valleys and on flat sections of the coast. The largest homogeneous agricultural area is the plain of Messara south of the town of Iraklion. It served as Crete's breadbasket even in ancient times. Great palaces stood here once, such as those of Phaestos and Agia Triada, and the Romans ruled the entire island from Gortyna.

Other areas under cultivation worth mentioning are those around the Gulf of Kastelli-Kissamos, around Platanias near Hania, the section of coast east of Rethimnon and the plains of Iraklion and Ierapetra. In recent years, however, the use of heavy agricultural machinery and the employment of both greenhouses and

CRETE IN THE MEDITERRANEAN SEA

modern irrigation techniques have altered the landscape considerably as well as increasing the amount of arable land. Olives and wine constitute the main staples of agricultural production; 42 percent of the arable land is covered with olive trees used mainly in the production of olive oil. Wine accounts for 14 percent of the area under cultivation and the rest is devoted to growing vegetables, citrus fruits and other products. Grain has lost its importance ever since the importation of cheaper grain from the vast plains of Thessalia.

Pastures also account for a sizeable portion of the agro-economy. Particularly hardy breeds of goat and sheep live on the sparse vegetation growing among the stones in the mountains and hills. Their milk is often made into tasty cheese locally. The most famous names are Graviera, Mizithra and Anthotiro. The island's own production of cheese, however, is not great enough to support the invasion of over 1 million tourists during the summer months.

Besides agriculture, tourism has become a major factor in the island's economy. It provides most of the hard currency and simultaneously spurs trade and the service industry. Crete has otherwise no large factories or industries worth mentioning. The most important economic center and the island's largest city is Iraklion, followed closely by Hania. Both are port cities servicing the Greek port of Piraeus several times daily. Ferries to Piraeus also leave from Rethimnon. A ferry leaves twice weekly from Kastelli-Kissamos to Githion on the Peloponnese. Ships also travel from Agios Nikolaos and Sitia to Karpathos and Rhodes. International car ferries to Cyprus, Israel and Egypt usually lie over in Iraklion where the international airport is also located. In summer chartered aircraft land at the inland airport near Hania. The road network on Crete has been well developed, especially along the northern

Right: Dusk as it has fallen for millenia upon the shores and mountains of Crete.

16

coast. On the southern coast the roads are not nearly as good, though those leading to the major administrational centers in the north are well built.

Crete is one of eleven administrational districts of Greece and is ruled by a "governor general", elected by the Council of Ministers in Athens. The island itself is divided up into four districts *(nomoi):* Hania, Rethimnon, Iraklion and Lassithi (Agios Nikolaos).

The last census, in 1981, gave Crete a population of 502,165. 75 percent of the inhabitants are concentrated in the northern half of the island, and 46 percent in the district *(nomos)* of Iraklion. Further, Crete is divided into 20 sub-districts encompassing 578 communities including 1450 villages.

Climate

Crete is dominated by a mild Mediterranean climate, with hot, dry summers and a rainy winter. The transitional seasons are short and usually more notice-able in the mountains. Cretans speak only of summer and winter. But spring is the most pleasant time for a visit. Bathing only begins in May, but the island's flowers in bloom are a splendid sight indeed. Particularly advisable during this period are long walks in coastal regions. Those who love the sun and the sea, surfing and night-life will find all they need in summer especially when the taverns come alive long after the sun has gone down leaving the night air cool. Daytime temperatures in summer usually hover upwards from 30°C (86°F). A gentle northerly breeze cools the northern coast throughout the month of August. The southern coast on the other hand has African climatic traits. The average annual temperature of the drier eastern and southern parts of Crete is generally higher than that of the western part and the northern coast. For most people autumn is warm enough. One can swim throughout all of October. Winter begins after Christmas and reaches its climax around January and February.

17

PROFILE OF
CRETAN CIVILISATION

"There is a kind of flame in Crete – let us call it soul – something more powerful than either life or death. There is pride, obstinacy, valor, and together with these something else inexpressible and imponderable, something which makes you rejoice that you are a human being, and at the same time tremble."

(Nikos Kazantzakis, *Report to Greco*)

A lot of things have been said about Crete and the Cretans – Crete is the most authentically Greek of all the Greek islands – Crete is the land of the Minoans – Cretans love liberty, refuse to accept enslavement, smash sacrosanct old molds – Cretans are liars, wicked men and lazy workers – but throughout this range of opinions there also runs the common theme of Cretan national pride, hardheadedness and honor.

Obviously, Crete is not just another Greek island. Situated in the center of the eastern Mediterranean, halfway between Europe, Africa and Asia, it was considered in ancient times as being at the center of the world. In such a position Crete could not escape contact with the foreign cultures of East and West. On the contrary, each new influence was first assimilated and then adapted to suit the needs of Crete itself, thus creating a unique culture that was unlike any other.

The peculiarities of Crete – its crucial geographic position, the succession of foreign domination and revolts – created their own mood, not found in other islands in the area. Its climate, people, and ways of life belong to the Aegean Archipelago, Greece, and Mediterranean

Europe. But it is unique in its long history and culture.

Its civilization is part of that of Greece and of Asia Minor. Lying between the last promontory of the Peloponnese and Cnidos in southwest Asia Minor, and framed in the north by the islands of Cythera, Karpathos, and Rhodes, it forms the southernmost bridge of the Aegean Sea between Greece and Anatolia, the link uniting continental Greece to Asia. "Crete is like a leviathan, pushed up by successive geological explosions" says Lawrence Durrell. "It is also like the buckle in a slender belt of islands which shelter the inner Cyclades from the force of the deep sea..."

Crete has gone through the same upheavals as Greece and has witnessed the arrival of the same waves of peoples while serving as a contact between the Near Eastern and the Greek world. It influenced the Mycenaean civilization, and during the classical period it inspired all kinds of legends. Its people traveled to Egypt, Anatolia and Syria, propelled by the winds of the summer, and brought back exquisite objects made of ivory, steatite, and semi-precious stones together with exotic foodstuffs that had all been traded for their own distinctive handicrafts.

Positioned between the Orient, Egypt and Greece, Crete eventually worked out a mode of survival. Throughout different periods the island was to play a role of paramount importance in the Mediterranean world.

Notwithstanding all the successive foreign occupations the character of Crete has not changed much throughout the ages. For four thousand years, despite all the invasions and oppressions, Crete has jealously guarded all its individual and unique identity. High in the White Mountains, ancient institutions and a love of tradition are still to be found among its blue eyed and blond haired people who speak an archaic Greek and, at times,

Left: The Koules fortress built by the Venetians stands in the port of Iraklion

men of all ages work silently on their farms, wearing their traditional high-boots, black shirts and baggy pants. One feels in the presence of an ancient and noble people, who have descended in a straight line from an unknown past, with minimal changes on the way; "eventually the grandeur of the place is forgotten; it only supports a background in whose foreground a huge Cretan stares at you". (Raymond Matton, *La Crete au Cours des Siecles*)

The Poets' Crete

And yet it is this "background" that helps to explain Crete and its people.

Crete, "the great island" as it is called, appears still larger, with tall mountains and deep valleys that dominate the countryside. Over the last three centuries these mountains have been immortalized by poets and songwriters, who in their moving Cretan songs – *mandinades* and *rezitika* – tell us of revolts of the chieftains of the island against the Turkish yoke. They have also inspired foreign artists, like Captain Spratt, who have tried to capture the shimmering light of the mountain tops in the morning, or the change of the pastel hues after sunset.

"... I sat watching its play of pink, purple, and golden hues, tinting the mountain tops or lower landscape as the light faded, with intense admiration and pleasure, until... the bright tints vanished, and all was gray..." (Captain T.A.B. Spratt, *Travels and Researches in Crete*)

look like the "golden Dorians". Rich in tradition and Homeric in its sense of hospitality, Crete, like Mani in southern Greece, has a sense of honor and a deep and abiding passion for independence. These are common traits in the two regions.

The Cretans have experienced everything – the disappearance of the Minoan Empire, the rise of Venice, Turkish Islamization, Nazi brutality, present-day tourism: nothing has been spared them. Under the Romans, the Venetians, and the Turks, they constantly rose in revolt, led by their chieftans – their famous *kapetanoioi*. During the early phases of the Second World War nowhere in Europe did one see such fierce fighting as in Crete and nowhere were there more martyrs to the cause of freedom or more widows and orphans left to lament.

The human element is rich in Crete. In the small villages, old women still weave,

The mountains are omnipresent in Crete's history, geography, and its art: "...The mountains of Lassithi and the rock of Sphakia and between them Psiloritis – the tallest, like a giant Patriarch – hold, engraved on their sides, their plateaus, their peaks, and hidden among the densely forested slopes, many centuries of vicissitudes, of lessons, and accounts of man's fate", sings the Greek poet, Kostis Palamas.

Above: Romantic moods on the southern coast. Right: Mountainous splendors.

It is in the isolation of these forbidding mountains and wind-haunted valleys that the Cretans became so self-sufficient, proud, and unique. It is in this island with its stretches of rolling hills and fertile soil, extravagant flora, and rich culture, that the people felt and still feel that they are Cretans first, Greeks second.

Spratt's sketch of Mount Ida is a masterpiece of landscape painting: "...I was captivated by this brilliant effect, and sketched the panoramic view of hill and dale, coastline and bays, ... as seen from my aerial position on Ida..."

The mountains rise "ironbound from the deep sea on the southern coast like great walls against which the sea pounds". Deep caves have also been found in most of the mountains; the one at Ida is believed to have been the birthplace of Zeus, while the Diktean cave is where the god was hidden and cared for as a child. And there is the sea which determined the development of Crete and the character of the people as much as the mountains. The slim silhouette of Crete is sandwiched between the angry Cretan Sea in the north and the vast, empty Sea of Libya in the south.

The Cretan coastline is irregular. From west to east there are many gulfs: Kissamos, Hania, Armyro, Mirabello, Sitia, with long stretches of beaches in between.

In the south lie the unique Bay of Messara and the three capes: Krios, Lithinos and Goutheron. There are deep gulfs in the north and narrow beachheads in the south, but the finest of them all is the Bay of Souda, the largest natural bay in the Mediterranean, a gulf of great beauty which captivated Spratt with "the intensity of its ultramarine blue, as it combines the azure reflected from the firmament above, with the blue hues arising from its own crystal-clear transparency and profundity beneath."

With natural ports such as these it is no wonder the Cretans became good sailors and explorers early on, even in the third millenium crossing the Aegean Sea to the north, to Sicily in the west and to Egypt

21

in the south, spreading their culture around the Mediterranean as they went.

Homer mentioned the richness of the island with its hundred cities and palaces. Its influence was so great that it could survive without any fortifications. But natural forces were stronger and more able to destroy fortifications than any human endeavor, although what remains of Minoan civilization will still impress today's visitor.

Digging up the Past

It was here that the oldest European civilization developed and flourished five millenia ago, almost simultaneously with the "river civilizations" of Mesopotamia and Egypt. This mysterious civilization was uncovered and studied by imaginative archaeologists at the turn of the century, led by the pioneer Arthur (later Sir

Above: Piecemeal past – archaeologist Sinclair Hood at work. Right: A copy of the bull jumping fresco from Knossos.

Arthur) Evans, who – like Heinrich Schliemann, the celebrated excavator of Troy and Mycenae – had not been trained as an archaeologist. Evans turned to archaeology later in life, after a successful career as a journalist, curator and antiquarian. He had a passion for the Balkan countries but above all Crete attracted his attention. He was certain that in Crete he would find a rich, prehistoric civilization, as reflected in the Homeric lines:

"Out in the dark blue sea lies a land called Crete, a rich and lovely land, washed by the waves on every side, densely peopled and boasting ninety cities... One of the ninety towns is a great city called Knossos, and there, for nine years, King Minos ruled and enjoyed the friendship of almighty Zeus."

Evans was familiar with the legends about Crete. He knew how Rhea, the mother of Zeus and wife of Cronos, had saved her son from his jealous father by hiding him in a cave on Crete where he grew up among the Corybantes and the Curetes. These ancient people were the

masters of fire and were the first to forge bronze weapons and armour.He had also read Apollodorus and knew the story of Theseus and the Minotaur.

As lord of the Aegean, King Minos demanded a tribute from the state of Athens. This tribute took the form of seven noble Athenian boys and seven girls whom he then sacrificed to the Minotaur, the monstrous offspring of his wife Pasiphae and a bull (no doubt some god in disguise). Some say that the Labyrinth the Minotaur lived in was the Palace of Knossos with its long corridors and complicated access.

Theseus, the son of the lord of Athens, Aegeus, decided to liberate Athens from this heavy tribute. He sailed for Crete where he met the daughter of King Minos, Ariadne, who fell in love with him. Ariadne gave him a spool of thread to roll out behind him so that he could find his way out after killing the Minotaur. Flushed with excitement, he set sail for Athens where he forgot to give the prearranged signal of victory – white

sails instead of black. His father, Aegeus, waiting impatiently at Cape Sounion, flung himself into the sea in his grief, believing that his beloved son was dead, and thus giving the Aegean Sea its name.

In March 1900, Evans started digging in Crete and found Knossos. The legend proved to have been based on historical events. The excavations found here were breathtaking.

There was a huge palace with a large central courtyard, a throne room, long corridors, many of which led to storechambers containing enormous jars *(pythoi)* for oil and other agricultural produce, official quarters, private quarters for the family of the king, bathrooms, gay frescoes in blue and red showing young princes, beautiful women, dolphins, birds, priests, bulls, double axes and seals, and most important of all, clay tablets bearing hieroglyphic scripts that Evans hoped to decipher.

Who were these people that left behind this amazing art and architecture? What was their cilivization? When did they live? Slowly, the mystery unfolded, but it still keeps many archaeologists busy.

The Minoan Period

The story of Crete begins shortly after 3000 BC, with the slow replacement of stone by copper, although earlier Neolithic settlements have also been discovered at many sites, most notably Knossos, Phaestos and Agia Triada, places that were to be important palace sites in the period that followed. It was these first settlers, who arrived in Crete between 6000 and 5000 BC, who introduced agriculture on the island basing it on the cultivation of cereals, olives, grape vines and the herding of animals. They also imported the cult of the fertility goddess, with her big buttocks and heavy thighs, a "steatopygous" figure of the African type. The Neolithic culture of Crete is like the Neolithic culture of mainland Greece and has left us some decorated pottery and clay figurines of animals but it is the next period that was most important.

Around 2600 BC, new people descended on Crete. The new settlers of Crete, as well as of mainland Greece, came from western Anatolia. They worked with copper and later with bronze. These new settlers did not destroy the culture already existing on the island. Rather they embraced and absorbed it and created the famous Minoan civilization, so called by its discoverer Sir Arthur Evans after the legendary ruler of Crete, King Minos. Evans, basing his chronology on pottery styles, divided the Minoan Age into three periods, which he called Early, Middle and Late Minoan, each further subdivided into three subperiods.

For over one thousand years the Minoans lived peacefully – weapons were scarce and no city fortifications have been found. A seafaring economy developed, trading in metalware and agricultural products. Traveling to western Anatolia, the Aegean and the West, the Cretans carried their pottery with its spiral designs, their carved seal-stones and also their oil, perfumes and wines, which they exchanged for the goods of their neighbors – leather from Cyprus, gold and silver from the Cyclades, stone from Milos. Its ports – Zakros and Palaikastro in the east, the little islands of Mohlos and Psira in the north – were its centers of commerce with Asia Minor. Increasingly, Crete welcomed and assimilated the influences of Anatolia and its art, starting in the EM III (2300 BC) period, spreading from the eastern part of the island to the central area of Knossos and Phaestos and to Kairatos in the west through a new route that ran from east to west.

In approximately 2000 BC, Crete experienced a profound change, probably due to the development of its pottery industry; the famous Kamares vases with their eggshell surface and polychromy were introduced at that time, as was the establishment of direct commercial relations with Egypt. This is the Middle Minoan period when the complex palaces of central Crete were built: Knossos, Malia, Phaestos and Agia Triada, together with other royal residences, as well as large towns. Many of the palaces were destroyed during the MM II (1850 - 1750 BC) period but were quickly rebuilt around 1700 BC. Life in the palaces seems to have been pleasant and carefree, the nobles affluent, the institution of kingship secure – a centralized government with a large civil service and a highly stratified society. Religion played an important role and was practiced within the courts of palaces as well as on mountain peaks and in caves.

After 1700 BC new and grander palaces were built on the ruins of the old

Right: Ivory carving depicting a bull jumper (Archaeological Museum of Iraklion).

with architectural innovations such as columns made of cypress trees, and skylights over patios. Art was freed from its oriental influences and a real renaissance began during this MM III period (1750 - 1600 BC). The Cretan navy ruled the Aegean and the Mediterranean – making Crete a real thalassocracy. Relations with the neighboring peoples increased while the "oriental trade" experienced a recession due to the invasions of the Hyksos in Egypt, the expansion of the Hittites in Asia Minor and the arrival of new waves of people in Greece proper.

King Minos (an individual monarch) reigned unchallenged. "Minos", writes the historian Thucydides in the fifth century BC, "is the first sovereign, as we hear, that possessed a navy and the control of the sea we now call Hellenic; his

Above: An Etruscan plate tells of the encounter between Pasiphaä and the Minotaur. Right: Gold coin left over from the days when the ancient Greeks lived in Knossos.

power spread to the Cyclades and other islands of the area which he held for a long time and where he appointed his sons as leaders. He purged the seas from the pirates as much as he could, obviously in order to better assure the safety of the revenues from these islands."

We find the name Minoa given to towns and whole areas in Laconia, Sicily, Syria, Arabia, the Cyclades – a real Cretan imperialism. A colony was established in Corcyra, commercial relations were strong with the XVIIIth dynasty of Egypt, everywhere we see signs of the Cretan thalassocracy and the spreading of the Cretan civilization.

But around 1450 BC the palaces of Phaestos, Agia Triada and Tylissos were destroyed by fire. Who set it? Rivals of King Minos or enemies from abroad? And why is it that Knossos flourished for the next fifty years? Had the Mycenaeans, called by Homer "Achaeans", taken Knossos and were they the ones who introduced new forms of architecture, new weapons, a new pantheon of

gods, a new social and political organization, a new calendar, adapting the Cretan writing to their own language and needs? It seems likely. But in 1400 BC Knossos too was destroyed through pillage and fire. Was this a result of earthquake, war or internal revolt? Scholars differ in their conclusions. What is certain is that this brings to an end the great era of Minoan history, while the ascendancy of the Mycenaeans continued on the mainland until the invasion of the Dorians, "the people from the North."

The Classical Period

The Minoan civilization did not die with the destruction of the palaces. Instead it blended with the newcomers and enriched their culture. Eventually, the coming of the Dorians to Crete created new circumstances and a new type of culture. The new conquerors were able to assimilate the native population so that by the opening of the classical period Crete had become fully Greek. During its long history, Crete has kept this Greek character despite repeated wars and foreign occupations and despite its occasional forced isolation from the mainland.

In Crete the retention of place-names throughout long periods of historical change is remarkable and by comparison with other areas, quite unusual. Prehellenic and ancient Greek place-names are preserved to this day all over the island. This phenomenon implies a stubborness and will to preserve the Greek element despite the geographic isolation of the island.

The era of classical Crete appeared first, separate from the Greek mainstream to which it eventually succumbed but not without passing on its deities and customs, legislation and institutions which were finally adopted by the other Greeks. The Cretan Zeus, the Gortyna legislative tablets and the Cretan Assembly are indications of this process. In this manner Crete slowly became part of the Greek mainstream.

27

Pax Romana

During Roman times Crete participated in eastern Mediterranean affairs, being an intermediate stopover on the way to the Roman Eastern Empire. Crete was the last Greek region to be conquered by Rome after considerable resistance. The Roman period was peaceful; in fact it brought to an end the internecine wars between Cretan cities. Christianity was introduced early in the island and easily triumphed over paganism. Tradition has it that the island was visited by St. Paul either in 61 or 47 AD. Paul stopped at Kali Limenes, met with Titus, and appointed him Bishop of Gortyna, asking him to continue his missionary work in Crete. Besides the remains of his church in Gortyna, many other churches in Crete are dedicated to Titus.

Above: Church of the Archangel Michael in Rotunde, a relic of the great Byzantine Empire. Right:The division of Crete into four districts under the Venetians.

Crete and Byzantium

As part of the Eastern Roman Empire, the island was just another "eparchy" of the Byzantine Empire and for a while it was little known. The next important event and one which produced a historical upheaval was the conquest of the island by a band of Saracen pirates from Spain in 824 AD. They made the city of Iraklion their principal fortress calling it Rabdh-al-Khandah, Handax in Greek, which means ditch – hence the name Candia given by the Europeans to the city and later to the whole island.

The Arab conquest did not leave any important legacy on the island although it lasted 133 years. The island was taken back by the Byzantines after a brilliant campaign Nikiforos Fokas – later Emperor Nicephorus II – who by 961 AD was able to throw the conquerors out. For another century and a half the Byzantines ruled again in Crete and tried to rehabilitate the island. This was a period of consolidation and strengthening of the Greek

element in the island through settlements. Twelve noble families from Constantinople – the twelve *archontopula* – were "imported" into Crete at the time thus creating a new aristocracy in Crete and importing new bloodlines to intermarry with the old Cretan families.

Crete and Venice

Soon a new calamity fell on the Byzantine Empire: the fourth Crusade, on its way to the Holy Land, veered towards the rich city of Constantinople to loot and conquer. Among the booty was the island of Crete "as a diamond in the midst of the Mediterranean", the link of the Near East with Western commerce. The island was eventually purchased by the Venetians, who considered it indispensable to their lucrative Eastern trade. Thus, starting in 1211 and for the next 450 years, Crete became part of the Venetian Republic. It is interesting to note that a modern traveler to Crete, especially if he arrives by sea at the port of Iraklion, as countless travelers

have done before him, will be faced with the double lions of Venice, set on the walls of the fortress. This is vividly described in the introduction of William H. McNeill's *Venice, the Hinge of Europe*, 1781-97.

The Cretans fought continuously and courageously against this new conqueror, and for the first three centuries rose in a series of bloody but unsuccessful revolts and revolutions in order to keep their Greco-Christian identity intact against the repeated assaults of the Roman Catholic enemy. It is actually said that all during this unbroken series of unsuccessful revolts, each generation of Cretan men married, raised a son to continue the line and went off to the mountains to fight the invaders.

With the fall of Constantinople into the hands of the Ottoman Turks in 1453, the hopes for liberation died and, by necessity, the two elements, the Orthodox Cretans and the Catholic Venetians, began a slow but steady rapprochement which became especially pronounced

29

It was during this period that important artists were born and raised in Crete: Domenico Theotocopoulos, named El Greco (the Greek) in Spain, George Hortatsis, a superb playwright of popular plays, which were performed both in Crete and in the rest of Greece, and Vincenzo Cornaro who wrote the masterpiece of the Cretan renaissance, the *Erotocritos*, the most popular work of Greek literature for two hundred years, a stereotypical Italian romance transformed into an original epic in Cretan dialect and still recited by Cretan shepherds from memory. In architecture and in art, the Venetian influence is strong in such masterpieces as the church of Saint Mark in Iraklion, the famous Loggia – the club of the Venetians – across from the Morosini fountain, and the lovely St. Titus church with its stone façade. The fortresses around the city of Iraklion – built by the famous Venetian architect Michel Sanmicheli – and its port are awesome with their thick battlements and recurring theme of lion reliefs.

among the middle classes of the larger cities. After the middle of the sixteenth century, we see a new, strong mixture that worked toward the creation of a common culture.

The old enmity receded, allowing the fusion of the two peoples which brought about a Cretan renaissance in literature and the arts, a renaissance that witnessed the fusion of Greco-Byzantine elements with Western European elements, a fusion seen for the first and last time in history – not just a sterile acceptance of foreign elements but the coming together of two cultures into one. Although it represents one of the greatest accomplishments of neohellenism, the astounding Cretan culture of the last century of the so-called Venetocracy has not yet been acknowledged by the modern Greeks, no doubt because of the bitter memories of a brutal occupation.

Although the Venetian rule in Crete had been a colonial rule of systematic economic exploitation, of intolerance towards the Greek Orthodox ecclesiastical hierarchy, demanding in the tone of its communications and cruel in the collection of taxes, it also proved intellectually stimulating in the fields of poetry and the other arts.

Crete and the Turks

This brilliant period ended with the coming of the Ottoman Turks in 1641. In a sudden change of course, they set foot on the outskirts of Hania as their fleet was ostensibly headed for Malta. The Venetians were taken by surprise. By then, the Ottomans had conquered most of the Greek mainland, and after a twenty-year campaign against the main cities of Crete they were able to take the last big bastion of Crete – Candia – by 1669.

Above: The Venetian Loggia in Iraklion.
Right: It was the Turks who introduced coffee drinking.

The twenty year siege of the fortress of Candia has been recorded and studied in great detail. Not only was it a question of siege tactics and suffering but also an important example of the balance of power in Europe where the players were France, Venice, the Ottomans, Genoa and Central Europe. Even Pope Clement IX. was involved, as well as the French king, Louis XIV. Molière's social satire, *Le Bourgois Gentilhomme*, ridicules the current fad for things of Turkish influence *(turquerie)*. This fashion was encouraged by the presence of various Turkish emissaries in Paris and to French equivocations in foreign policy: they needed the Turks as a political balance.

A recent account of the siege of Candia, of the "Cretan War" in general and its parallels with the siege of Vienna by the Turks is given by E. and R. Eickoff in *Venedig, Wien und die Osmanen*. The siege was also recorded by a Cretan poet – Marinos Zane Bounialis – in his moving epic *Cretan War*. Bounialis implicates – apparently not without reason –

a Venetian traitor, the engineer Andrea as having supplied details about the fortifications and their weak points to Koprulu, the Turkish general. The Turkish leaders met with Barozzi just outside the fort.

"They descended there, were they were instructed by him, and they saw and measured and he said to the vezir that this is the easy way: from here they can pierce the fort and get inside."

Indeed, during the last months of the siege, the Turks abruptly changed objectives: the fort was stormed from Sabionera (Sandy Place), the side near the port, and St. Andrea where the fort abutted on the sea. A truce was signed and soon the island was abandoned for ever by its Venetian conquerors and most of its native population.

These Cretan refugees filled the intellectual centers of Western Europe and western Greece and taught philosophy, painting, drama and poetry. For Crete, though, this was the beginning of a steady and dramatic decline, a dark period of sacrifice and struggle.

The peasants in the countryside, too poor and illiterate to leave their island, received the brunt of the fight. They began a long resistance against this new and cruel conqueror, a conqueror of different culture, religion and habits.

We now have a period of violent change in the political, social and economic life of the island plus dramatic events in religious affairs, since the earlier sporadic conversions to Catholicism were followed by an extensive Islamization of the Cretans, sometimes through the soft path of economic incentives and other times through forced conversion. These Islamized Cretans were not only lost to the Orthodox church but to Hellenism as well. As we shall see below, the so-called Turco-Cretans emigrated to Asia Minor and still speak Greek.

Once being under Ottoman domination, Crete became an *eyalet* (or *vilayet*),

Above: Even priests did their duty as freedom fighters in those days. Right: The erstwhile mosque of Pasha Hassan.

a province governed by a *vali* as governor general, and a large staff which included the *mufti* (the chief justice), the *reis effendi* (the recording secretary), the *defterdar* (the treasurer), and a considerable number of clerks.

The eyalet of Crete was divided into three smaller units, the *sanjaks* of Hania, Rethimnon, and Candia. Within the social and economic structure of Crete under the Turks, the non-Muslim population represented the class most liable to suffer from taxes, duties, impositions, and general insults. Since the *pashas* were rarely stationed in their post for a long time, they showed little interest in reforms and a just administration; in any case, an effective vali could not survive the pressures exerted on him from below by the *janissaries*, the *beys*, and the *aghas*. It was the latter who really set the tone, and any administrative higher official could easily lose his post by being deposed by the undisciplined janissaries, the élite group of the sultan's army. In between, the Christians of the island remained poor and unprivileged since in return for taxes paid they received practically nothing in the way of roads, public services or improvements in communications. The only consolation to them was that the Turkish system, loose and disorganized as it was, allowed them to follow their religion, conduct their own affairs, and educate their children in the Greek language.

Cretan Revolts

No wonder, then, that the history of Crete in the period of the Turkokratia (Turkish occupation) is a story of maladministration, cruel oppression, continuous terrorism and frequent massacres. It is also a story of successive revolts by the Christian population against the Muslim overlord. The Cretan revolts have been chronicled by folk poets, narrated by novelists, and sung in the *rizitika* songs

by the inhabitants of the highland villages of the White Mountains who expressed their desire for revolution against the Turks and for their freedom, through these allegorical and symbolic songs. Among these folk songs, the most important deals with the revolt of Dhaskaloyiannis in 1770 and recounts in over a thousand lines the heroic revolt of a teacher, John, who fought against immense odds, relying on promised help from Orthodox Russia. This support did not materialize and the revolt collapsed. John was finally caught and flayed alive by the Turks. The best known song about him is the version dictated by Barba-Pantzelio, an illiterate cheese-maker, to an amanuensis in 1786.

"They handed him over to the torturers; afterwards they flayed him, right up to his eyes and his nose: bitterly he screamed at the tortures they inflicted. When they had done the worst with him, the mercy of death came on him."

Other superb accounts of the Cretan rebellions have been given in the fictitious histories of Nikos Kazantzakis and Pandelis Prevelakis, who have described so well the physical, racial, and social make-up of these revolts. *Capetan Mihalis* by Kazantzakis (translated as *Freedom or Death* in English) is the story of the author's father who fought in the 1889 revolt, while the trilogy of Prevelakis, *The Cretan*, describes the uprisings from 1866 to 1906 and has as a sequel *The Tale of a Town*, the town being the birthplace of the author, Rethimnon, the quiet, magical town in the middle of northern Crete, which witnessed the expulsion of many Creto-Turks in 1923 with the exchange of populations.

Until the end of the nineteenth century all the Cretan revolts failed, but they do compose a unique story of blood and heroism, legend and romance. From 1770 to 1898, Crete was periodically in revolt. Each revolt has its own history, its colorful personalities, its heroic battles, perhaps some elements of cold-blooded manipulation by the Great Powers, but they all follow a well-defined course.

33

The Christians, chafing at the discriminatory rules of law and the unequal conditions of life under Ottoman rule, petitioned the Porte, and often the Great Powers, for reforms. These reforms usually involved taxation and civil rights. Often one Great Power or another supported the rebels for its own reasons of higher strategy, but usually only verbally. As it became clear that upheaval was imminent, the Muslim inhabitants of the countryside, being at the mercy of the Christians, flocked to the walled towns of Iraklion, Rethimnon and Hania; Christian inhabitants of the towns, being at the mercy of the Muslims, attempted to flee to the mountains but were often trapped inside the towns to face massacre.

Committees were formed in the mountains followed by a number of assemblies of the people. The leaders of the villages *(demogerontes)*, or the chieftains *(oplarhigoi)* with their private bands came into contact with the Cretans working for the cause in mainland Greece.

Once the opposition forces were mustered, the course of the rising involved the landing of ammunition, if not volunteers as well, from Greece, to provision the insurgents. The sultan's forces poured into the mountains, and skirmishes followed, but the real hope on the Greek side seems to have been not so much to defeat the superior Turkish forces singlehandedly but to attract the attention of the Great Powers to Crete's plight so that they would finally intervene decisively, winning new concessions from the Porte and, eventually, driving the sultan's troops out of Crete and uniting the island with Greece, which had won its independence from the Turks in 1829.

The bloodiest and longest revolt took place in 1866, as a result of the failure of the Ottomans to introduce reforms in the island. The Turks attacked the monastery of Arkadi, which the Cretans were using as their headquarters and camp. As the Turks stormed the monastery, the abbot, Igumenos Gabriel, set fire to the powder magazine and hundreds of men, women and children were blown up. This dramatic suicidal defense of the monastery aroused public opinion in Europe and America. Well-known revolutionaries, novelists, and poets such as Garibaldi, Victor Hugo, and Swinburne spoke with admiration about it and wrote fiery poems to commemorate the event. In his *Ode to the Insurrection in Candia* of January 1867, Swinburne notes that:

"...In the hundred cities of Crete... Such glory was not of old... Though her name was great upon earth... And her face was fair on the sea... So fair, who is fairer now... With her children dead at her side... Unsceptred, unconsecrated... Unapparelled, unhelped, unpitied... With blood for gold on her brow..."

Greek interference and growing escalation of the fighting led to the Great Powers' intervention, resulting finally in the acceptance of the Organic Statute of 1868, under which Crete was to be administered for the following ten years. If the statue had been complied with, the conditions of the Christians in Crete would have improved. However, this did not happen until 1878, when the Pact of Halepa inaugurated a more satisfactory regime for the Christians and gave them virtual self-government. The pact became the Magna Carta of the Christians from that day on. If it had been executed in good faith, the results would have been satisfactory, despite the fact that it was full of ambiguities that could alter its meaning.

Under the first Governor General of Crete it was interpreted in a broad spirit and worked well but under his successors the imperfections of the pact became apparent, the directives of the governors were vague, the agreement between the

Right: Ships from the international defense forces in Hania harbor.

Chania. Ships of the International Forces in the medieval harbour.

Cretan Assembly and the government ceased to be clear, and the authority of the General assembly was undermined by the veto powers of the Sultan which turned the Assembly into a consultative rather than a legislative body. The result was agitation, new petitions and endless friction, ending with the revolutionary movement of 1896-98, when the Great Powers intervened in a direct and decisive way.

Crete and the Great Powers

As noted earlier in reference to the Venetian occupation, the island of Crete had posed difficult political problems for the Great Powers since the seventeenth century. In the center of the eastern Mediterranean, halfway from Europe to Africa and halfway from Malta to Syria, Crete commanded then as it still does today the strategic sea lanes from north to south and from west to east. Its mixed population of 50 percent Muslims at the end of the eighteenth century and the sen-

timental importance it had for Greeks only heightened the sensitivity of its foreign relations.

Greece, Turkey, England and Russia had direct interests in Crete. Greece, committed to the "Great Idea", the vision, that is, of incorporating the unredeemed Greeks of the Ottoman Empire in a single Greek state, was looking forward to the redemption of the Greek majority of the historically Greek island of Crete. As a consequence, Greece unconditionally supported *Enosis* (union to the mother country).

Turkey, unwilling to relinquish those territories which formed a connecting link between the European portions of the empire and Egypt, but also acting as the defender of the large Muslim population in Crete, wished to retain Crete as a province. England was the least favorable to Cretan aspirations. For England, Crete, along with Gibraltar, Malta, Cyprus and the Suez Canal, controlled the sea lanes that led to the riches of India; it was essential to the "internal communications"

35

of the British Empire. Russia's attitude fluctuated. For Russia, Crete was a strategic outpost needed to protect her access to the eastern Mediterranean. All the powers, but especially Turkey, were concerned that concessions to Greece on Crete could lead to demands for similar concessions in other parts of the Balkan peninsula and possibly widespread war. The other European states formulated their politics following the demands of treaty obligations, sentiment, and power politics.

France, her idealistic philhellenic notions influenced by her revoluntionary and Napoleonic ideology, now supported Greece in her Cretan policy.

Italy was ambivalent. Crete was of no immediate interest to her but the Venetian occupation of Crete and of other Aegean islands in the past made her speak of certain "historic rights" in the area.

Above: Commander of the international forces on Crete. Right: Cretan delegates in 1911.

The European powers had played an important role during the Turko-Venetian war and especially during the siege of Candia. Prodded by the Holy Sea and ambiguous in their policies the French had led in numbers but other nations sent their armies against the "infidel Turk" too. Armies from the Papal, Italian and German states took part in the twenty-year siege.

The British did not, but followed events closely because of their economic interests in the area. They had already established the first foreign consulate in Hania in 1520.

Ten years after the fall of Candia, in 1679, the French opened a consulate too and French commerce flourished all through the eighteenth century. Russia's development lagged behind the Western Powers. As Russia consolidated its position in European affairs after the rise of Peter the Great, the continuing expansionary forces led her to try to extend her influence in the Balkans and the Mediterranean under Catherine the Great.

The orthodox unity provided a motive and a rationale for this expansionist movement. This culminated in the instigation by the Orloffs of the Dhaskaloyiannis revolt, mentioned before. After that fiasco and the Russo-Turkish war of 1770-74 the Treaty of Kutchuk-Kainardji imposed on the Porte "the protection of the Christian religion and its churches" and defined Russia's role as the protecting power of the Balkan peoples who looked towards her for guidance from then on.

In the period 1770 to 1821, the European powers considered a variety of schemes for acquiring the more attractive territories of the Ottoman Empire – the Ionian islands, Rhodes and Crete. For example, the Treaty of Tilsit of 1807 between France and Russia promised Crete to France, while in 1809 the English ambassador to Vienna was suggesting to his government the occupation of Crete and

Οἱ ἐγκαθειρχθέντες εἰς τὰ Εὐρωπαϊκὰ πολεμικὰ Κρῆτες Βουλευταὶ κατὰ τὸ ἔτος *1911.*

Les Deputés Crètois gardés sur les vapeurs de guerre Européens en 1911,

Cyprus as territories of great strategic importance.

The Greek Revolution of 1821 changed the Powers' calculations. It preempted their schemes for Crete, but, simultaneously, it began a new era of foreign interference in Cretan affairs.

During the Greek Revolution of 1821 the Cretans fought long and hard. However, the Great Powers decided to exclude Crete from the new kingdom of Greece and their approaches to the Cretan problem took different paths. France, although interested in ultimate unification, was unwilling to take any initiatives on her own. England, on the other hand, opposed unification, first because of fears that Greece would act as an extension of Russian influence and second because of her own ambitions in Crete. Russia wished to preserve the status quo if only to be allowed to pursue her interests elsewhere.

Thus came about a series of bloody revolutions culminating in the 1866-68 Great Revolution, followed by the revolts

of 1878 and 1889, when the Cretans were, obviously, the great losers since they had no policy and thus always resorted to action which was effective only in dramatizing their plight, not in changing it. Change was impossible without a combination of revolutionary (destructive) forces with conciliatory (constructive) forces. The Cretan and Greek action, confrontational and ineffective for so long, only became productive when Eleftherios Venizelos, a young Cretan leader, relying on the developing political maturity of the Cretans – nurtured by increasing participation in their own government – realigned their policies towards a pragmatic combination of "guns and negotiations" *(toufeki kai pazari).*

Venizelos and Crete

The entrance of Eleftherios Venizelos in the active politics of his island came at a difficult time. This was the post-Khalepa period which saw the gradual solution to the Cretan Question after a

37

A. B. Y. Πρίγκηψ Γεώργιος
S. H. R. Le Prince Georges

great deal of negotiation and infighting. Four elements characterized this period: 1. Turkey showed a reluctance to implement the Pact. 2. The Cretan parties started intense infighting. 3. The Greek government and the Greek powers played an increasingly important role in directing Cretan affairs and policy. 4. The Great Powers' position vis-à-vis Crete was confused and confusing.

Venizelos was born in Hania on the north-west coast of Crete, educated at the University of Athens and then returned to Crete where he opened a law firm, coedited an influential local newspaper, and at the age of twenty-four won a seat as a liberal in the Cretan Assembly. He was superbly trained as a lawyer, well-read in European literature and political thought, and was a born leader.

He played a very important role in the series of intricate and interlocking steps by which Crete passed from Ottoman

Above: Prince George of Greece. Right: The spirit of Venizelos is alive and well.

domination to autonomy and then to union with Greece and went on to become the most important statesman of modern Greece from 1909 to 1936 when he died in exile.

The inevitable failure of the reforms of the sultan led to increasing insecurity and sectarian violence on the island and culminated in the great fire of the Christian sector of Hania on January 1897 which started a new revolt on the island – the famous Akrotiri revolt – followed by a new demand by the Christians for union with Greece. The Greeks landed a force but the admirals of the European powers, who were stationed in Souda Bay, also sent an international landing party and put an end to the fighting by occupying Hania and bombarding the positions of the insurgents. Finally, through a series of intricate negotiations – during which Venizelos played an important role – the powers imposed a settlement, with all four holding Hania: the British held the Iraklion area, the Russians the area of Rethimnon, the French the Sitia area in the east, and the Italians the southeastern area of Ierapetra.

They also tried to introduce necessary reforms. The powers' intent was to negotiate autonomy under Ottoman suzerainty but a tragic incident changed the situation. In August 1898 fourteen British soldiers and the British viceconsul were murdered by the Turks in Iraklion. In the wake of the Iraklion "massacres" the powers decided that all Turkish influence had to cease. On November 3rd, 1898, the troops of the sultan started withdrawing from the island, ending 253 years of Ottoman rule.

A new arrangement was agreed on. Crete would become independent under the nominal suzerainty of the sultan and the protection of the four powers and would be governed by Prince George of Greece as High Commissioner of Crete. With the new autonomy, a legal structure had to be drawn up for the island, so a

committee of sixteen was chosen. Not surprisingly, given his political and legal background, Venizelos was made a member of the committee and played an important role in the drafting of the legislation. On January 24, 1899, in the new elections, Venizelos became the representative of Hania in the Cretan Assembly, which accepted the Constitution of the Cretan State *(Kritiki Politia).* In April, he was appointed Councillor for Justice in the primary Greek cabinet of Prince George.

Prince George, in late 1900, began to lobby the powers for union with Greece, but Venizelos strongly disagreed, believing it more important to perfect Crete's autonomous government. After a short but acrimonious clash with Venizelos, Prince George dismissed Venizelos from the government on March 18, 1901.

Venizelos' position was interpreted as being for autonomy and against union, whereas he had simply intended an orderly transition to union. His alleged autonomist position led to virulent public

denunciations and a war of words between Venizelos and the Prince in the newspapers of the island.

In protest against the Prince's futile policy of attempting to persuade the Powers to proclaim *enosis* – union – and in protest against the Prince's despotic rule in Crete, Venizelos and a group of his friends established on March 10, 1905 a new revolutionary camp at Therissos, a virtually inaccessible village south of Hania. Amazingly enough, he was able to persuade the representatives of the powers to meet with him and discuss Crete's political future, and even more amazingly, he was able to persuade them to withdraw their support from the Prince. The revolutionary camp was disbanded in November.

During 1906, power shifted from the Prince to the powers and then to the elected Constituent Assembly. The Prince left Crete in September.

In the wake of the Young Turk Movement in the Ottoman Empire and the loss of Bosnia-Herzegovina and Eastern Ru-

melia to Turkey, the assembly attempted to proclaim union, but again the Powers vetoed it.

In March of 1910, after elections, Venizelos became President and Prime Minister of Crete, but not for long. Venizelos was called to Athens by the leaders of the Military League in Greece, a reform group which had executed a coup d'état in August 1909. On September 12, Venizelos resigned his Cretan positions and on October 5 he became Prime Minister of Greece.

An October 14, 1913, Crete finally achieved union with Greece. At the fort of Firka in Hania, on December 6, Venizelos, together with King Constantine of Greece, ceremonially raised the Greek flag over Crete. Venizelos' Cretan period had ended and his position as head of the Greek government propelled him to the rank of international statesman.

Above: Invaders come, invaders go, but here it's business as usual. Right: Nazi medallion depicting their landing on Crete.

Crete and Greece

With its union with mother Greece, Crete finally realized its dream – to be part of the Greek nation. Now, the Cretans were ready to offer even more to their new country – their talented sons, the Greek statesman of international fame, Eleftherios Venizelos (1864-1936), and the superb novelist and philosopher, Nikos Kazantzakis (1867-1957), the author of *Zorba the Greek* and of the modernized version of Ulysses, *Odyssia*.

Now, governed as one of the Greek provinces, Crete had its own Governor General to coordinate its diverse services – agriculture, education, public works, justice. The island was cut into four *nomes* (districts) Iraklion, Hania, Rethimnon, and Lassithi, governed by a nomarch nominated from Athens, with a mayor for each commune.

Following the defeat of Greece by the Turks in 1922, an exchange of population took place and Crete received 13,000 Greek refugees from Asia Minor while

approximately 11,000 Turco-Cretans (Cretans who had been Islamized) left Crete and were resettled in the area of Smyrna where one can find them today dressed in Cretan fashion, using the Cretan dialect, and mourning their lost life on their beloved island.

The feeling of "lost paradise" created by the expulsion and exile of these islanders is beautifully and movingly portrayed in the masterpiece of the Cretan novelist Pandelis Prevelakis, *Tale of a City*.

The Battle of Crete

With the coming of the Second World War and the occupation of Greece by the Germans, the Cretans again rose to the occasion and started the famous Battle of Crete, a fight against another brutal conqueror that cost them many lost lives and long guerilla warfare against the German forces immobilized in the Cretan mountains. For a moment it seemed that Crete was going to be spared the occupation.

British, Australian and New Zealand forces descended on Crete, driven from the Greek mainland by the invading Germans. The Greeks were jubilant. The king and the government were in the hands of their allies and the brave Cretans!

Winston Churchill stated, "We intend to defend to the death, without thought of retirement, both Crete and Tobruk... Let there be no thought of cutting our losses." Yet Crete was attacked and taken by the Germans after twelve days fighting only. What had happened?

According to C. M. Woodhouse, General Bernard Freyberg, who took over command of the Allied forces in Crete, had received important information regarding the German plans to occupy Crete. He was ordered, however, to ignore the information relating to movements of German forces so as not to betray its source. This was the reason, that the Maleme airport west of Hania was inadequately defended. The decision was fatal.

41

On May 20, 1941, the Germans attacked and 7,000 parachutists and glider troops of the Seventh Parachute Division began to land around the Maleme airfield. It was an impressive sight as the northern skies blackened with a multitude of airplanes dragging gliders and filling the space below with descending parachutes. For the local population it evoked biblical comparisons with the plague of locusts in Egypt. Next day more troops landed along the north coast. Iraklion was attacked from both the east where paratroopers landed amidst the vineyards, making their way towards the fortress, and the west near the airport. The British troops, including the Australians and New Zealanders, helped by Cretan citizens, put up a magnificent resistance, using at times knives, clubs, and their bare hands and causing casualties among the enemy. But the Germans

Above: The German military cemetery in Maleme near Hania. Right: Peace finally, after years of war and occupation.

continued to pour forces onto the island. Soon, 20,000 troops had arrived. By May 31, it was all over. Almost half of the force of British, Australian and New Zealand troops was left behind, either killed or captured on the island. The loss for the Allies approximated 15,000 men while the count for the Germans varies from 6,000 to 15,000. Some of the Allied soldiers and officers who were left behind, and were not captured, were able to reach the south coast of Crete and, eventually, Egypt. Others were sheltered by the Cretan fighters in the White Mountains and the Psiloritis for the duration of the war where they were cared for by Cretans who risked their lives to save them.

The loss of Crete by the Allies has been severely criticized by British and other commentators. Although the major reason for the defeat was without any doubt the lack of enough air power on the side of the British and a commitment of 1,200 planes by the Germans, other questions remain. Why, for example, had the defences of Crete not been improved?

Why were the forces so badly armed while the Cretans had not been armed at all? Unforgivable mistakes? Simple miscalculation? We will never know. We know, though, that the strong restistance of the island disrupted Hitler's plans for the invasion of Russia which thus started later than anticipated. This delay had serious consequences for the outcome of the Russian campaign and the war in general. Moreover, according to Churchill, this was a Pyrrhic victory for Goering "for the forces he expended there might easily have given him Cyprus, Iraq, Syria and perhaps Persia."

Soon the Germans brought the necessary military material (tanks, trucks, artillery) to organize the occupation and the defense of the island. A guerilla campaign started immediately in Crete from the first day of occupation. The Cretan fighters were helped and supplied by the British from Egypt, who also provided officers and agents. The situation was dismal in the occupied island, with insufficient food, forced labor and raids and executions by the German and Italian troops. But acts of heroism and bravado by both Cretans and Allies are also recorded. The most famous of these incidents was the kidnapping of the German Commandant Karl Kreipe, who was taken from his headquarters (the famous Villa Ariadne, from which Evans worked on the excavations of Knossos) to the mountains of Crete, shipped to Egypt by the British agents on the island and later flown to London by the Allies. The Allies' agents were often helped in their communications by Cretan messengers. One of these messengers was the George Psychoundakis who later wrote his memoirs in a book called *The Cretan Runner*. The book has been translated by another famous fighter of the island, the Englishman Patrick Leigh Fermor, who, as the peasants recall, "was a giant who could reach a mountain peak with only one big jump!" The guerilla warfare immobilized a large number of German troops in the mountains and so slowed down other attacks by the Germans.

Crete was finally liberated on May 23, 1945, almost exactly four years after its fall. The count was chilling: one out of every six villages was destroyed, her large cities had lost 35 percent of their populace, the economy of the island was in ruins.

Crete Today

After all these bitter experiences, how can Cretans today go to Germany as workers, own VWs, speak German, serve German tourists, even erect a German memorial outside Hania and take care of the German cemetery at Maleme?

What a strange people the Cretes are, and what a strange place is modern Crete! Old men sip their coffee at a mosque turned into a cafe, unaware of the history of the place, or probably pretending to be.

Above: Looking into the future between progress and tradition. Right: Campaign poster rhetoric, from right to left and growing heated.

Strong odors emanate from a raisin-processing plant next to a garden with the heavy smell of jasmine. Young Cretan girls in mini-skirts stroll past an ogling old Cretan in baggy pants and knee-boots. Markets are full of fresh fruit, vegetables and mounds of herbs from the Psiloritis – some you buy for their medicinal properties, some to flavor food, and others to use as aphrodisiacs – aromatic erontas, thyme, oregano, basil and chamomile fill the air with their heady scent. This is the atomosphere of Crete, whether approaching the port of Iraklion, looking at the White Mountains that rise all around Hania or making one's way along the winding roads of gentle Rethimnon. At the end of a long day of exploration, which has included an exhilarating excursion in the Malaxa Mountains for an aerial view of Souda Bay, sip *tsikoudia*, the pure Cretan raki, at the Venetian port of Hania, and eat sea urchin salad or unique *staka*, a distillation of pure butter. It is an unforgettable experience. And when night comes and the

noises of the city subside the lines of Prevelakis come to mind:

"... let me simply pray that you may one day drop anchor off Rethimnon some summer evening at the hour when the sea is sweet-scented as a water melon and the women are anointing their hair with oil of jasmine and coming down for a stroll along the quay. Then rest your elbows on the gunwale and gaze form afar at the magical city, which will itself be looking at you through thousands of eyes and will make its waters a mirror to the lights streaming from your boat and will wink back at you from its own innumerable little lamps ..."

But these hours of peace and romantic introspection are rather rare in the island these days. Tourism has arrived in Crete – somewhat late, but in full force – in the last fifteen years. Roads have been built, innumerable hotels and pensions have sprung up in every corner of the island, package tours have been promoted, and hordes of Germans, Swedes, Italians und British have descended on the island. The Venetian Morosini Fountain, in the center of Iraklion, is surrounded by hundreds of mopeds whose owners drink espresso while asking for the traditional *bouyatsa* at Kir Kor's "modernized" cafe. Music pours out of tavernas but it is seldom the traditional *mandinada* anymore. To see the wild *pentozali* dance one has to be invited to a Cretan wedding since it is seldom performed in public places anymore. Cretan baggy pants and high-knee boots have been exchanged for "Athenian finery". *Tsikoudia* is being offered to the tourists while the local population prefers its whisky straight. Does this mean the end of tradition in Crete? Let us hope not.

Behind all this façade, a brisk export trade of tomatoes, grapes, raisins (the major crop of the island), olive oil and flowers, keeps the economy of the island strong. The ferry-boats that continuously work the lanes between the ports of Crete and mainland Greece (and Italy on occasion), carry not only full loads of passenger cars but heavy multiwheeled intercontinental trucks – many refrigerated

– that reach all the major cities of Europe. There is an infrastructure that supports all this agricultural production and trade; machine shops, repair shops for cars, trucks, buses, tractors and ploughs, plastic pipe factories, the ubiquitous noisy and sputtering motorcycles; and there is a work force with greasy clothes, hands and faces, that struggle for their daily bread. The demand for scarce agricultural labor remains high and during the olive gathering or grape picking seasons one can find many tourists and foreigners for hire in the market.

The resulting traffic congestion, pollution and population pressure in the cities makes life difficult. The resources of the island (fresh water, game, beaches, forests) are under extreme pressure by the increased industrial, tourist, recreation, and agricultural demands. The ecology of the island is seriously threatened by over-hunting, pesticides, fertilizers, herbicides (especially those used to combat cane brush), disposal of factory wastes from olive presses into scarce and valuable streams, and lowering of the water table by irrigation. The introduction of mechanical rotary cultivators and small diesel driven water pumps has permitted the cultivation of otherwise useless land on hills. Sadly, the construction work involved in building the new roads to reach remote villages and fresh pastureland has left ugly scars on the virgin landscape. This development has enormously increased the cultivated acreage of grapes, adding to the problems created by monoculture and the subsidies required to support it. It is said that the population of noisy cicadas has increased because of the overhunting of birds.

But the pressure to survive on the local farmers is so intense that these problems seem non-threatening for the moment and the state is powerless to enforce

badly needed environmental measures. But, high up on the rugged mountains, in remote beaches and villages off the beaten path, there is still magic. Whether one sits on a deserted beach as the fishermen bring in their catch of the day or, in a quiet corner of a monastery listening to the evening chants of the esperinós, heavy scents come to you of orange, almond and lemon, mixed with the odors of olive oil and garlic, the cicadas sing on into the dusk – wild and uncontrollable like the Curetes' cymbals in the cave of Zeus – not to hide the cries of a baby god, but to signal the presence of an island that has produced and nourished rough mountaineers, gentle poets and shrewd merchants – brave people who fought and suffered to keep their freedom, individuality and love of life.

Five thousand years ago, Crete created the first maritime empire of the world. Today, it is only a province of a developing country, with all its problems. However, due to its place in the Mediterranean world, its people and its history, it has not ceased playing an important role in the world. As the main US military base in the eastern Mediterranean Crete has found a strange destiny, which it shares with the other large islands of the Mediterranean – Cyprus, Rhodes, Sicily.

"A precarious, a restricted, a menaced life, such is the common fate of these islands. Their private life, if you will. But their outside life, the role that they played in the foreground of the stage of history is of an importance which one would not have expected from such miserable worlds. History in the large – the so-called grande histoire – washes the shores of these islands. You could say that it abuses them... Those islands on the path of powerful maritime routes are inevitably linked to the history of the Great Powers. Thus, an aspect of the grande histoire will always superimpose itself on their daily existence." (Fernand Braudel, *The Mediterranean*)

Right: This Cretan villager surely has a great deal to tell.

HANIA

HANIA CITY

AKROTIRI

SAMARIA GORGE

SPHAKIA / GAVDOS

SOUGIA / PALAEOHORA

KASTELLI KISSAMOS

GRAMVOUSA

WEST COAST

The westernmost part of Crete is dramatically isolated from the central and eastern part of the island by the massive ridge of the **Lefka Ori** or **White Mountains** which, for most of the winter months, are covered with snow and all but inaccessible. On the southern side of the island this ridge drops precipitously into the sea making a great barrier with few, if any harbors. One part of this ridge runs to the nothern sea coast at **Kalami** where the modern national highway cuts slightly inland. The older highway can still be followed, and affords the opportunity to visit many small and interesting villages.

The nothern coast is marked by three great promontories jutting out into the sea. One of them, **Akrotiri**, forms the nothern side of the great **Bay of Souda,** the largest natural harbor in the Mediterranean. The other two, uninhabited and desolate, form the **Gulfs of Kissamos** and **Hania**. Between the nothern and southern shores run a number of valleys and ravines that link the two coasts and are occasionally quite forbidding. It is not surprising that the *kri-kri*, or Cretan ibex, the animal symbol of the independent and stubborn character of the Cretan

Preceding pages: Goats. A dialogue. Venetian port in Hania. Left: In a cafenion.

people, has taken its last refuge in these isolated regions of the island.

Despite all the formidable mountains Hania is comparatively rich agriculturally. Apart from winter rains there is an abundance of springs. The valleys are carpeted with great groves of orange, lemon and grapefruit and in the more mountainous areas these groves give way to walnut trees. Olive groves are found und everywhere and many different varieties are grown. Hania's vineyards are excellent, and the cheeses of this region are duly famous.

To a certain degree, the Prefecture of Hania is less well known to tourists as there are comparably few Minoan ruins and even fewer well-ecxavated sites. Some sites have been identified with famous ancient cities of considerable reknown such as **Aptera**, **Pergamon** (Platanias), the city mentioned in the Aeniad as having been founded by the Trojans after the fall of Troy, or **Diktyna** on the **Rodopou Peninsula**. Many of the ruins are spread out over fields and valleys and afford good opportunities for hikes into the countryside and surrounding mountains. There is a reliable public transportation system that makes most of the sites accessible but by far the best manner of travel is by renting a car or motorbike.

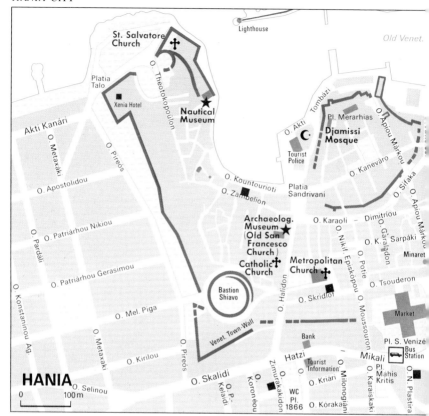

Hania City

There is something magical about **Hania** quite apart from its minarets, Venetian palazzi, and the narrow streets of the old town. It is full of extremes and contradictions. Its dramatic backdrop of mountains face out towards the vast Cretan Sea. Its climate is determined by hot winds rising from Africa that are confronted by less temperate winds from the north. These extremes have had an effect on the volatile character of Haniotes. In the winter Hania is decidedly Gothic, an ambience that gives way to a sensually sun-drenched atmosphere in the summer. In antiquity Hania was known as Kydonia and extensive Minoan remains have been found on **Kastelli**, which was then, and was to remain until well into the Middle Ages, the acropolis. During the Roman period Kydonia was, along with Knossos and Gortyna, a major administrative city. It remained so until the Arab conquest of the island in 828, when it was initially sacked and then reconstructed and renamed al-Hannim, from which Hania was derived after the Byzantines retook the city. Little if anything remains from these centuries to indicate the importance of Hania.

In the late thirteenth century the Venetians took Hania and under them it became the administrative center for the west of the island. The acropolis, now known as the Kastelli, was heavily for-

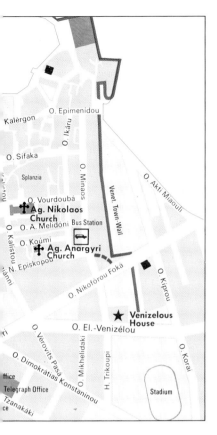

The Cretan revolts against Ottoman rule in the nineteenth century culminated first in the independance of Crete and then in its absorption by Greece in 1913. Since then further dramatic changes have affected Hania. The great Venetian walls that circumscribed the old town, were, for the most part, torn down and Hania began to expand in every direction so that today it is a sprawling urban complex and the center of economic life for the western part of Crete. In World War II it suffered severe bombing and the old town was heavily straffed for several days prior to the Nazi occupation. The Kastelli, with its pallazzi and the memories of centuries, if not millenia, has remained almost a ruin since then. Despite this old Hania still evokes the past and its twisting lanes and winding backstreets, dominated by Ottoman lattices and Venetian frontages, have seduced more than one visitor with their magical aura.

Getting Around

Quite apart from its many neighborhoods Hania is really two towns: the old and the new. The old town also has two parts: one older and one comparatively newer, and is built around and behind two harbors: the inner and the outer. Since visitors coming to Hania inevitably reach the new town first it is probably best to orient oneself from there. New Hania has as its center an enormous cruciform-shaped **market** that was erected after the union of Crete with Greece in 1913.

In the early hours of the morning, huge quantities of meat, poultry, fish, vegetables, fruit and cheeses are piled up ready for sale. It is the perfect place to get a sense of the busy and volatile Haniote and its little shops are stocked with spices, herbs, great jars of honey and pickled vegetables. It is a wonderful place to browse.

Until late in the nineteenth century to the east of the market there was a per-

tified and a working harbor was constructed with arsenals and administrative offices. After the daring sea attacks of the Ottoman corsair Barbarossa in the sixteenth century Hania was completely rebuilt and expanded. A new, or outer harbor was built and great walls marked the new limits of the town which held out until its final conquest by the Ottomans in the early seventeenth century. The Turks loved Hania and quickly transformed what must have been lively noisy quarters into quiet lanes dotted with fountains and centered on neighborhood mosques. The old Venetian palazzi were soon renovated to provide the quiet solitude of the harems and gardens for which Hania was so well known.

manent encampment of Bengazi Arabs who, for some obscure reason, had been exiled to Crete. Old prints of this encampment show its palm trees and tents in between which are tethered camels and goats. The old market (this was a commercial center even before the present building was put up) also had large numbers of Abyssinian *hamals* or porters and the minaret of their mosque can still be seen slightly east and to the south of the present market. Off the square in front of the market runs **Tsanakaki Street** on which the post office and telephone service are located and slightly farther on are the gardens and zoo. There is an old-style coffee shop here as well as an open air cinema: a favourite spot for families until late in the evenings during the summer and fall.

To reach the old town the most convenient approach is to walk down **Hali-**

Above: Folkloric wares and chess games. Right: Restaurants and cafés in the Venetian port.

don Street on which is located the **Metropolitan Church** of Hania built in the late nineteenth century by a Muslim as a votive offering to the Virgin Mary after the cure of his son due to her intercession. Behind the cathedral and to the right sprawls a section of Hania that was put up shortly after World War II after the old houses that crowded against the city wall that cut across Halidon Street were razed through the ill-directed energies of a local mayor. To get an idea of the old character of the town in this area one should wander through the narrow streets to the left of the **cathedral** and behind Halidon Street to the east. Elegant Venetian facades still stand as well as the defaced stone surfaces marking wall fountains that almost inevitably indicate the proximity of a neighborhood mosque.

Directly across from the cathedral and down a small alleyway, is the **Catholic Church** of the Capuchins and not far from it, also on Halidon Street, stands the **Archaeological Museum** of Hania which is housed in what was formaly the **Mosque of Yusuf Pasha** and prior to that the Venetian church of **St. Francis**. The museum is small but well worth a visit as it contains sarcophagi, pottery and other artifacts dating from Minoan down to Late Roman times, all from the Prefecture of Hania. The building itself is exquisite and adjacent to it is a small garden filled with interesting fragments as well as an old fountain dating from the Ottoman period. Almost directly across from the Museum is a small **Turkish bath** that is now being used as a foundry.

Halidon Street opens out into the harbor area. To the right rises the **Kastelli**, the oldest part of the old town, and to the left is the newer part, mostly built up in the sixteenth century. The Kastelli can be reached by walking up **Kanevarou Street** to the right of the square. Another approach is from **Karoli-Dimitirou Street** – also to the right. The latter approach skirts some of the oldest walls of

the citadel. Embedded in them can still be seen the columns and rubble of 3000 years that were incorporated into their fabric. Once on the Kastelli there is little to see today other than the ravages of the last world war but some of the cleared areas contain the foundations of Minoan houses and pavings that reveal Hania's most ancient past.

Continuing along this street will lead one into a quite different quarter known as the **Splantzia** or **Chiones** as well as the Koum Kapi. Rising above it is the single minaret of the old **Mosque of Ibrahim Sultan** which is now once again (as it had been before the Ottoman period) the church of **St. Nicholas**. At the entrance to its square is the small, elegant, and derelict fifteenth century church of **San Rocco**.

The Splantzia is a fascinating place to wander through, with many tiny streets and cul de sacs. From here almost any street to the north will take you down to the inner Venetian **working harbor**. All along it are the **arsenals** and worksheds

built by the Venetians, and central to them is the still majestic façade of the **rector's palace**. At its western end the harbor opens up into the outer harbor and the newer part of the old town.

The **outer harbor** has a wonderful frontage of Veneto-Ottoman houses and shops marking its entire course. It is a beehive of activity in the evenings and certainly the touristic nerve center of Hania. In some ways this is unfortunate as it means that it has lost its natural life. Houses have been converted into pensions, hotels, bars and discos that make it noisy and quite unlike the quarter that had a unique life of its own until very recent times. This part of Hania, behind the harbor front, is still known to many as the **Colombo** and there are still a few Haniotes who speak a dialect that was peculiar to this part of the city. It has two landmarks: the old **Mosque of Hassan Pasha** with its great bulbous dome, and the **Pharos**, or lighthouse. The mosque was built in the substructure of the old Venetian "dogana" or customs house and

59

until very recent times a small cemetery linked it to the adjacent building. This now houses a hotel as well as some restaurants, but was once a local *medresse,* or school where Muslim children studied the Quran. It functioned as late as 1900. The other landmark, the Pharos, marks the end of the protective mole. Renovated by Ali Pasha in the mid-nineteenth century, it is built on old Venetian foundations. A walk out to the Pharos early in the morning provides one with a spectacular view of the old town bathed in limpid colors, backed by the majesty of the White Mountains.

The Colombo was once divided into two main quarters: the **Ovraiki** and the **Top Hana** – both of which had different names during the Venetian period. The Ovraiki is the first of these quarters and its limits are marked by the **Halidon**, **Zabeliou** and **Kondylakis Streets**. This

Above: The Turkish lighthouse on the Hania pier. Right: The Katholiko Monastery near Gouverneto.

was the old Jewish quarter of Hania in medieval times and the old synagogue of Etz Hayyim, formerly the Venetian fifteenth century Church of **St. Catherine**, can be seen on Parados Kondylaki.

Past the Ovraiki is the Top Hana which was the principal Muslim quarter until the nineteenth century, and before that an elegant Venetian neighborhood as can still be seen from the fronts and high structures that mark the narrow streets. On Zabeliou Street an old *hamam*, or **Turkish bath** marks one corner and a short distance from it, to the east, is a corner house with a base for a minaret and nearby fountain that indicates its former life as a neighborhood mosque. As in the case of many places of worship in Crete it was, prior to its conversion to Islam, a Venetian chapel.

At the end of the outer harbor, facing the lighthouse, is the **Firka**, an old Ottoman fortress that was built into the ruins of the Venetian bastion. It is now the **Naval Museum** and in the spring and summer months occasional concerts of

Cretan music, dancing and theatrical performances are given in an outdoor theater.

If one continues along the sea front, the Venetian bastion to the left marks the end of the sea wall. Rising above the sea is the **Xenia Hotel**, built on the uppermost part of the fortification. The street that cuts between these two sections of the old fortifications is known as Theotoko-poulou (El Greco) and just to the left of the entrance it is the old Venetian church of **St. Salvadore**.

It is in the process of being restored and has a fine Venetian interior with delicately groined arches as well as a small arched recess that, according to its Latin inscription, is dedicated to an image of the Virgin Mary. The floor is set with stone slabs that covered the burial places of Venetian notables.

During Ottoman times the building was converted into a mosque and its *mihrab*, pointing to Mecca, is still in situ. In the course of the restoration an earlier, and most likely Byzantine apse was found imbedded in the later Venetian additions.

A walk up Theotokopoulou street leads one into an old **Veneto-Turkish quarter**. One of the more interesting houses is the wooden structure just to the left on entering the street. Though not very old (mid-nineteenth century) it is a very good example of the type of Ottoman house that characterized certain parts of the old town of Hania but has been, for the most part, either razed or destroyed by fire.

The road that continues past the front of the bastion supporting the Xenia Hotel continues along the sea front to **Nea Hora**. Here are found some of Hania's finest fish restaurants as well as a small beach that attracts locals as well as considerable numbers of tourists in the summer months. Directly across from the beach is the island of **Agii Theodori** which is today a nature reserve on which the Cretan ibex is allowed to live.

Akrotiri Peninsula

(Unless otherwise stated all distances are calculated from Hania.)

The promontory of **Akrotiri** can be seen from Hania and is easily reached by following the road marked for the airport or the village of **Kounoupediana** (6 km). At the left turn into Akrotiri a signpost marks the way to the **tomb of Eleftherios Venizelos**, the great statesman of modern Crete and Greece. From here there is a magnificent view west over Hania and along the entire coast.

Akrotiri is currently being developed and there are fine tourist facilities and a very good beach at **Kalathas** and farther on at **Stavros** both of which are on the western side of the peninsula. If you continue straight on at the Venizelos turn-off, the road leads directly to the airport, skirting **Souda Bay**. An interesting diversion can be taken to **Sternes** which is a very old village. Just after entering, to the right, is a large Venetian country house, now in ruins, and adjacent to it the sub-

AKROTIRI PENINSULA

0 2 4 6 km

structure of a Byzantine church dating from the sixth century.

The airport turning, just before Sternes to the left, passes an abandoned Venetian monastery of the fifteenth century and then continues on to the Greek Orthodox monastery of **Agia Triada** (16.5 km) which has a very fine church of the seventeenth century. Beyond it, to the north, the road leads to the **Gouverneto Monastery** the church of which is small and has an elegant Venetian renaissance façade (20.5 km).

After Gouverneto a short walk leads to the cave of the **Panagia Arkouditissa**, or the Bear Virgin which, while dedicated under this name to the Virgin Mary, has revealed artifacts indicating that it was once dedicated to the bear goddess Artemis. Not far from this cave is another cave that was used by a famous Cretan saint, St. John the Hermit.

Right: A monk sounding the vespers at Agia Triada Monastery.

Omalos Plateau

The journey to the **Plain of Omalos**, high in the White Mountains, is best made by car. It should be kept in mind that a later excursion to the Samaria Gorge necessitates passing through the same terrain but the return, once through the gorge, is via the sea and alternative routes from either Hora Sphakion or Palaeohora. Thus, to see the gorge as well it will be best to join one of the tours, take local transportation, or hire a taxi.

The road for Omalos (39 km) leaves Hania to the west and ascends through rich fertile countryside. A stop should be made at **Alikianos** where there is a finely frescoed church of the fourteenth century – **Agios Georgios** –, as well as the remains of an old Venetian country manor that belonged to the Damolino family. Not far from this village is **Fournes**, where a left turn will take you on a short trip to **Meskla**, on a road that winds through orange groves. In this village there are two small fourteenth-century churches that are among the most important in Crete – the **Transfiguration** and the **Church of the Saviour**. Both have wall paintings of the same period.

Returning to Fournes, continue on to **Lakki** which is worth a stop if only to take in the breathtaking views of the White Mountains. It is also the last petrol stop. After leaving Lakki the ascent leads through increasingly wild, stark, and barren mountain country until the Plain of Omalos is reached. For centuries the plain and its produce fed the lower villages and the surrounding mountains provided rough grazing for herds of goats. In the last century it was here that the initial stages of the Cretan rebellion against the Ottomans began and one of the great leaders, Hatzimichaeli Gianari, rests in a small tomb on the hill of **Agios Panteleimon**. (To reach the entrance to the Gorge of Samarias one continues on the Omalos road marked for **Xyloskala**.)

The Omalos Plateau has an eerily deserted atmosphere; for most of the year it has few inhabitants. When the tourist throng heads towards the Samaria Gorge in the summer, shepherds and the few farmers move to the overhead plateau.

At an altitude of 1080 m, Omalos is surrounded by a formidable granite mountainwall. It is snow-covered in the winter, marshy in the spring melt and refreshingly cool on summer evenings.

The tiny hamlet of **Omalos**, the only settlement on the plateau, has a restaurant and a few rooms to rent. It could serve as a base for travelers who want to take their time exploring the gorge, as camping inside the park is now forbidden, or for those who want to walk the plateau. It has a wide variety of wild flowers, many rare, endangered species of birds of prey and *kri-kri* on neighboring slopes.

This wild area in the heart of the White Mountains is a paradise for hikers and nature lovers.

Serious hikers should get information from the Greek Mountain Club (EOS). It

operates the **Kallergi Hut**, a one-and-a-half hour walk from Omalos at the base of the peaks. A caretaker rents beds and serves meals, as well as giving information about climbing the peaks in winter and slopes suitable for advanced skiers.

Pahnes, at 2453 m just shorter than Mount Psiloritis, is a two-day hike from the Kallergi Hut. **Mount Gingilos**, beginning at the top of Samaria Gorge, is lower than Pahnes but its near vertical slope makes it more formidable. Its path is marked sporadically with orange paint and it is best to stick to it, for peculiar rock formations and powerful winds make it hazardous. The payoff for those who do conquer it is a splendid panoramic view, perfect for observing larger birds of prey or *kri-kri* who have taken refuge on upper levels to escape the crowds walking the Samaria Gorge.

Samaria Gorge

Hikers should probably receive badges at the end of their trek through the

Samaria Gorge which say "I can't believe I walked the whole thing!" Every evening in the tavernas and bars of Hania, conversation between people of all ages and countries, most rubbing their shins and thighs, consists of anecdotes about their different experiences along the 18-km route of the longest gorge in Europe.

The walk through the Samaria Gorge can be one of life's more awesome experiences, a journey to what looks and feels like the veritable navel of the huge island of Crete. To enjoy it fully, wear sturdy, waterproof walking boots and carry only light provisions, binoculars and water. Allow at least six hours to walk and explore the gorge and its environs. Severe leg strain and accidents occur most often when people are rushing down the steep path at the beginning of the walk from Omalos.

Take the early morning bus from Hania or wherever one has stayed overnight so that the walk from Omalos is begun by at least eight o'clock. This allows enough time to have a refreshing swim, take photographs or sunbathe on a rock and still get back in plenty of time to be sure of catching the last boat from Agia Roumeli at the end of the day's hike. It is a tiring day, but the spectacular scenery makes it all worth while. The gorge is a huge ravine caused by the erosion by surface water. A light jacket or pullover will protect against the morning chill, although you will probably be carrying it by the time you reach the bottom in the hotter months.

The descent begins on the "xiloskala", wooden steps once made of logs, a dizzying walk that carries you down a 1000-m plunge in the first couple of kilometers. Nevertheless, it is a safe walk on a wide path that has a hand railing. During the summer, as many as several thousand people a day cross the gorge. The hectic

stampede down this first section may not seem conducive to a spiritual atmosphere but the hordes will spread out over the length of the track.

Agios Nikolaos is a whitewashed chapel which sits in a clearing between massive cypress trees, about 2 km after the beginning of the trail. In this area, there is a terrace of coniferous trees. Herbs such as sage, thyme and Cretan dittany as well as wild orchids, irises and peonies are found here but some of these are rare species, so look but don't pick. Numerous lizards and occasional snakes glide in the undergrowth. The Cretan ibex or *kri-kri* is too elusive to be seen – sometimes the bearded vulture can be seen soaring overhead.

Shortly before the 7-km marker stands the deserted village of **Samaria**, reached via a bridge crossing a stream. You should note that each marker gives the distance between it and the next marker. When one reaches the 0 marker, there are still a couple of kilometers before the end of the trail.

Left: The Samaria stream pushing its way through the "ron Gate" of the gorge.

The village of Samaria, slowly eroding with time, was inhabited by the Viglis family, descendants of one of the 12 aristocratic Byzantine clans. The residents were all relocated in 1962 when the area was offically made a park. The church of **Ossia Maria**, named for a converted Egyptian courtesan, was founded in the late twelfth century. The Venetians called this church the "San Maria", which was corrupted to become "Samaria", also the name of the gorge.

The most interesting artifact in the chapel, now on Mount Athos, was an icon showing Ossia Maria brandishing a claw-hammer in order to slay a terrifying beast in the Samaria Gorge. The dragon's lair was probably on Mount Gingilos, the other imposing peak north of **Mount Volakias**. The mountain has a sinister reputation in local folklore, and is said to

Above: View of the so-called Xiloskala steps above the gorge of Samaria. Right: Shrine in the White Mountains above the gorge of Samaria.

be the abode of Satan, and of various demons, including vampires.

After this point, the cliff faces become higher and the rocks crossing the stream closer together. Just before the "Sideroportes", the famed "Iron Gates", sits the little church of **Aphendis Christos**, built as a shrine by Sphakiote mountaineers. The Sphakians proudly state that in two and a half centuries of Turkish rule in Crete, they never got past the Iron Gates into the gorge. One such attempt by the Ottomans was crushed by 200 Sphakian soldiers under the leadership of Yannis Bonatos during the 1770 rebellion led by Dhaskaloyiannis.

The highlight for many walkers is the passage through the "**Iron Gates**", where the sheer rock walls rise on either side to just less than 300 m. The path has disappeared under the wildly swirling water of the stream and the two walls are only 2.5 m apart at the narrowest point. Looking up, the feeling is of being in an abyss, with only the far-off rays of the sun faintly glinting far, far above.

After the narrowest of the "Iron Gates", the path emerges into a broader valley and gentler landscape covered with olive trees, pines, oaks and platenos. Past this is the now-deserted old village of **Agia Roumeli**, whose residents were also displaced when the park was opened in 1962. Near this site is a ruined Turkish fortress and a Venetian church. The church is reported to have been built on an ancient temple to Apollo belonging to the city of Tarrha. Tarrha has had excavations which show that it was inhabited from the fifth century BC until about the fifth century AD. During the Hellenistic period, it banded together with half a dozen cities on the southern shore to form the Confederation of Oreioi. The temple of Apollo must have been one of the most important shrines of the ancient Cydonians, the predecessors of the modern Sphakians.

After this point, it is a short walk to today's **Agia Roumeli**, where there is some accomodation, a few tavernas, and facilities for swimming in the Libyan Sea. It is from here that a return to Hania can be made by small motor-boats that ply between Agia Roumeli and Palaeohora via Sougia, to the west, or Sphakia to the east. From both of these ports one can return to Hania via motor coach. Itineraries vary during the year and can easily be checked on in Hania.

Sphakia and the Askyphou Plain

Hora Sphakion and its forbidding mountainous terrain have an almost mythical quality about them. It has been claimed that no one has ever conquered this region of Crete nor its fierce inhabitants. This may be questionable but is quite believable as one enters the passes that climb up to Askyphou. The port was quite important until the last century, as ships docked there from North Africa and Egypt, bringing goods that were carried by donkey and camel caravans up to the markets of Hania and Rethimnon. If you have reached Hora Sphakion by boat after passing through the gorge you have

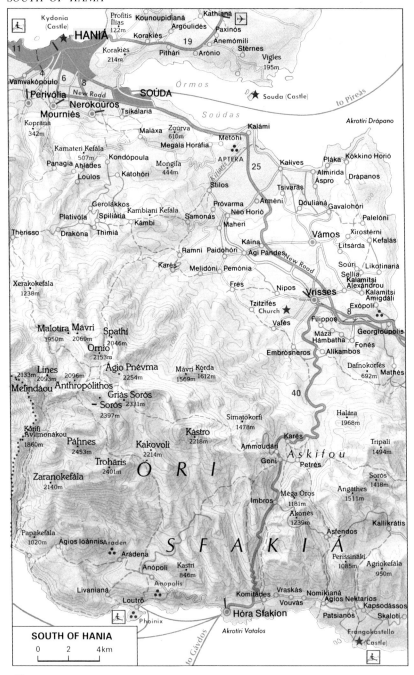

SOUTH OF HANIA

0   2   4km

no alternative but to take a coach back to Hania. This obviates the possibility of exploring the countryside and villages at leisure, and on foot. By far the best way to see Sphakia and the Askyphou Plain is to rent a car or motorbike from Hania.

Take the road from Hania marked for either Souda or Rethimnon to the east. Just before reaching Souda (6.5 km) you can choose to take either the old highway that goes through Souda or go on the new national highway which bypasses it.

The Venetian fortress on the **Islet of Souda** in the Bay of Souda was built in the late 1500s but didn't fall to the Turks until 1715. It played an important role during World War II, first in the evacuation of the Allied Forces in 1941 and later in supplying the troops during preparations for the Battle of Crete. The village of **Souda** and its harbor area is the main port of Hania as well as an important naval base and photography is forbidden for security reasons. The village is of little, if any, interest and can easily be skipped.

Shortly after passing Souda the road begins to skirt the flank of a large promontory. In order to ascend the promontory for a breathtaking view out over the Bay of Souda and Akrotiri take the right turning marked for **Aptera**. The site of ancient Aptera is sometimes called Paleokastro after the huge Venetian fortress which dominates it today. Scattered in every direction around it are the ruins of the city which was founded in the fifth century BC. Dominating as it did the entrance to the Bay of Souda it was important during Roman and Byzantine times until its destruction during the Arab conquest of Crete in 828 AD. From Aptera access to the old highway can be gained by taking the route marked for **Stilos** or **Agii Pantes** and then on to Vrysses.

Alternatively you can take the route down to the national highway on the coast. Shortly after getting onto this road two other routes to Vrysses (and on to

Sphakia) are feasible. The old road with access to fine beaches and tourist facilities is that marked for **Kalami/Kalives** to the left. Otherwise the main national highway can be followed and at the sign for Vrysses a right turn should be taken. The drive along the new highway from Kalami to Vrysses passes the **Drapano** promontory which has several interesting villages and at **Georgioupolis** (38 km) follows the coast to Rethimnon. There are tourist facilities as well as access to a fine beach. Should you be interested in fresh water swimming, shortly after passing Georgioupolis there is a sign marked for Kournas to the right.

Lake Kournas is reached after a short drive (4 km). This is the largest fresh water lake in Crete and the water is quite refreshingly cool even in the mid-summer months. There are restaurant facilities and opportunities for quiet walks in the vicinity of the lake. After this diversion return to the Vrysses turn-off and drive on to the village of that name. In the summer **Vrysses** is a refreshing place to stop and rest, as it is surrounded by great plane trees and watered by many springs. There are some good cafes and tavernas, selling local specialities, one of which is yoghurt and honey.

Out of Vrysses continue on the main road. Shortly after leaving the village the road divides. The road that continues on is marked for Sphakia and to the right it is marked for **Embroseneros**. This village is in itself of little interest other than for the castle of "Ibrahim Alidakis", a local Muslim who was active in the defence of the area against Christians during one of the rebellions in the nineteenth century. The drive to it, however, is very beautiful and if continued to its terminus provides many opportunities for hikes into the foothills of the mountains of Sphakia.

Having taken this diversion, return to the road marked for Sphakia. From this point the terrain begins to change quite dramatically as one ascends up to the

Askyphou Plain through the Katre Ravine to Kares. Side roads, marked for **Maza** and **Alikambos**, lead to small villages with Byzantine churches, both painted in the interior by the fourteenth-century Cretan painter Ioannis Pagomenos. The church in Alikambos is dated to 1323, that in Maza was painted two years later. Pagomenos is somewhat of a rarity in Byzantine art as he signed his paintings and consequently it is possible to follow not only his development as a painter, but also his travels, as several churches in the region of Kandanos are signed by him. He had a highly personal style and, as he was a native Cretan, it is through him that we obtain an insight into a still relatively unknown school of painting that developed on the island under strong influences from Asia Minor and the monastic in painting, rooted in Cappadocia.

Above: The coast at Hora Sphakion. Right: The old donkey path from Anopolis to Aradena.

Returning to the main Sphakia road, the route ascends sharply through rugged mountain country to the **Askyphou Plain** and the towns of **Kares** and **Goni**. If there is time to stop, these villages are worth visiting, as they have good examples of local architecture and there are also some good tavernas. From the Askyphou Plain it is also possible to climb up to **Mount Kastro**.

In the winter months the green lush valley gives way to snow and this is a favorite outing for Haniotes. On leaving **Goni** the road begins a sharp and tortuous descent along the **Imbros gorge**, one of the most dramatic drives in Crete, cutting through the heart of the Sphakia region. The road terminates at **Hora Sphakion** on the Libyan Sea. The village is usually bustling with arrivals from the Samarian Gorge waiting to take coaches back to Hania. There is some accommodation of a modest nature and several good tavernas. Out of Hora Sphakion to the west there is a small road that leads to the ancient sites of **Phoeniki** and **Loutro**, its port. According to tradition it was here that St. Paul was shipwrecked. Further inland and accessible by tracks are sites of other ancient cities that were destroyed in the nineteenth century AD and in many of the villages there are quite fine Byzantine churches.

A good road leads from Hora Sphakion to **Anopolis**, where there is the Church of the Transfiguration. From here a rough road leads to **Aradena**, with the church of St. Michael, dated to the early Byzantine period. Farther on from Aradena is the village of **Agios Ioannis**, built high above the Libyan Sea and backed dramatically by the Sphakiote Mountains. In the vicinity of the village are several important caves, one of which, called Drakolaki or the Dragon, is said to be inhabited by Neraidis even to this day.

To the east of Hora Sphakion the road leads to **Komitades**, a village known for being the meeting place of Sphakiote revolutionaries in the nineteenth century. Beyond Komitades the road leads into the Prefecture of Rethimnon. The return to the nothern coast can be made from this direction via Plakias and Rethimnon. The shorter route by far is simply to return to Hania by retracing the route from Hora Sphakion through the Imbros gorge and Askyphou Plain.

Gavdos

Out of Hora Sphakion there is a boat service to the island of Gavdos and its sister island, Gavdopoula, some 40 km off the Cretan coast. Gavdopoula is uninhabited, save for a few shepherds. **Gavdos**, the larger of the two, has a good number of villages and was known in antiquity as Clavda. It was here, according to some, that Calypso seduced Odysseus and held him prisoner in her "vaulted cave" for seven years. This island was a Saracen pirates' nest long into the Middle Ages after Crete had been returned to Byzantine hands.

Gavdos, little more than a barren rock except in its interior which is covered in dwarf pines and herbal brush, is the home of about 35 year-round residents, most of them fishermen or shepherds. A few families spend the summer in Gavdos but return to Crete in the fall because employment is scarce. Emigrants have formed the community Gavdiotika in Palaeohora.

Daytrips are possible on the boat from Palaeohora or Hora Sphakion during the tourist season. The boat trip takes about two hours. Those who want to stay overnight on the islet can book a room through Brown's Travel in Palaeohora or can look for one in the port of arrival, **Karabe**, or in the capital **Kastri**, reached on foot in about an hour from Karabe, or in other small settlements. 90 percent of the overnight guests are Greek.

Gavdos was probably inhabited as early as Neolithic times, though the first permanent settlement dates from the post-Mycenaean era. **Kaudos** was the name the Romans gave to Gavdos and

71

GAVDOS

0   2 km

this is the name of the islet which St. Paul blew past during a storm which eventually shipwrecked him in Malta. During Byzantine times, Gavdos had a population of almost 8000, and was the seat of a bishopric, which probably included the villages of Sphakia. It was abandoned during the later Byzantine era when pirates used the eastern side of the islet as one of their lairs.

It's hard to imagine that Gavdos was once a thriving island when **Kastri**, its capital, is almost a ghost town with six families remaining. Camping is possible almost everywhere but bring bottled water and basic provisions because these supplies come from the mainland and there are shortages of both.

Activity in Gavdos centers around the beaches during the day and the few tavernas or a campfire at night. The north and east of the island have a low coastline with good beaches at **Potamos** and

Right: Fishing with tried and true means on the south coast.

Sarakiniki in the north and **Korfos** in the east. The south and west coasts are high and rocky.

Gavdos is a good place for lovers of solitude and a simple life style. Temperatures can be oppressively hot during July and August but a gentle evening breeze usually makes the evenings pleasant. The Libyan Sea is warm enough to swim in most of the year and is very clean. Snorkeling and spearfishing are fairly good here because the inhabitants have not dynamited all the fish away, as has happened off the coast of Crete.

Talk has been bandied about for some time about building a hotel and paved roads, but no definite plans have been made for either. The natives of this southernmost part of Europe have felt overlooked in the general improvement plan for Crete. Requests have been made for upgrading of the sanitary facilities, electrical hookups (there is no main generator) and medical care (a doctor is on the island only in the summer).

If Gavdos is still too "civilized" for

your taste, an excursion can be made to the tinier islet of **Gavdopoula**, uninhabited except for a few shepherds and their flocks.

West and South of Hania

If possible, try trips to Omalos, Sougia and Therissos. All provide magnificent views of the mountains and begin by taking the turn-off marked for Omalos/Therrissos just west from Hania.

If there is time, it is worth while to take a left turn marked for **Meskla**, where there is a fine church from the fourteenth century. If you continue on, the road leads up into the mountain foothills through orange groves to **Therissos** and its gorge. By far the best way of making this day trip is to hike, as the countryside and gorge are breathtaking.

West of Hania, the Libyan Sea and southern coast can be reached by three main routes: 1. via Alikianos to Sougia (70 km), 2. via Tavronitis to Palaeohora (74 km) and 3. directly west through

Kastelli-Kissamos (42 km) and then down the western coast of the prefecture to Elaphonissi (57 km). All three trips are more than worth the time and effort as the countryside and terrain passed in each are quite different and striking. They also offer opportunities for some energetic hiking on the surrounding mountainside, swimming, and visits to several ancient sites of importance. Most of the latter have been only partially excavated, if at all, and the remains of theaters and other buildings protrude out of fields and hillsides. There are, as well, a great number of medieval Byzantine churches that are especially prevalent in the region around **Kandanos** (57 km).

From Hania to Sougia

Of the three trips to the south this is certainly the most arduous but also very beautiful. It passes the western flank of the White Mountains and twists and winds down to the sea past several ancient sites that are seldom visited. Take

73

the south-west road from Hania, marked for **Agia** or **Alikianos**. Just before Alikianos there is a small church off a left turn, called **Agios Georgios**, that was decorated and signed in the early fifteenth century by Pavlos Provatos whose work is quite different from that of the earlier painter Pagamenos who also worked in this area.

After leaving Alikianos the road begins to ascend the White Mountains and continues on, passing many small villages until, at **Apopigadi** (1331 m high), it begins its descent to the sea. At **Rodovani** the road cuts to the east and arrives at the ruins of **Elyros** which during Roman and Byzantine times was one of the most important cities in south-western Crete. It was an important bishopric and there are remains of what must have been a fine fifth-century Byzantine church with a floor mosaic. Elyros was destroyed during the Arab conquest of

Above: A Shrine by the wayside. Right: A friendly encounter.

Crete in the early ninth century and never recovered its fortunes, and today it is possible to make out only the remains of its aqueduct, a few remnants from the walls, and a theater. In the village are the remains of basilican church of the sixth century with a fine floor mosaic.

From Elyros the road passes **Moni** in which there is a church dedicated to St. Nicholas with frescoes from the fourteenth century. At Moni the road takes a sharp bend and then descends south to **Sougia** which was the port of Elyros.

There are only few remains from before the period of its destruction in the ninth century. There are also some tavernas, and reasonable places to stay though with limited facilities.

Should you wish to take a short hike, it is possible to walk west along the sea coast road to another ancient sea port at **Agios Kyrkos**. In antiquity it was known as Lyssos, which was the port for Hyrtakina, a city located slightly to the north. While not as famous as Elyros, it was well known for its Asklepion, some of the remains of which have been identified and can be seen today. Of special interest is a section of floor mosaic from the temple to Asklepios.

A further hike northwards will take you to **Prodromi**, which is built on the site of the ancient Hyrtakina. If you are driving, it is possible to return to Rodovani and from there continue on westwardly to **Maza** and **Temenia**. At the junction take the road south to Palaeohora.

From Hania to Palaeohora

The road leading directly west out of Hania skirts the sea as far as the Rodopou Peninsula. The entire coast is in the process of being heavily developed touristically. Many of the accessible beaches are now lined with pensions, hotels and tavernas, though there are still several open and relatively undeveloped beaches near **Kato Stalos** and just after leaving Platanias. One should be wary of strong undertows in the sea. Just beyond Agia Marina on the coast west of Hania, one can see the islet of **Agii Theodori**, which was known in ancient times as Akytos. Legend holds that its craggy form is the distorted head of a prehistoric monster petrified by the gods when it tried to eat the islet.

A cave on the island, dated to 2000 BC, was thought to have been used as a sanctuary, along with one of a slightly later date at Agia Marina, one of the few Minoan sites unexcavated on the main land. Excursion boats from Agia Marina sail around Agii Theodori, now used as a preserve for the ibex, so that one has a chance to see them.

At **Tavronitis**, just before reaching the **Rodopou Peninsula**, there is a major turn-off to the left marked for Palaeohora. This road leads through the region of Selinos down to the Libyan Sea. The main road out of Tavronitis goes on to Kastelli-Kissamos and out of there farther west to unite with a road that follows the western coastline, also down to the Libyan Sea.

This itinerary to the south and Palaeohora runs through the eparchy of **Kydonia** and then into that of **Selinos**, the principal village of which is **Kandanos**. It provides many opportunities for side trips, hiking and visits to some of the many small but important churches that are occasionally not too easy to find – but well worth the effort by the adventurous.

Initially the road out of Tavronitis passes through rich and verdant agricultural land. **Voukolies** is an interesting place to stop and investigate. After the Ottoman conquest of Crete many of the Cretan (and Venetian) families in this region and that of Selinos converted to Islam and the village became an important center for marketing local produce. There are two churches of some interest: St. Constantine (1452) and that of the

Archangel Michael dating from 1392. There are also some Venetian remains including a tower with a spring credited with having curative powers.

After Voukolies a steep ascent begins through the harsh mountains of the region. A worthwhile side trip out of Voukolies leads off toward **Kato Kefala** after which it passes between two ridges. At **Ano Kefala** (just before Platanes) there is a side road to the left that leads to **Sembronas** through terrain being quite magnificent and deserted. Through this region it is possible to feel some of the grandeur and solitude that pockets of Crete still retain. This road, at Sembronas, joins the major road that goes to Sougia from Alikianos.

Should you wish to visit the more isolated and typical villages of this region, the road to **Platanes** (which has a small church dedicated to St. Demetrios, with wall paintings from 1372) can be taken at Ano Kefala. At **Palea Roumata** you can continue on – in circular route – around the valley and, returning to Palea Rou-

mata, take the road marked for Kako-petros, which will get you back on the main route to Kandanos and Palaeohora.

The road to Kandanos from **Kako-petros** passes through typical, but less harsh landscape than that met with in the diversion to Platanes, and begins a sharp ascent at **Floria**, where there are two churches, located in the upper and lower parts of the village. One, that of St. George (in the lower village) dates from 1497 with frescoes painted by Georgios Provatopoulos. The other church, Agion Pateron (in the upper village) has unfor-tunately lost its paintings. The mountain ridge that this road passes over marks a sharp north-south division after which one is in the region of Selinos. After pass-ing the peak, the road begins its descent to the Libyan Sea. This is a compara-tively rich countryside, marked with many small villages out of which one can take fine walks into the hills. Many of these villages give access to more or less isolated churches of great importance, in-terest, diversions and stops throughout this region are well worthwhile.

Kandanos is surrounded by magnifi-cent olive trees with low, writhing, age blackened trunks. Although accommoda-tion is limited and sparse, this is a good place to stay if you wish to hike in the surrounding hills, explore the many small churches dating from the fourteenth to the sixteenth centuries or even to visit the ancient site of Kandanos which is located in the hills above the present village (to the south). Around Kandanos, as far as **Kakodiki** and **Kaniskades**, the villages are more in the nature of compounds and the churches are small and intimate and have not been systematically studied. In Kandanos there are Agios Ioannis and Archangelos Michael – the oldest, and both dated to the early fourteenth century. **Skoudiana** has an especially interesting

church, the Panagia, which is one of the few extant churches in Crete dating to before the Arab Emirate (sixth century).

Kakodiki has several dependent vil-lages in all of which are small churches. **Veidika** has a church painted in the early fourteenth century by Ioannis Pagome-nos (the Panagia) and in **Tzinaliana** is Agios Isidoros which has a magnificent *pantokrator* and decorations reminiscent of Monreale in Sicily, dated to the fif-teenth century. The road south from Kan-danos descends through olive groves and the Libyan Sea can be seen stretching toward Africa.

Palaeohora is located on a small isth-mus – the promontory of which is domi-nated by one of the very earliest Venetian monuments on the island. This fortress, known as **Selino Castle**, has only in re-cent times been abandoned. Palaeohora itself is a pleasant enough village with a good beach and reasonable facilities that are being developed for tourists.

West of Palaeohora there are two possible itineraries that lead one back

Left: This village priest has found a quiet spot. Right: Plain and simply beautiful.

77

into the mountains and valleys of **Selinos** and to some of its most isolated villages. It is not advisable to attempt to reach the most western part of the island from this direction.

Leaving Palaeohora to the west there is a turn-off marked for **Agia Triada** and at **Kondokinigi** it divides. The most interesting villages to visit are those reached by taking the route to **Agios Pavlos** and from there to **Sklavopoula** where several Byzantine churches appear to have been erected not long after Crete was re-taken by the Byzantines in the tenth century. Most of this region of Selinos was settled by Bulgarians, Slavs and Armenians who were brought in to re-populate isolated pockets of the island. Agios Giorgios in Sklavopoula is one of the very early churches with remnants of frescoes dating from the late thirteenth century. At **Voutas** there is another church with fourteenth century frescoes, Agia Paraskevi.

Above: Everyday life in a Cretan village.
Right: The south coast and the Libyan sea.

Returning to the northern coast from Palaeohora it will be necessary to retrace the route north through Kandanos on to Tavronitis.

From Hania to Kastelli-Kissamos

As the most western part of Crete cannot be reached from the south coast, it is necessary to go west and then south along the western coast. This region of Crete is known as **Kissamos** and was named after its principal city. It lies on the coast between two great promontories that jut out into the Cretan Sea to form the Gulf of Kissamos.

The first of these, **Rodopou**, is a mountain ridge that is for the most part uninhabited, except for the village of **Afrata**, near which recent evidence was found of human remains dating back 20,000 years. It is possible, though not recommended, to hike to the tip, where only a few remains of the ancient city of **Diktyna** can be seen. The road is quite pitted and the some 12 km distance that it

covers is barren and of geological interest, but, after the first kilometer or so, quite repetitious and marked by nothing extraordinary. It is perhaps best, should one wish to visit the tip of the promontory, to take a local boat. The **monastery of Gonia**, located not far past **Kolimvari** on the east side of the promontory, is relatively late and most of what remains is from the late seventeenth century. There are a few fine icons in the monastic church, also of this period.

Out of Kolimvari an interesting diversion can be made by taking the road south out of the village leading to **Spilia**. There are several fine churches here. Especially noteworthy is Archangelos Michael which has an ornate carved wooden ikonostasis dating from the sixteenth-seventeenth century.

At **Drakona**, not far from Spilia, there is a very ancient church with decorations from before the Arab Emirate in the ninth century. The nearby village of **Episkopi** got its name as a result of being the residence of the Bishop of Kissamos. The cathedral church of Archangelos Michael is especially interesting in having a rotunda built over the nave in the style that was typical of churches in Crete prior to the ninth century. The area around Episkopi has several villages and sites that have been identified with ancient cities – though remains are scanty and of little interest.

To return to the main highway and Kissamos, the road north can be taken from **Vassilopoulo** to **Nohia** which was apparently a Minoan site. Some scholars have even identified it with Pergamon, the city founded by Aeneas after he fled burning Troy.

Once past the isthmus of Rodopou, the road descends to Kastelli-Kissamos and in the distance can be made out the second promontory, Gramvousa. The town of **Kissamos** was originally the port of an ancient city to the south called Polyrrhenia. During the sixteenth century Kissamos was reconstructed by the Venetians and given a large fortress from which it got the name **Kastelli**. The countryside

79

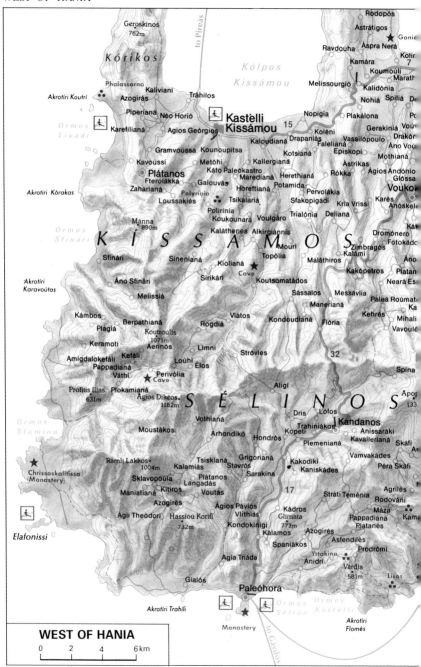

WEST OF HANIA

0   2   4   6 km

Ágii Theódori

around it is very rich and some of Crete's finest wines come from its vineyards. Out of the town, **Polyrrhenia** can be reached by taking the route marked for Palaeokastro on an ascending road. Polyrrhenia itself is a jumble of ruins that range from Ottoman to Venetian and far back into Roman and Dorian times. The site is very beautiful and well worth a trip.

Directly to the west of Kastelli-Kissamos, and reached by a somewhat circuitous route, is the ancient site of **Phalassarna** (59 km). This city was a serious rival to Polyrrhenia in antiquity and while little remains of it today the site dominates a magnificent beach and views of the sea as well as the western coast of the Gramvousa Peninsula. The ruins of the city are found inland today, as this end of Crete was thrust upwards by about 9 m during the sixth century AD as a result of a massive earthquake. It was this, rather than rivalry, that caused the decline of the city.

An interesting sea trip can be made by hiring a boat at **Trahilos**, not far to the west of Kastell-Kissamos, and going round the northern the northern tip of the coast at Gramvousa. Here you can see the massive fortifications of the Venetian castro. There are some beautiful and almost completely isolated beaches along the coastline.

Gramvousa

Gramvousa, a triangular islet north of Phalassarna Beach in the northwest corner of Crete, is attached to the mainland by a series of shoals and reefs. To visit uninhabited Gramvousa and its wilder and larger northern neighbor, **Agria Gramvousa**, hire a caique in Kastelli.

Flat-topped Gramvousa is historically important because the Venetians built an impressive **fortress** on the rocky northwest tip in 1579, after they had conquered Crete. They refused to relinquish

it or their other strongholds at Souda and Spinalonga. Gramvousa fell in 1692, twenty-three years after the surrender of Iraklion, when two Neapolitan commanders sold Gramvousa to a pasha and absconded with the money.

After some years when the islet was deserted, 900 Cretan veterans captured the fortress. They installed refugees there, mainly women and children, who were joined by islanders from Psara and Kasos, driven off by the Turks. Without any source of income, they were forced to turn to piracy. Eventually Capodistria was compelled to intervene and the matter was turned over to the European powers. They restored the islet and the rest of Crete to the Turks who used the islet to blockade boats of Cretan rebels fleeing to the independent island of Antikythera. The high walls of the ruined fortress have a romantic profile, espe-

Above: Cloister steps. Right: The cloister of Chrysoskalitissa in the southwest of the island.

cially when seen in moonlight. The slope up to the fortress is pitted by bullets and shells from the many conflicts, and the characteristic escutcheons of the lion of St. Mark were removed from the walls by the Turks. Families from the nearby mainland often make excursions to the cove on **Cape Tigani**, south of the islet and cross to Gramvousa to fish, for its waters are known for abundant fish and seafood, such as crab.

The West Coast

It is feasible, though the road is less interesting and more difficult, to reach the south-west coast of Crete by taking the road south from **Platanos**. This inland route affords access to the west coast at several points but follows a mountainous ridge. By far the more interesting route is that which runs south out of **Kaloudiana** to the east of Kastelli-Kissamos. This road follows the bed of the Tiphlos river and passes two villages of note: **Voulgaro** and **Topolia** (46 km); in and near

both of which are fine churches still decorated with frescoes. At **Latziana** the church of Agia Varvara was constructed almost entirely from the antique ruins of a temple that once stood there.

Not far from Topolia the road enters the **Koutsomatados Ravine**. Not long after entering it care should be taken to watch for the signs for the **cave of Agia Sophia** which is one of the largest caves on the island. Out of the ravine the road runs on to **Elos**. This village may well have been part of the ancient Inachorium and today is included in what are called the Nine Villages or *Enneahoria* – though there are, in fact, more than nine. The countryside is magnificent and great forests of chestnut trees thrive here. At **Kefali**, one of the nine villages, the road flanks the eastern side of Mount Elias. After reaching **Vathi** it begins to degenerate rapidly and the last few kilometers to the coast are difficult. Both Kefali and Vathi have fine churches and afford rich opportunities for hikes in the nearby hills.

The road reaches the sea at **Ormos Stomiou** and continues south to the Monastery of the Virgin of the Golden Stair – or **Chrysoskalitissa** (57 km). There is a legend that of the ninety steps that lead up to it, one is made of gold, but it has never been discovered as only a person who has never sinned will be able to recognize it.

Past the monastery, the road leads down to the coast at **Elaphonissi**, an island located just offshore that can be reached by wading and swimming from what is certainly one of the most beautiful beaches in Crete, washed by the Libyan Sea and warmed by the winds of Africa.

Offbeat Beaches

Crete is 260 km long; so if you are willing to wander off the beaten track, secluded beaches can be found at any time of the year. Those craving isolation might prefer to visit in the spring or fall. The seas surrounding this southernmost of the

Greek islands are warm enough to swim in from April to October.

Nudism is prohibited on the beaches of Crete except in the specifically designated areas but some of the remote beaches are unofficially allocated for skinny dippers. If bathers are discreet and do not offend other families or conservative islanders, chances are they will not run into trouble.

The **town beach of Hania** is a ten-minute walk west of town and other, better beaches lie in the same direction. A bus goes as far as the sandy beach of **Kalamaki** but it is better to get off before this and go to one of the less populated sandy stretches. Better yet, head to **Akrotiri Peninsula** in the east, dotted with isolated beaches, many within walking distance of ancient monasteries for those who get bored with lying in the sun. In between Kounoupidiana and Stavros, especially in the **Bay of Kalathas**, are

Above: A camper's paradise on the beach of Elaphonissi.

sandy coves that attract more locals than tourists.

Stavros, at the end of the Akrotiri Peninsula, is the locale used in the last scene of *Zorba the Greek* when the Englishman dances with Zorba. The beach is lovely, in a circular bay with a shelving bottom that makes it safe for children. A mountainous mass dominates the far side of the bay. Behind the beach is the **Cave of Lera**, known for its interesting stalactites and said to have been used as a sanctuary as early as 1200 BC until the Hellenistic period.

East of Souda there are fine beaches at **Kalyves** and some kilometers farther on in the idyllic village of **Plaka** which has not yet been inundated with tourists.

One of the thrills of swimming at **Georgioupolis's** gently curving beach, is to wade through the ley streams of bubling fresh water that flow into the sea.

Phalassarna beach near Kastelli Kissamos stretches for many kilometers and is used mainly by campers. It is undeveloped, has some ancient ruins and nice sand, unfortunately marred by an oil slick. If you opt for complete isolation, hike for three hours from the village of **Kaliviani** to the lovely white sand beach opposite the islet of Gramvousa. It's a pity it is also plagued with patches of tar and torn plastic.

Tempting beaches lie below the spectacular cliff off the winding coastal road leading to Palaeohora. The road drops at **Kambos**, making it easier to reach the small beach there, as well as the one at **Sfinari**. The small islet of **Elaphonissi** can be reached by wading from the coast. An idyllic retreat, mellow pink in tone due to coral fragments in the sand and good for snorkeling, the atmosphere can be marred by garbage left by picnickers.

Compared to the northern coast of Crete the southern coast is still less accessible. With the exception of the area around Ierapetra you will not find the kind of big hotels typical of the northern coast. Your compensation for that, however, will be remote and tranquil inlets.

Palaeohora, flanked by Venetian ramparts, has been discovered by younger travelers but the place is still lowkey. The beaches to the east tend to be nicer than the western ones, which are spoiled by plastic greenhouses. To the east, the beaches are often pebbly but more isolated and favored by nudists.

There is also a popular beach at **Sougia** with rooms for rent, some tavernas and even a discotheque.

The beach near (now deserted) **Agia Roumeli** is usually frequented only by hikers trekking through the Samaria Gorge, because otherwise this village is only accessible by boat. The scenic fishing village of **Loutro** is also only accessible by boat. From here a 20-minute walk takes you to the beach of **Phoeniki**. Near **Hora Sphakion** the sea offers crystalline water but is more rewarding to make a side trip to **Frangokastello** with its beach of fine sand, hospitable tavernas and moderately-priced accommodations.

CRETAN WEDDING

Although weddings in Crete in recent years have become less elaborate than they once were, much of the tradition is still maintained. "Thus, for the families involved, the marriage negotiations have the quality of participation in a kind of ritualized contest" (E. Friedl, *Vassilika*, 57 ff.) where boy meets girl, intermediaries get involved, marriage contracts are drawn, courtship and engagement follow, and, finally, the wedding ceremony takes place.

In Crete, in earlier generations, it was possible for a woman and a man never to have seen each other until the first formal occasion for meeting. Most of the times today, though, a young man may have met a girl in a feast *(paniyiri)*, and may have asked his father to look into the financial and social status of her family. In turn, a young girl may have seen a young man at a local festival and may have asked her family to investigate the situation. But neither of the two young people is supposed to know anything about the negotiations between their families. Secrecy is important since the families do not believe they can get accurate information if the villagers know they have an interest in the matter.

Once information is at hand, the father of the would-be groom or bride sends three to four well-respected members of the community as intermediaries, to start the negotiations *(proxenia)*. Sometimes, these intermediaries *(proxenitades)* use socks of different colors as a sort of sign for their intentions without openly declaring them from the outset. At times, they also wear their cloths upside down for good luck!

After the first pleasantries, the aim of the visit is stated and the group gets down to serious business, exploring the amount of dowry the family is willing to give. In transmitting later the information to the interest parties, both the size of the dowry

and the qualities of the young people are exaggerated by each group. The game, then, is to find out the actual truth.

Once the main parts of the marriage contract are agreed upon, the two young people meet formally and, if they feel that "the chemistry is right" the formal engagement takes place at the home of the bride, usually on a Saturday night, while during the previous day gifts are sent by the groom to the bride in big baskets full of dried fruit, liquor, food, dresses, and cosmetics.

Saturday afternoon the friends of the groom pick up the groom and march in procession to the bride's house to "give her the groom" *(tis piyenoun to yambro)*. A priest is always present to give his blessing. The party lasts from Saturday night through Sunday, sometimes. Next day, the bride sends sweets to the groom and his family *(ta boxalíkia)* wrapped in

Above: Even modern couples maintain traditional marriage customs. Right: Again and again typical specialities are served up.

special clothing, the so-called *boxádes*.

When the house of the groom is ready and the bride has finished preparing her dowry, the formal date of wedding is announced and the whole village is invited, together with the relatives of the young people. The week preceding the wedding, family and friends are at hand to help with the preparations. The dowry is exhibited – sheets, pillow case, blankets, curtains, towels, carpets, tablecloth and napkins, embroideries and, most importantly, a mattress filled by a happily married couple. Friends throw on the mattress walnuts, sugared almonds *(koufeta)*, coins, and place a little boy on it, so that the first child is a male.

In between, the mother-in-law prepares ring-shaped biscuits with special care for the bride's cake *(kouloura)* which she decorates with sculptured birds, animals, fruit and abstract disigns. The dowry is complete when items of furniture are purchased consisting of a bed, a table, some chairs, a wooden wardrobe, and cooking and serving utensils. On Friday, before

the wedding, the dowry is collected in a small pickup truck and taken to the couple's house accompanied by young men singing and laughing. While on Saturday, the house of the bride is decorated and dinner preparations are made.

On the afternoon of the wedding day the young men prepare the groom while young women help the bride dree in her white wedding gown, a gift of the groom. Both the groom and the bride have to wear one used old item to avoid "the evil eye". The groom is supposed to place in his right shoe a coin so that he may become wealthy while the girlfriends of the bride write their names on the bridal shoes to secure a good groom too.

By late afternoon all is ready. The bells start ringing, the priest with the marriage sponsor arrive at the groom's house and the procession starts towards the bride's house to pick her up for the church ceremony. As the procession marches towards the church, friends and relatives sing Cretan songs written for the occasion *(mantinades and rizitika).*

During the ceremony, the marriage sponsor *(koumbaros)* holds the limelight together with the couple. He is responsible for the decoration of the church, provides the large white candles which are held at the ceremony, the wedding crowns, and the *kufeta,* the sugar covered almonds arranged in small packages of white netting, tied with a white ribbon, which are distributed to each of the guests after the ceremony. Immediately after the church ceremony a pomgranate, the symbol of fertility, is thrown down and as it breaks up in pieces family and friends wish the couple a large and happy family. Then, the whole procession forms again and moves towards the bride's home, with the bride and groom often on horseback with family and friends following on foot, amid songs and music played by musicians, hired for the occasion, in their *laouto* (lute) and *lyra* (Cretan lyre). At this point, the young men start shooting blanks to express their hapiness and virility. Their "balothies" are heard all over the area and signal the

87

TASSOULA MAMALAKIS, LYRA

Dressed in a long black dress, Tassoula Mamalakis has a delicate Victorian air, emphasized by the serious expression on her pale face. This image is dispelled when she picks up her lyra and begins to sing classical Cretan songs with great conviction. Her eyes glint and the power of her voice and instrument increases as she continues, giving a glimpse of the determination that propelled her to achieve her dream of becoming a professional lyra-player, the only woman performing today.

Tassoula began studying the violin but switched nine years ago to the lyra because she feels it gives a more authentic expression of the spirit of Crete. This is not unusual because many young Cretan women study the lyra. But she surprised everyone by beginning to play in *kentra* (clubs with music).

Her parents had supported her in playing the lyra as a hobby but did not approve of their only child playing in nightclubs. Their attitude changed five years ago, when she married Stratis Mamalakis, a *laouta* player. She admits, "If I hadn't married Stratis and started to play with him, my family never would have accepted my profession."

Tassoula is from Amari near Rethimnon, once the stronghold of lyra music in Crete. She spends her summers in Crete, playing together with her husband at weddings, *panigyria* (festivals), and at *kentra*, including Zamania, Lefka Ori and Kondaros in Hania. In the winter, she stays in Athens because "the music scene in Athens is more lively than Crete during the cooler months. Most Cretan clubs are closed."

Tassoula encountered prejudice from both men and women who felt only a true *pallikari* (brave man) could play the lyra. Those that spend an evening listening to her spirited playing, usually overcome their prejudice.

beginning of the *glendi* (feast). The wedding feast goes on for hours and sometimes days with a lot of singing *(ta tragoudia tis tavlas)* dancing (the famous complicated dances of *sousta* and *pentozali*) and eating (young roast lamb - *rifaki* –, entrails – *gardouba*, stuffed cheeses, sweets, and to top it off, the wedding cake.)

Eventually, the wedding feast ends and the bride ist accompanied to the groom's home by her brothers. All cry as they leave the girl with her new husband.

Although some of these customs have slightly changed over the years, one has the feeling that there is a continuity in Crete that ties the joyful Minoan frescoes with their scenes of games and feasts to the medieval poems of courtly love, like the national poem, *Erotokritos,* to the wild and rowdy songs of courtship and marriage of modern Crete.

Above: Souvenirs of Crete. Right: Tassoula Mamalakis with her lyre.

HANIA
Accommodation

LUXURY: **Amphora**, Tel: 42998. **Casa Delphino**, 19 Theophania St., Tel: 42613. **Kontessa**, 15 Theophanus St., Tel: 23966. **Porto Del Colombo**, Tel: 50975. **Kydon**, Tel: 26190.
MODERATE: **Doma**, El. Venizelou 124, Tel: 21772/3. **Enetiko Limani**, Tel: 29311. Domeniko, Zambeliou 71, Tel: 55019. **Xenia**, Theotokopoulou St., Tel: 24561. **Domenio**, Tel. 53262. **El Greco**, Tel: 22411. **Lissos**, Tel: 24671. **Porto Veneziano**, Tel: 29311. **Samaria**, Tel: 51551.
BUDGET: **Meltemi**, 2 Angelou, Tel: 40192. **Stella's**, 10 Angelou, Tel: 43756. **Loukia**, Akti Kountourioti, Tel: 21821. **Manos**, Akti Kountourioti, Tel: 29493. **Peraieus**, Zambeliou 14, Tel: 54154. **Amphitriti**, Tel: 22980. **Aptera Beach**, Tel: 22636. **Diktynna**, Tel: 21101. **Hellenis**, Tel: 28070. **Kriti**, Tel: 21881. **Kypros**, Tel: 22761. **Canea**, Tel: 24673. **Avra**, Tel: 23654. **Nea Ionia**, Tel: 22706. **Averof**, Tel: 23090. **Phidias**, Tel: 52494.

Post / Telegraph / Telephone
Hania: area code 0821.
General Post Office: Tzanakaki St. 3, open: 7.30 a.m.- 8.00 p.m. Central Telephone/Telegraph Office (OTE): Tzanakaki St. 5.

Museums
Archaeological Museum, Halidon St. (Tel: 0821/20.334) Open: Daily 8:45 a.m. to 3 p.m. Closed on Tuesdays. **Naval Museum**, on the Old Harbor. **Historical Museum** 20 Tsanakakis St. **Folk Museum**, Kydonias St. (Hours of opening should be checked with Tourist Association)

Tourist Information
The Greek Tourist Association is in the old mosque on the outer harbor, Tel. 26426.

Churches
Metropolitan church, venetian church of St. Francis, church of San Rocco, church of St. Nicholas, church of St. Catherine, venetian church of St. Salvadore

Restaurants
The **Karnagio** in the old Venetian Harbor (next to the Rector's Palace), **Akrogiallia** in New Chora. There are also a number of good and reliable restaurants in the backstreets of the harbor areas. **Kytarro** (chinese and vegetarian), **Oleander** (international cuisine), **Tamam** (eclectic menu), **Zorbas Cafe Ouzeria** (appetizers), **Jimmis** and **Faka's** (simple tavernas).

Greek Mountain Association
EOS Hania, Akti Tombazi 6, Tel. 24647. Refuges in the White Mountains at Kalergi and Volika.

Travel Agencies
Canea Travel, Karaiskaki St. 46, Tel. 24780. **Akrotiri**, Ver Pascha St. 8, Tel. 26610. **Kriti**, Fotiadov Pascha 10, Tel. 23212. **Patris** 1866 Place, Tel. 23751

Taxi
Place Dikastirion, Place 1866, Central Market, Sintrivaniou Place, Place Kotzambassi, Venizelos St., 1897 St., Iraklion St., Souda St., Markopoulos St., Zymbrakakidon St.

Rent a Car
Avis, Karaiskaki St. 26, Tel. 21196. **Blazakis**, Fotiadou Pascha St. 6, Tel. 24618. **Zouridakis**, Hatzimichali Jannari St. 12, Tel. 24403. **Canea Travel**, Karaiskaki St. 46, Tel. 24780. **Manolikakis**, Fotiadou Pascha St. 10, Tel. 21837. **Spanoudakis**, Ver Pascha St. 52, Tel. 23427. **Hertz**, Tzanakaki St. 21, Tel. 20366. **Kontadakis**, Konstantinou St. 31, Tel. 25583.

Banks
National Bank, Chatzimichali St. **Bank of Greece**, Venizelos St. **Commercial Bank**, Chatzimichali St. **Ioninan and Popular Bank**, Tzanakaki St. 4. **Credit Bank**, Chalidon St. 106. **Trapeza Kritis**, Pl. 1866.

Cinema
Apollo, Botsari St. **Asteri**, Skalidi St. **Olympia**, Konstantinou St. **Pantheon**, Pl. 1866. **Rex**, Skalidi St.

Shopping
The **Covered Market**, Halidon St., with many shops selling Cretan handicrafts. **Top Hanas**, Angelou St., Antique Cretan embroideries and carpets. **Carmela's**, Angelous St., modern ceramics and silver work.

Beaches
WEST OF HANIA: **Agioi Apostoloi (4.5 km)**, **Galatas (5.5 km)**, **Agia Marina (8 km)**, **Platanias (11 km)**. AKROTIRI, Stavros (14 km). EAST OF HANIA, Kalami (16.5 km), Kalyves (20.5 km), Almirida and Plaka (25 km).

Access & Local Transport
Olympic Airways has several flights to and from Hania and Athens each day. Schedules vary according to season and should be checked with Olympic Airways. Tel. (0824) 27701.
There are several daily ferry boat services connecting Hania (Souda) with Piraeus (Athens). These normally leave in the evenings and arrive in the mornings. Exact times and companies vary and should be checked.
From Hania to Rethimnon (58 km) and Iraklion (137 km) there is a public coach service several times a day. There are also services to Omalos (39 km), Palaeochora (75 km), Hora Sphakion (72 km) and Kastelli Kissamos (42 km).

From Hora Sphakion to Rodakino, Plakias, and Agia Galini, there are daily coach services. The central bus station in Hania (KTEL) is located on Kydonias St., Tel. (0821) 23052.

There is a ferry-boat service out of Kastelli- Kissamos two times a week that connects with Antikythera, Kythera, Neapoli Voion, Monemvasia and Gythion. There is also a weekly service to Elaeraka and Kyparissi. Tel. (0822) 22024.

From Palaeohora, there are three sailings a week to the island of Gavdos. There are also boats out of Hora Sphakion for Gavdos. For information call: Palaeohora (0823) 41214, Hora Sphakion (0825) 91292.

OUT OF HANIA
Provinces
Kydonia (capital: Hania), Kissamos (capital: Kastelli), Selinon (capital: Kandanos), Apokoronas (capital: Vamos), Sphakia (capital: Hora Sphakion).

Accomodation at:
MALEME: **Chandris** (0821) 73100.
GALATAS: Panorama (0821)54200.
Delphini (0821) 68507. **Ariadni** (0821) 31621. **Creta Maria** (0821) 51335.
AGIA MARINA: **Santa Marina** (0821) 68460. **Amalthia** (0821) 68542.
KASTELLI-KISSAMOS: **Elena Beach** (0822) 23300. **Castron** (0822) 22140. **Kissamos** (0822) 22086. **Morpheus** (0822) 22086.
PALAEOHORA: **Elyros** (0823) 41348. **Elman** (0823) 41412. **Lissos** (0823) 41266,
STALOS KATO: **Delfini** (0821) 68507. **Pavlakis Beach** (0821) 68528.
SPHAKIA: **Xenia** (0825) 91202.
SOUGIA: **Pikilassos** (0825) 51242.
GEORGIOUPOLIS: **Gorgona** (0825) 22378, **KOLYMVARI : Rosmarie** (0824)21220. **Dimitra** (0821) 22244.
MALEME: **Crete Chandris** (0821) 91221.
OMALOS: **Xenia** (0821) 93237.
PLATANIAS (0821): **Villa Platanias**.
RAPANIANA: **Olympic** (0824) 22483.
SOUDA: **Knossos** (0821)89282. **Parthenon** (0821) 8924.

Camping at:
HANIA (0821) 51090, persons 100, tents 33.
AGIA MARINA / HANIA (0821) 68555, 68565, persons 240, tents 80.
PALAEOHORA, Loupassis Camping (0823) 41225), 41130, persons 120, tents 40.
KISSAMAS, Mythimna (0822) 31444-5, tents 54.

Small Islands
NORTH COAST: Agii Theodori, Agria Gramvousa, Imeri Gramvousa. **WEST COAST**: Elaphonissi. **SOUTH COAST**: Gavdos, Gavdopoula.

Beaches
WEST OF HANIA: Kato Stalos, Platanias, Maleme, Phalassarna, Elaphonissi. **EAST OF HANIA**: Kalyves, Plaka, Georgioupolis. Akrotiri: Kalathas Bay, Stavros. **SOUTH COAST**: Palaeohora, Sougia, Loutro, Frangokastello

Festivals
Ther are many local festivals in the villages as well as in Hania. It is best to contact the Tourist Association for exact dates as they vary. Many of them feature Cretan music and dances.
HANIA: during August theaters, concerts, exhibitions.
AGIA MARINA: church festival 17.7.
AKROTIRI: Horafakia 15.8.
VAMOS: Summer music festival with famous artists from Greece and Crete.
VOUKOLIES: Commerial festival on Good Friday.
GEORGIOUPOLIS: Church festival Tou Sotira 6.8; church festival in Kournas 29.8.
ELOS: chestnut festival 20.10.
THERISSOS: festival of Holy Mary 15.8.
KALIVES: church festival Agia Paraskevi 26.7.
KANDANOS: Memory day for the battle of Crete 20.5.
KASTELLI-KISSAMOS: Wine festival begin of Aug.
KOLIMVARI: church festival 15.8., in Tavroniti church festival 14.9.
OMALOS: church festival of Agios Pantelimonas in Fourni.
PALAEHORA: music festival 1.- 10.8.
PERIVOLIA: church festival tou sotira 6.8.
PLATANOS: festival of Agios Akinitos 12.8.
PHALASSARNA: festival of Agia Paraskevi 26.7.
POLYRRINIA: festival of Agion Pateron 7.10.
SOUDA: navy week in June.
FRANGOKASTELLO: festival of Agios Nikitas 15.9.

Gorges
Samaria gorge, Eligias gorge, Aradhena gorge, Imbros gorge (all South coast), Topoliano gorge (Kastelli-Kissamos), Therissos gorge (near Hania), Agia Irini gorge (near Hania).

Caves
Lera (Stavros), **Agia Sophia** (Topoliana gorge), **Spilia Panagias** (Gouverneto), **Drakolakkos** (near Anopolis), **Chonos** (Omalos).

Mountains
Pahnes (2453 m), Troharis (2401 m), Castro (2218 m), Volakias (2116 m).

RETHIMNON

RETHIMNON CITY
ARKADI
PREVELI / PLAKIAS
FRANGOKASTELLO
AMARI VALLEY
AGIA GALINI
BEACHES

The district of Rethimnon lies just to the west of the center of Crete, occupying a broad swathe of north-south territory between Mount Psiloritis to the east and the foothills of the White Mountains in the west, its northern and southern coasts, on the Aegean and Libyan seas respectively, fringed with expanses of fine sandy beaches.

On the north coast, the capital city of **Rethimnon** is conveniently situated midway between Crete's major sea- and airports of Iraklion in the west and Hania in the east. Lacking a natural harbor and being traditionally a center for artistic and intellectual activities rather than commercial ones, Rethimnon has escaped much of the development that marks both Iraklion and Hania. Its old city is still its main city, and the charm of its post-Byzantine past, principally that of the medieval Venetian occupation, is thus alive and ever-present.

Rethimnon rests on a wide isthmus of land, joining the mainland at the high rocky promontory that is now the site of a sixteenth-century **Venetian fortress**. Ever since Late Minoan settlers began to arrive in the area in the thirteenth century BC, the promontory seems to have had

Preceding pages: A view of Rethimnon. Left: An idyllic spot for an antique.

something of importance built upon it. In the fourth century BC, temples to Artemis, Apollo and Athena were raised there and after that, sometime during the Byzantine, Saracen, and Genoan possessions of Crete, a fort of some sort was erected, as is indicated by the traditional name for the hill, **Paleokastro**.

When the Venetians took control of Rethimnon in 1210, they occupied this old castle and immediately began building a line of walls, towers and gates across the entrance to the isthmus in order to protect the city on its landward side. These fortifications and the old castle also were eventually reduced to rubble by a series of mid-sixteenth-century pirate and Ottoman raids, some led by the notorious Greek mercenary, Barbarossa, scouring the Aegean for the Turks. In 1573, the Venetians began constructing the present fortress, which was completed in 1583. In 1645, after a 23-day seige, it was overrun by the Ottomans, who would occupy it until forced out by the allied powers of Britain, France and Russia in 1898.

While virtually no trace of the Venetian walls remains today, their invisible presence nevertheless continues to define the "real" city of Rethimnon as distinct from its somewhat colorless modern extension rising along the east-west high-

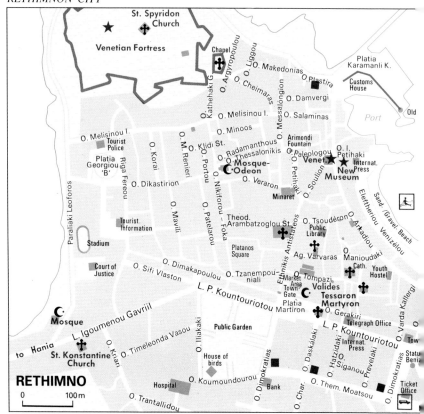

way between Iraklion and Hania. The only extant part of the original fortifications – a piece of an arch from the Venetian gate of Goora – is still considered to be Rethimnon's main entrance. This is also the very best place to begin a tour of the city.

Getting Around

The Goora Gate is located just off the Iraklion-Hania Highway as it passes Rethimnon's **Church and Square of the Four Martyrs** and its **Public Gardens**. Here the traveler can find agencies selling tickets for ships embarking from the ports of Hania and Iraklion. The square marks the spot where, in 1824, four Rethimniots were beheaded and hung on plane trees for refusing to convert to Islam, while the gardens, built on the ground of the old Turkish cemetery, are a wonderfully verdant and refreshing refuge from the heat and dust of the summer as well as being, in July, the nightime site of the city's annual **Wine Festival**. The **Goora Gate** is still known as the "Big Gate" (Megali Porta) even though it is now not a gate at all, but a street, and that barely wide enough for a modern truck to negotiate a passage through. Spanning the entrance from above is a portion of an arch that is now the only existing trace of the Venetian walls.

As in the old days, the gate leads immediately into the **market area**, a small,

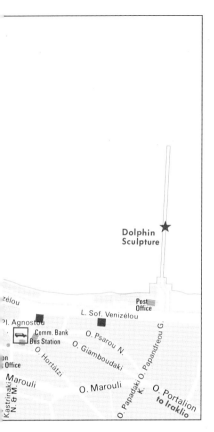

Dolphin
Sculpture

Post
Office

zélou

L. Sof. Venizélou

Pl. Agnostou

Comm. Bank
Bus Station

O. Psarou N.

O. Giamboudaki

O. Papadaki

K. Papandreou G.

on
Office

O. Hortátzi

Marouli

O. Marouli

O. Portalion
to Iraklio

Kástrinaki
N. & M.

the Four Martyrs and the market street, but its entranceway closed off by encircling private houses and impossible to get to. Further down the main market street, however, and just to the west of tree-lined Platanos Square, is the very accessible **Neratzes Mosque and minaret**.

The finest of its kind in the city, the Neratzes Mosque is believed to have originally been built as a church during the Byzantine era and subsequently converted by the Ottomans. Today, it serves as both a tourist attraction and a concert hall and offers an excellent 360-degree view of Rethimnon from the top of its minaret's 120 stairs.

At the far (northern) end of **Platanos Square** and the line of plane trees, restaurants, cafes, diving, antique and leather goods stores that make up its length is the **Rimondi Fountain**. Named after the Venetian rector, Antonio Rimondi, who had it built in about 1629, it is architecturally a virtual time capsule of the city's history in the last 2000 years, the pillars being Corinthian, the lion heads Venetian, and the back wall a Turkish restoration. In 1930, its overhead vault was torn down to allow motorized vehicles to penetrate more deeply into the residential area around the fortress, the most beautiful part of old Rethimnon.

When the Venetians built the present fortress to withstand continuing Ottoman assaults, the Cretans disdained to enter and rebuild their houses outside the fortress walls, refusing to seek protection inside until the final Ottoman attack made death the only other alternative.

These houses are, for the most part, those that visitors see today lining the defensive warren of streets that is the old quarter. Built in Venetian times, some have wonderfully sculpted marble portals and superb interior courtyards and fountains. Quite a few also display the subsequent addition (by Turkish overlords) of overhanging projections of second-storey living rooms, built to allow the la-

but bustling cornucopia of fish, meat, cheese, bread and fruit and vegetable stores as well as tourist shops, leather goods, clothing, hardware, photography, music and book stores, a library (with books in English), antique shops, saddle makers and metal working establishments. There are very good workers' cafes and tavernas in the area, and also, just outside the Goora gate and on the street to its left before entering, a musical instrument maker's shop specializing in Cretan *lyras*, the long-necked, three-stringed type of violin that is the principal sound and instrument in Cretan music.

To the east of the gate is the **Valides Mosque**, the spire of its minaret tantalizingly visible from both the Square of

97

dies of the house to observe, from behind latticed screens, the goings-on in the streets below without themselves being seen.

The **fortress**, built by the Venetians with forced labor and unilaterally surrendered by them to the Turks, has long been a blot on the communal memory of Rethimnon, a symbol of anguish and enslavement as well as, in August 1944, martyrdom as Rethimniot women leapt to their death over its walls rather than be taken as hostages during the German withdrawal. Hence, until recently, the fortress was allowed to fall into ruin, with the devastation wreaked upon it by the retreating Nazi army in 1944 left virtually in situ. It is now in the process of being extensively restored and is very much worth a visit if only for its view of the city and the sea. In summer, concerts by popular Greek singers are often given in its lovely, pine-bedecked amphitheater.

Above: Aphrodite in marble in the Archaeological Museum of Rethimnon.

Opposite the fortress entrance is the new **museum**. Originally the site of a Venetian prison and maintained as such by the Turks, it was allowed to fall into disuse after the latter's departure. Recently restored, it replaced the Loggia (see below) as the city's new museum in 1986.

Although there has been little systematic archaeological digging in the area of Rethimnon, the museum does have a representative collection of items from all periods since human habitation began in Neolithic times.

There are tools, jewelry, pottery and votive idols from the Neolithic period, pottery from Minoan times, and various vases, figurines, statuettes, seals, jewelry, weapons, tools, coins, sarcophagi, gravestones and architectural fragments from the Classical period of Roman and Byzantine rule on the island. Also included are certain pieces from Egypt.

The fact that only little exists from the days of the Turkish occupation is yet another indication of how thoroughly the

Rethimniots went about obliterating that part of their past.

The lovely **Venetian harbor** is but a five-minute walk away from the fortress east along the northern sea wall. Colorful and intimate, ringed with caiques and cafes and restaurants specializing in grilled meats and seafood, it is a world unto itself and a perfect place to retreat from the bustle of the city in day or night.

Begun by the Venetians in 1300 (the lighthouse was restored in the mid-1980s), it has yet to be completed to the satisfaction of any seafarers but the owners of the smallest types of fishing and pleasure craft. The problem is one of continually accumulating sand and silt that requires constant dredging to keep the channel to the interior of the port open, a truly Sisyphean endeavor.

At approximately the center of the curve of the harbor, there is a narrow street lined with Cretan handicraft and jewelry shops which leads back into the city towards one of Rethimnon's most cherished landmarks – the **Loggia**.

The Loggia, recently the city's Archaeological Museum until that was moved to the old prison outside the entrance to the fortress (see above), was built in the sixteenth century as a club for Venetian gentlemen.

Opposite it to the north was a large clock tower, built, say the locals today, so that the gentlemen would know when to stop their gaming in order to arrive home at a decent hour, presumably for lunch, since the clock was a solar one. At night, apparently, the time didn't matter. This tower formed the last substantial part of the original city walls to remain standing into the present century. Unfortunately, in 1945, the day after the German occupation of Crete ended, it was razed to the ground in the middle of the night by a property owner wanting to gain access to Arkadiou Street, then as now the main shopping street running behind the beachfront and past the Loggia.

The wide expanse of Rethimnon's **public beach** is a comparatively recent but welcomed addition to the attractions of the city, having achieved its present excellent state only after the construction of a second jetty to the south of the city center in the 1960s. Before that, as old photographs testify, the sea came virtually up to the windows of the beach-front houses.

In the center of the curve of the beach is a relatively new single-storey structure containing a snack bar, showers and bath houses as well as the city's Government **Tourist Office** or "**EOT**" (eh-ot) as it is known to the Greeks. This is an invaluable source of information on all aspects of both the city and district of Rethimnon, including the availability of rooms in hotels, pensions, and private houses.

At night, the road along the beach is closed to traffic, a practice formerly observed only on Sundays, when the Rethimniots still observe the time-honored Mediterranean custom of displaying marriageable daughters and sons on an evening stroll *(volta)* along the seafront.

Another stroll that is especially recommended, particularly in the evenings, is on the road around the fortress promontory to its western side. There you can sit and watch the sun sink into the Aegean Sea from an *ouzeria* just below the fortress and the curious **church of St. Spyridon**. The facade of this church is flush with the rock face of the promontory, its interior built into a blast hole dynamited by beseiging Turks in an unsuccessful attempt to tunnel under the fortress walls during their assault on the Venetians and Rethimniots in 1645.

Within the city, there are many other sights to see and opportunities for rewarding walks, particularly through the old quarter. The city has a lively and genial warmth that is best absorbed by encountering the Rethimniots themselves, young and old, as they go about their daily lives in a manner that must be

as little changed over the centuries as the streets themselves.

Outside the city, with Rethimnon as a base, there are numerous extremely rewarding excursions to be made.

To the Monastery of Arkadi

Nearest to Rethimnon is the **Monastery of Arkadi**. This is the most renowed monastery in Crete, particularly as the site of the 1866 martyrdom of hundreds of Cretan rebels and their women and children, who blew themselves up in the monastery's gunpowder room rather than be captured by the beseiging Ottomans. You can see a drawing of the monastery on the 100 drachma note.

Located on a plateau in the foothills of Mount Psiloritis, the monastery is only 22 km to the southeast of Rethimnon, but

Above:The weather-beaten Renaissance monastery of Arkadi. Right: The monks appear to have gotten used to the hordes of visitors.

takes some 50 minutes to reach, the road narrow and winding and, in its final ascent, skirting the edge of a precipitous ravine so that it must be traveled with care.

The present-day monastery is principally a memorial to the 1866 martyrdom and is made up of four separate clusters of buildings. Sitting among a grove of trees to the left (or west) of the parking area is a **pavilion**, dedicated to the fallen heroes of the rebellion. Within is an ossuary, containing the skulls of several of the martyrs.The building at the far, northern, end of the parking area is a **tourist rest center** with a souvenir area and a dining room, from the balcony of which there is a fine view of the valley leading north down to the Aegean.

The huge gate and front wall of the monastery itself, destroyed by cannon in 1866, were rebuilt in 1870. Inside the gate are arcades leading to the monks' cells, most of them now no longer in use.

Opposite the entrance is the magnificent façade of the monastery's main

church of **S. Helen and Constantine**. Built in about 1587 during the Venetian occupation of Crete, the façade is an ornate Renaissance blend of Roman and baroque elements which seems, like many things Venetian, to be imperceptibly levitating. Certainly, it is an enchanted anomaly in the rough and earthy Cretan landscape. On the other hand, the scars in its stonework made by the Turks when they stormed the monastery, bear testimony to the fact that it is all too firmly grounded in the island's often brutal historical reality.

To the left of the church, and behind the present-day refectory, is the famous **Gunpowder Room**. It was here that nearly a thousand men, women and children gathered on November 9, 1866, and, when the Turks broke through the stiff resistance at the front gate, died in the explosion which ensued when Kostis Giambudakis, the renowned hero of the event, fired his pistol into a barrel of gunpowder. It was truly a shot heard round the world, and the international furore it aroused over the continuing enslavement of the Cretans was of great significance in the eventually liberation of the island ten years later.

The monastery's **Historical Museum**, to the right of the main church, contains many mementoes of this martyrdom, including a three-dimensional reconstruction of the surrounding topography, showing how the Ottomans approached and encircled Arkadi.

Hike from Arkadi to Thronos

If you don't have an automobile, you can reach the monastery of Arkadi from Rethimnon using public transportation. The way there is lined with beautiful old olive trees, their trunks twisted into gnarled and imaginative knots. The olive harvest takes place between the beginning of December and the end of January. Usually a net is stretched under the tree and the fruit allowed merely to fall into it. Sometimes the tree is also hit with a stick, a tedious job. More recently they have

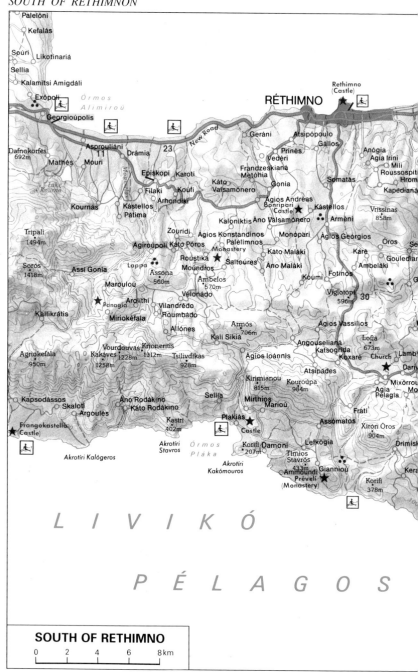

SOUTH OF RETHIMNON

0 2 4 6 8 km

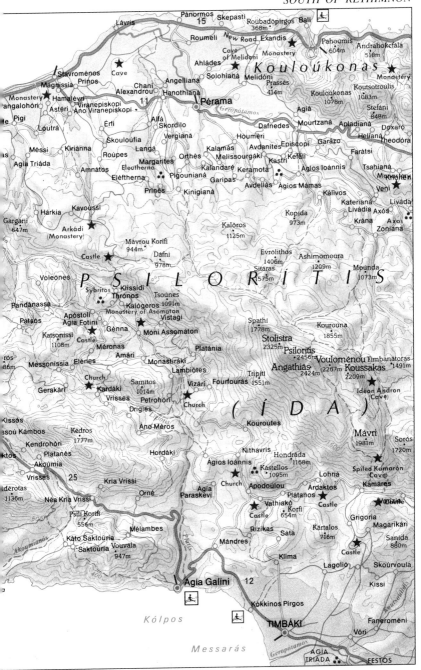

started using compressed air to blow the olives off the tree. Anyone needing a job to survive in Crete over the winter will have no difficulty in finding work hitting trees. The pay is about 20 US$ a day.

The final section of the road goes along a deep gully and then up to an elevation of take over 500 meter where you'll find the monastery.

The visit to the monastery is followed by less a hike on a gravel road to Kavoussia/Charkia. The monastery still owns some property in the area. After a couple of hundred meters you come to a pretty pinery and about a quarter of an hour later to a cement bridge where you turn left. (The road straight ahead leads to Kavoussi.) 20 m later a wide road turns off to the right. However, follow the small gravel road that runs along a stream lined with oaks. This road is seldom used. It climbs gently through pastures dotted

Above: Winds of hurricane strength often pound the island. Right: A donkey waits patiently while the vines are pruned.

with rocks and low bushes. A herd of goats will take flight on your arrival. Stay on the main road, disregarding any forks to the left or right. After about an hour's walk, just before reaching the top of the plateau, turn for a last look at the monastery. The road forks, but head right. The gravel road twists and turns down the mountain until you can spot the terraced hillside that gave Thronos its name (it has a broadcasting antenna on it). After about a quarter hour you once again encounter the wide road that you left behind at the cement bridge after the monastery of Arkadi, which girds the mountain with the width of a highway. The huge aisle that was cut to build the road is one of the great eyesores in the landscape. The piles of rubble that were merely pushed to the side of the road have been deeply furrowed by rain and wind and appear like a lunar landscape in an otherwise homogeneous picture. Follow the new road for a bit, and after a long right-hand curve you come to the spring **Petra sto Nero**. Its water is supposed to heal kidney and

gallstone problems and on weekends people often come to take some of the water home in large canisters. Take a break at some small benches and tables. Stay on the road until, after another long curve, a mule path forks off to the right. A few minutes later you arrive in the borough of **Klissidhi**. Turn right at the next intersection (a covered bus stop) and walk for 10 minutes into town. Here you have a view of the **Amari basin**, while to the left the houses of **Kalokairi** village sprawl on the mountain slope with the Psiloritis range in the background.

The modern village of **Thronos** was founded on the remains of a Graeco-Roman city named *Sybritos*. The church of the Panagia in the center of town merits a visit, for it is built on the ruins of a much larger early Christian basilica and floor mosaics can still be partly seen on the square on front of the church. The view from here or from the neighboring *kafenion* is of the village's luxuriant gardens and the peaks of the Psiloritis that remain snow-covered until spring. The

bus from Thronos to Rethimnon runs only once a day (mornings) and returns in the evening, so you must go back the same way on foot.

West of Rethimnon

There are two fine swimming areas bordering the New Road to Hania just west of Rethimnon: the beaches of Gerani and Petres River. **Gerani Beach** is 7 km to the west just below a small bridge over the Gerani River. Here, next to a tiny chapel nestling in a grove of tamarisk trees, is a small camping area and an unpretentious taverna. There is also a **cave**, discovered during the construction of the New Road and immediately locked up to protect its Neolithic finds. Permission to visit can be obtained from the proper authorities. Ask at the Rethimnon Tourist Bureau (EOT) on the beachfront.

The **Petres River Beach**, 16 km to the west of Rethimnon, with the often snow-covered white mountains (Levka Ori) in the background, is a 7-km stretch of almost undeveloped seafront, all of it covered by fine sand interspersed with clusters of shady trees. One of the reasons, perhaps, for its lack of development is the strong offshore currents, which are dangerous for even the best of swimmers, no matter how placid the sea might seem. There are two tavernas as well as camping facilities located just off the main road at the beach's center.

Turn south at this point, off the New Road to the village of **Episkopi**, from which side trips can be made to the rarely visited areas around the village of Argiroupoli or to Lake Kournas, the only fresh water lake on Crete.

Argiroupoli and its environs formed a retreat for Cretan aristocracy during the Venetian occupation from the thirteenth to seventeenth centuries, a fact evident in some of the local architecture, while in the nearby village of **Miriokephala**, the church of the monastery of the Panagia offers some of the earliest Byzantine frescoes on Crete, from the eleventh and twelfth centuries.

Further into the mountains is the village of **Assi Gonia**, birthplace of George Psychoundakis, author of the *The Cretan Runner*, and the site on St. George's Day (April 23) of a highly recommended village festival at which the sheep are blessed.

West of Episkopi is **Lake Kournas**. Said to be bottomless, it covers approximately 65 hectares of the relatively arid Cretan landscape with pure, fresh water. There is a taverna just up from the water's edge serving fish from the lake, but swimming in its waters is strongly discouraged. Sudden whirlpools have claimed the lives of several people foolish enough to ignore the warnings, one of them having been a professional scuba diver attempting to reach the bottom of this dangerous water.

Right: The idyllic Preveli monastery overlooking the sea.

As with similar phenomena elsewhere, the site has also given rise to various legends. Bullets fired from one side are said to be swallowed up by some mysterious force before they can reach the opposite shore. In addition, the lake is believed to be haunted by the ghost of a young girl who was raped and killed by her father somewhere in the vicinity.

From Kournas, a reasonably good road, paralleling the north coast New Road, eventually crosses this road and leads further east to the lovely tree-shaded fishing village of **Georgioupolis**, nestling at the mouth of a river at the far western end of the above-mentioned Petres River Beach. From here, the traveler can proceed further west on the New Road to Hania or south along the road through the enchanting riverside village of **Vrysses** to Hora Sphakion and the fortress of Frangokastello.

South of Rethimnon

The main road to the south begins at the Square of the Four Martyrs in the center of Rethimnon. Signposts direct the traveler along the side of the Public Gardens and, at the southern edge of the city, into the foothills which span the area between the western range of the White Mountains and the eastern massif of Mount Psiloritis (Ida).

The village of **Armeni** lies only ten minutes' drive into the hills outside Rethimnon and offers a pleasant and easy-to-reach respite from the summer crowds of the city. There are several tavernas and cafes along its shady main street, and some interesting old houses off the eastern side of the road. About 2 km before reaching the village from Rethimnon there is, on the right, about 100 meter after the turn-off for Somata, a **Minoan necropolis**. Uncovered in 1969, it has yielded many artifacts including several painted sarcophagi now on display in the Archaeological Museum at Hania. About

4 km south of Armeni, the traveler can turn eastwards towards the village of **Kare** and cut over to the beautiful valley of **Amari** (see below) or continue on to the southwest or southeast of the district of Rethimnon.

The Southwest Route

Another 12 km further along the main road to the south from Armeni is the turn-off to the west leading to the monastery of Preveli and the beaches of Plakias and Frangokastello, plus the fortress.

The monastery of Preveli is about a 15-minute drive directly south of a turn-off to the left, as the main road passes through the village of **Asomatos**. On the way, along the side of the winding, tree-lined **Megapotamos river**, one comes to the ruins of a sixteenth-century monastery, now abandoned but still impressive.

Here, taking the bridge across the river to the left and following the road south (over another tiny bridge) will lead you to the sea, where a small taverna has re-cently been established. From here, it is a 10-minute clamber over the seaside rocks to **Preveli Beach**, isolated and idyllically fringed with palm trees, but suited only to those willing truly to rough it.

Continuing past the ancient monastery but staying on the right side of the river leads one to the present-day **Preveli Monastery** (Moni Preveli). Rebuilt after the Ottomans burnt it to the ground in 1866 for supporting resistance move-ments, it sits on a bluff on the southern side of the mountain and has a magnifi-cent view of the Libyan Sea.

It was from here that hundreds of British, Australian and New Zealand sol-diers were evacuated following the 1941 German invasion and transported to safety in Egypt by Allied submarines. A marble plaque on the wall outside the main church testifies to this event as do a pair of silver candlesticks donated to the monastery after the war by the grateful survivors of the Allied troops.

Preveli Beach may be reached from a curve in the road about 200-300 m before

107

you come to the monastery and from here there is a twenty-minute downhill trek over rocky fields and walls, the return being much more difficult than it would be from the mouth of the Megapotamos River.

Hike to the Palm Beach of Preveli

The departing point for this five-hour round trip is the village of **Asomatos**. Leave the village on the asphalt road leading to Rethimnon. 800 m from the village limits a dirt road leads to the right toward the **Kourtaliotiko Gorge**. At a sharp turn is a cement road leading downward that soon becomes a gravel road. Go straight along the orographical right bank of the Megalopotamos that flows from the Kourtaliotiko gorge. The hitherto trafficable road ends in about one km in front of a small chapel. A little

Above: Wilderness near the palm beach of Preveli. Right: Crystalline waters off the coast near Preveli.

further on you will find a path leading down to the river. The village of Asomatos is now behind you.

A five minute hike leads to an abandoned olive mill with an inscription indicating the year 1890. A young Greek couple have turned the inside into a little camp, with sleeping-mats, covers, sleeping-bags and various cooking utensils. At the old mill take the dirt road to the right. After about 300 m you will come to a wide asphalt road leading right along the Megalopotamos to Preveli monastery. The narrow strip of land between the road and the river is covered with olive and citrus trees. After about five minutes you can leave the road and rejoin the footpath on the river bank, which reveals a luxuriant vegetation of planes, reeds, high myrtle bushes and ivy.

About a quarter hour after having left the mill, you come to a Venetian arched bridge gracefully nestling against the backdrop of the massive cliffs of the Kourtaliotiko Gorge. To the south lie the ruins of the old Preveli cloisters also known as *moni mega potamou*, the cloisters of the great river. Cross the river and take the gravel road that stretches along its left bank. The ruins are now on the other side of the river.

A quarter of an hour after leaving the first bridge you arrive at a second arched bridge bearing an inscription which takes you across the stream. Disregard the fork off to the left and follow the gravel road on the orographical left bank of the Megalopotamos. You soon arrive at the dilapidated buildings of cloisters with a chapel intact. The road forks 25 m after the chapel. The right-hand path takes you in five minutes to an olive grove. Go to the left, up the slope on the left bank of the river. The river itself carves its way deeper and deeper into the rock. The path you follow, on the other hand, continues gently above the gorge between low scrub growth. About an hour after having crossed to the left bank over the Venetian

bridge, you pass under some telegraph lines. An exclave on the cliff about 200 m further offers the first superb view of the palm-covered estuary of the Megalopotamo. A little further miles and miles of the coastline come into view before the path loses itself between jagged rocks on its way down to the estuary. After a solid two-hour walk from Asotamos you have reached the palm beach of Preveli. The trees are protected.

At the foot of the cliff one local has built a small hut where he sells drinks and sandwiches during the summer months. The sign saying "Mini Market" suggests that the place is jumping in summer and certainly without much concern for nature conservation. Even in winter one group of Greek beach "bums" never leaves the beach. These fellows, all with dreadlocks, spend their days lying on the beach, drawing Socratic circles in the sand with their toes and defining their philosophical horizon by staring out to sea. They surely find all the peace and quiet needed for meditation during the winter months. According to reports from other travelers, the beach tends to look like a garbage dump in summer and the police have even raided the place on occasion.

You can wade across the estuary to the other side using a small sand strip between the river and the sea. The road leads upward here. After about a twenty-minute climb, a path branches into a gully leading right into the wall of the gorge. If you go straight ahead, the path leads to an asphalt road and from there to the upper Preveli cloister which is worth a visit. On the orographical left of the gorge is a path leading after approximately a quarter hour to a small cleft with a few scattered palms. Shortly thereafter you come across the telegraph wires you already passed under on the other side of the gorge. The path then remains about halfway between the edge of the gorge and the road further up (that passes under the third and fourth telegraph poles counting from the gorge). It is in good repair. After bypassing a few great rocks it

leads down an incline into the river valley. On the way down, after crossing a stone wall, you suddenly come across the **Agia Fotini** chapel hidden amongst olive trees. The interior of this inconspicuous little church is decorated with frescos from the fourteenth century. The road continues through an olive grove, down to the river, and upstream to the ruins of the Kato Preveli cloister and the Venetian bridge. After the bridge you can walk along the path between the road and the river, then on the road itself for a while and finally rightward on the gravel road leading to the olive mill. When you have reached the building there is a mule path that climbs leftward up to the little chapel from which you can now return to Asomatos as you came.

Accessible swimming is to be enjoyed at the seaside village of **Plakias**, some 10

Above: The fine sands of Frangokastello beach, once a Venetian stronghold. Right: Fortress walls in the scorching sun of the southern coast.

km further along the main southwest route from the turn-off for Preveli at Asomatos. The road leads through the small but spectacular **Kotsiphou gorge** and the hillside village of **Mirthios**, with good tavernas and an excellent view of Plakias below. It is worth a pause to admire the spectacular view.

Long a favorite of the people of Rethimnon, Plakias is now experiencing a considerable boom as a tourist center, with new hotels and rooming houses springing up every year. The best bathing area is on the left or eastern side of its lengthy beach, while the majority of tavernas and cafes are on the western side in the tiny tree-shaded fishing hamlet that is Plakias itself. In addition, there are many small and secluded beaches and coves over the rises to the east and west of the central area. It is also possible to walk from here eastwards to the monastery of Preveli; it takes about two hours, but the wonderful scenery en route makes it well worth the effort you have made.

To the west of Plakias, another 24 km

over a rather rough road along the coast, is the famous fortress and beach of **Frangokastello**. The fortress was built by the Venetians in the fourteenth century in a misguided attempt to subjugate the fiercely independent locals of the wild and mountainous area of Sphakia and was subsequently used by the latter in resisting the Turks.

A monument commemorates an 1828 battle in which hundreds of Sphakians died. The fact that their ghosts are still said to haunt the area has not discouraged flocks of tourists from descending upon its fine beach in summer to camp and party. Recently, several rooming houses and a taverna-bar have been erected, but the area is still basically unspoilt, although one is warned to look out at night for farmers' trucks, parked with dangerous casualness in the middle of the road as if the possibility of oncoming traffic was inconceivable.

From Frangokastello, the road to the west continues on to the fishing village of **Hora Sphakion**, from which it is possible to take a regular caique to **Agia Roumeli**, the fishing village at the southern mouth of the **Gorge of Samaria**. The road north from Hora Sphakion leads to the New Road along the coast between Rethimnon and Hania.

The Southeast Route

Instead of turning off the main north-south route towards the southwest, the traveler can continue along this road towards Agia Galini. The first stop en route, the picturesque hillside village of **Spili,** lies on the main road just 7 km south of the eastern turn-off towards Preveli and Plakias. Anyone accustomed to the aridity of Greece in summer will be both astonished and delighted by the torrent of water continually gushing out of the mountainside in the center of the village. There it is channeled through a **Venetian fountain** and drinking trough, its nineteen spouts marvelously fashioned in the form of marble lions' heads. Spili is, needless to say, a wonderfully re-

freshing place to stop on the way south. On the left-hand side you see the **Kedhros range** (1177 m). To climb up, start in Kendrahari or in Ano Meros in the Amari Valley.

The lovely fishing village of **Agia Galini** is some 25 km further to the south. Like similar villages in France and Italy, it clings picturesquely to the side of a cliff face, its main street making a winding descent down from the headland to the sea. Along and near the spacious concrete pier are numerous cafes and restaurants and tourist shops, as well as a small beach around the point to the east of the harbor.

From above Agia Galini the main inland road offers a connection northwards through lovely Amari Valley (see below) or continues curving eastwards through a fertile farming valley and the commercial center of Timbaki to the spectacular beach of Matala. The wonderful Minoan

Above: Village life in Amari Valley. Right: What does this ass have to do with Mitsotakis?

excavations at Agia Triada and Phaestos are only a matter of minutes away, along the main road leading north to Knossos and Iraklion.

Via the Amari Valley to Agia Galini

Situated only 30 km southeast of Rethimnon, the **Amari Valley** is one of the most beautiful in all of Crete: a soft and fertile Shangri-La tucked away between the rugged ranges of Kedhros to the west and Mount Psiloritis to the east.

To reach the valley, you turn off the new road 3 km to the east of Rethimnon, following the sign to Amari. From here it is approximately a 27-km drive to the village of **Apostoli**, which stands at the nothern approach to the valley. Along the way, a worthwhile detour is to the village of **Hromonastiri** and its church of Agios Eftikhios. The remains of the rare eleventh-century frescoes are meagre but superb. Beyond Hromonastiri can be seen the peak of **Mount Vrissinas**, the highest in the area and site of one of the finest Minoan peak sanctuaries on Crete.

From the village of **Apostoli**, Amari Valley extends some 50 km south to the main road linking the port of Agia Galini with the beach of Matala and the archaeological site of Phaestos. As there are roads running along both its sides, a complete circuit of the valley from north to south and back again to Rethimnon – about a 120-km drive (bends included) – is easily possible in one day.

The valley, fertile and well protected from sea invasions from the north and south, used to be one of the most important in Crete, particularly during the Byzantine periods, and is thus sprinkled with numerous churches, castles and various other edifices from other epochs. Take a trip south along the eastern side of the valley. About 1 km beyond Apostoli, with its fourteenth-century church, the tiny village of **Agia Photini** offers a view of the whole valley. East of here is the village of **Thronos** in the center of which stands a fourteenth to fifteenth-century church and, on an acropolis 10 minutes' walk above the village, the remains of the Greco-Roman city of **Sybritos**, with its magnificent view of the valley.

Some 5 km further on, near the turn-off to the village of Amari, is the former **Monastery of Asomaton**, now an agricultural school. Just outside the charming village of **Amari** is the church of Agia Anna with frescoes dating from 1225, the earliest found on Crete. At **Vizari**, there are remains of a Roman town and a Christian basilica (eighth century).

At **Fourfouras,** the jumping-off point for walks in the Psiloritis range, is a fouteenth-fifteenth-century church with the remains of some frescoes of the period, while above the nearby village of **Platania** there are three caves: Digenes (820 m), Kissospelios (1000 m), and the Cave of Pan (1750 m). Just north of the village of **Apodoulou** are, on the right, the church of Agios Giorgos, with mid-fourteenth-century frescoes by Iereas

Anastasios and, up the hill on the left, late Minoan *tholos* tombs.

Just after Apodoulou, the road divides. A left or eastward turn leads along a secondary road through the village of **Kamares** with its cave and eventually joins up with the main north-south route to Iraklion. A right turn leads south to a juncture with the road running up the western side of the Amari Valley. From here, one can either return to Rethimnon via the western side or continue south to the lovely port and beach of Agia Galini, and then drive back to Rethimnon via the mountain village of Spili (see above).

The western Amari route skirts the slopes of **Mount Kedhros** and, for those not driving, offers superb views to the south and west of the valley and the Psiloritis range. There are also fine churches and frescoes at the villages of **Agia Paraskevi**, **Kardaki** and **Meronas**, with the latter offering a rare fresco of the Christ Child as the Eucharist and a four-teenth-century one of the Virgin Mary that is one of the earliest on Crete.

113

East of Rethimnon

Another rewarding trip to the east of Rethimnon offers the opportunity to visit, in one day, a mountain pottery-making village, an ancient Dorian city, a prehistoric cave, and a charming fishing village on the north coast between Rethimnon and Iraklion.

Margarites is the village, about an hour's drive (27 km) east along the New Road to Iraklion and then south up into the foothills of Mount Psiloritis via the Old Road. A typical Cretan mountain village that would be worth visiting in its own right, it has a long tradition of pottery making that has in recent years seen a vigorous revival, much of it due to the presence of foreign buyers. During summer, shops selling local wares are open in the mornings and evenings and some all day long.

Above: A cove near the little fishing village of Bali on the northern coast.

The remains of the ancient Dorian city of **Eleutherna**, inhabited from the ninth century BC until the Middle Ages, lie just outside the village of **Prines**, about five minutes' walk from a parking area 200 m to the north. While little systematic archaeological excavation has been done since the 1920, the site, on a promontory between two river beds, is superb, and the **Hellenistic bridge**, another twenty minutes' walk to the north a marvellous example of its kind.

The large, many-chambered and wonderfully stalactited **Cave of Melidoni** is located directly south of the village of Melidoni, about 10 km east of Margarites, on the Old Road southeast of the commercial center of Perama. To reach the cave, follow the signs through the village and out to a small chapel just to the right of the cave's entrance.

In ancient time the cave was said to be the habitat of Talos, King Minos'giant, bronze, bull-headed guardian of Crete. In the Hellenistic period (300-67 BC), the cave was the site of worshippers of

Hermes. Today, just inside the entrance, there is a stone altar commemorating yet another martyrdom of Cretans at the hands of the Ottomans. In 1824, hundred people escaping from marauding soldiers in nearby villages, were trapped in the cave by the Turks, who blocked the entrance with brushwood and set fire to it, suffocating the villagers who all died.

The pocket-sized fishing village of **Bali** is just a 7-km drive north across the new costal road and down a rather precipitous road to the sea. Bali (the name comes from the Turkish word for honey) has considerable charm, a small beach and often not enough tavernas and cafes to accommodate the many visitors in recent years. Its beautiful natural setting and rustic warmth remain, however, as yet unspoiled.

Our final tour east of Rethimnon is one which might best be taken on a trip which continues to Iraklion. Some 53 km (about a two- hour drive) over the Old Road east of Rethimnon and into the mountains is the village of **Anoghia**, yet another site of Cretan martyrdom, this time at the hands of the Nazis.

It is here that the German commandant, General Kreipe, was briefly hidden after being kidnapped by British and Cretan resistance fighters. As a result, the Nazis killed every male in the village and razed all of its buildings, except the church of St. John the Baptist, to the ground, hence the rather unpicturesque, poured-concrete look of the village today. Nevertheless, it houses a thriving tourist industry, producing numerous handicrafts and holding various music festivals. In addition, it is one of the main jumping-off places for a journey to the upper slopes and peak of **Mount Psiloritis** (Ida) and its famous cave, said to have been the birthplace of the Zeus.

Most of the 20-km journey from Anoghia to the **Cave of Ideon Andron** can be covered by car over a winding asphalt road which passes through a land-scape dotted with picturesque stone cheese huts *(mutato)*. Some of these are hundreds of years old and still serve shepherds not only as repositories for curing goat's cheese but also as refreshingly cool summer sleeping quarters.

The road up to the slope of Psiloritis ends at the tourist pavilion on **Nidha Plateau**, from which it is only a twenty-minute walk to the cave. The cave's immense entrance (about 27 m wide by 9 m high) and the size of some of the interior chambers (the largest being 34 by 36 m) certainly justify it being thought of as the birthplace of Zeus. Discovered in modern times by E. Fabricius, it has since yielded up archaeological evidence from the ninth to eighth century BC, indicating cult worship of Zeus by dancing Curetes, one of whose clashing shields can be seen in Iraklion's Archaeological Museum.

Offbeat Beaches

Plakias, close to Frangokastello, is a calm area with a long beach fairly littered right near the town but cleaner as one walks to the west. The little settlement attracts young wayfarers many of whom camp out on its beaches. The setting is lovely, backed by flowering shrubs and herbs and jutting mountains. The beach has a few hotels and tavernas. At the end of a gorge at **Preveli**, you will also find a splendid beach.

Three lesser known beaches, known as **Damoni**, lie around the coast in the sparkling water of the eastern section of Plakias Bay. The middle one is nudist. A little further is **Ammoudi**, a dignified family beach with a taverna and rooms to rent. Ammoudi is close to the inland village of **Lefkogia** which has a few rooms to rent. East of Rethimnon, the sandy beaches with flat rocks circle three coves, with Paradise Beach the nicest. **Bali** is a small resort with the Bali Beach Hotel offering rooms to rent. East of Rethimnon there are nice beaches at **Panormos**.

A PROFILE OF EMMANUEL SKOULAS

On the way to Psilioritis, a picturesque village can be found nestling in the mountainside. **Anoghia** is justly proud of its exquisite woven articles and handicrafts. However, its main attraction is a 75-year-old primitive artist, Emmanuel Skoulas.

The self-taught painter and sculptor was originally a shepherd, but at the age of 37, he sold his flocks and devoted his life entirely to his art. He started to draw quite accidentally, imitating an artist whose work he saw in Iraklion, and discovered that he had a natural talent for it. "At first people said I was crazy," he recalls, "but when I started selling my paintings, they began to respect me."

Skoulas freely admits that he knows nothing about technique and is not even remotely interested in learning. "I like to

Above: Tableau by the native painter Emmanuel Skoulas from Anoghia.

have my own personal style," he says. "I've lived what I paint; I've seen it with my own eyes." And the dignified old man has certainly seen a great deal with his own eyes. His paintings are a vivid and colorful depiction of Crete's history and everyday village life, executed in naif style. The topics range from war scenes to weddings and other typically Cretan events such as parachutists, a Cretan couple drinking a glass of wine, and the gun-powder explosion at Arkadi. The sizes also vary greatly from small pictures to enormous wall paintings. The very large ones are not for sale. Also a skilful sculptor, Skoulas carves any pieces of wood he can find, using the form to determine the subject matter.

Skoulas's son sells his work since the proud old artist shies away from haggling over prices. "I'd like to give them away for free," he maintains. "I paint so that my grandchildren will see my work and thus keep alive things of the past. When I work I forget about everything. It makes me feel happy and fulfilled."

RETHIMNON
Accommodation

LUXURY: **Creta Star**, Rethimnon, Tel. (0831) 21896. **Rithimna Beach**, Rethimnon, Tel. (0831) 29491. **Europa , Kalypso Cretan Village**, Plakias, Tel.(0832)31296. **El Greco**, Rethimnon, Tel. (0831) 71102. **Rethymno Bay**, Rethimnon, Tel. (0831) 27512. **Oassis**, Perivolia, Rethimnon, Tel. (0831) 44705

MODERATE: **Adele Beach Bungalows**, Rethimnon, Tel. (0831) 71047. **Amnissos**, Rethimnon, Tel. (0831) 71502. **Kriti Beach**, Rethimnon, Tel. (0831) 27401. **Rea**, Agia Galini, Tel.(0832) 91390. **Neos Alianthos**, Plakias, Tel.(0832) 31280. **Bali Beach**, Bali, Tel.(0834) 94210. **Xenia**, Rethimnon, Tel. (0831) 29111.

BUDGET: **Golden Beach**, Adele, Rethymnon, Tel. (0831) 71012. **Ionia**: Rethimnon, Tel. (0831) 22902. **Steris Beach,** Rethimnon, Tel. (0831) 28303. **Livykon**, Plakias, Tel. (0831) 31216. **Miramare**, Aghia Galini, Tel. (0832) 91221. **Miramare Beach**, Rethimnon, Tel. (0831) 71012.

Hospital
State Hospital, Rethimnon (behind Public Gardens), Tel. (0831) 22261.

Local Festivals
Epiphany (Jan.6). Blessing of waters in Venetian harbor by Bishop of Rethimnon. *Carnival Parade* down main Iraklion-Hania road past Public Gardens, 3 Sundays before Lent, the dates changing every year relative to the moveable feast of Easter. *Feast Day Of St. John The Theologian* at Preveli monastery, May 8. *Anniversary Of The Battle Of Crete*, May 19-22, with wreath-laying ceremony in suburb of Perivolia on May 21. Also on May 21 is the *Feast Day Of Sts. Helen And Constantine* at the monastery of Arkadi. At Hora Sphakion, the *Anniversary Of The 1821 Revolution Against The Turks* is celebrated on May 26-27. In July, Rethimnon holds both its biennial *Cretan Handicrafts Exhibition* and *Rethimnon Wine Festival*, the latter a two-week affair in the Public Gardens from 8:30 p.m. to 2 a.m. with much eating, drinking, dancing and entertainment. August 15 is the feast day of *The Annunciation Of The Virgin Mary*, the second biggest religious holiday of the year outside of Easter. On November 7-9, the monastery of Arkadi commemorates *The 1866 Gunpowder Room Explosion* with ceremonies at Arkadi and Rethimnon.

Museums
The new **Rethimnon Archaeological Museum** in the former prison, opposite entrance to the Venetian Fortress. Timings: 8:45-15:00. (Sundays 9:30-14:30); closed on Tuesdays and national holidays. **The museum at the monastery of Arkadi**. Timings: 8:00-19:00 every day (closed 1 hour at various times for midday break).

Post / Telegraph / Telephone
General Post Office (ELTA), Kondourioti St., Rethimnon. **Central Telephone/Telegraph Office** (OTE), Kondourioti St., Rethimnon. (Long distance dialing phones also available at many cafes and cigarette kiosks).

Restaurants
SEAFOOD : All restaurants in the Venetian harbor, Rethimnon. *BASIC GREEK:* **Tassos'**, beachfront, Rethimnon, Tel. (0831) 24615. **Socrates'**, Rimondi Fountain, Rethimnon, Tel. (0831) 24365. **Pantheon**, beachfront, Rethimnon Tel. (0831) 29026.

Shopping
Handicrafts: Shops on Nearchou St. off of Venetian harbor and Arkadiou, Platanos Square near Neratzes Minaret; **Leather goods**: Giorgos Psathakis, Rimondi Fountain, Rethimnon; **Jewelery**: Cretan House, 222 Arkadiou St., Rethimnon and Gamma Gold-Silver, 81 Eleftherios Venizelou St., Rethimnon.

Tourist Information
Greek National Tourist Organization (EOT) on beachfront, Tel. (0831) 24143, 19148.

Access & Local Transport
Connecting buses to and from airport and docks at Hania for planes and ships to Athens and Piraeus. Local buses to Iraklion for ships and international as well as local flights.
Olympic Airways, Rethimnon, Tel. (0831) 22257, 24333.
Buses to all local villages, beaches, etc. Numerous automobile and motorbike rental agencies. Various sightseeing tours including day trips to Knossos and Gorge of Samaria.

Cinema
Kartalion, Voulgaroktonou St.,**Oassis**, Georgiou St.,**Pantellis**, Potaliou St., **Evrosini**, Arkadi St.

Taxi
Martyrion Pl., Agostou Statioti Pl., Dimitrakaki Street.

Rent a Car
Avis, Arkadi St. 196 (Tel. 29409). **Kaklidakis**, 4 Martyrion Pl. (Tel. 28316).

Monasteries
Arkadi, Preveli, Arseniou, Roustika.

Caves
Idaion Andron (Nidha Plain), Melidoni, Sentoni (Zoniana), Marathospilios (Margarites), Spiliostou Digeni (Platanias), Kranaios Hermes (Patsos), Trypiti (Ano meros), Gerani.

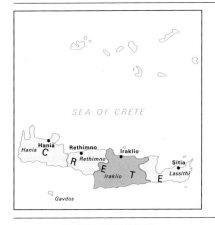

IRAKLION

IRAKLION CITY
ARCHAEOLOGICAL MUSEUM
KNOSSOS
ARKHANES / TYLISSOS
SOUTHEAST OF IRAKLION
MESSARA PLAIN
PHAESTOS / MATALA
AGIA TRIADA / MALIA

IRAKLION CITY

Iraklion, the biggest city in Crete and the island's capital, brims over with a noisy vitality that helps compensate for its sprawling, unplanned outskirts and the endless traffic jams in the alleys inside its Venetian walls. Its population, swelled over the past twenty years by migration from the surrounding villages, is now over 110,000, making it one of Greece's half-dozen largest cities. The province of Iraklion is among the richest in the country in per capita income terms, thanks to traditional agricultural products such as olive oil, sultanas, table grapes and wine and a healthy tourist industry which brings more than one million visitors a year to Crete.

A port for Knossos in Minoan times, the settlement was called Heraclium by the Romans and then El Khandak by the ninth century Saracen conquerors, after the great fortification ditch surrounding the town. Under the Arabs, Iraklion became a major Mediterranean slave market. But Byzantine rule was restored in 964 AD after a long siege by the army of Nikiforos Fokas.

Preceding pages: Fishing nets drying on the docks of Iraklion. Left: Detail of the 17th century Lion Fountain.

The city – and often the whole island – was known as Candia to the Venetians, who bought Crete in 1210 and sent colonists to establish feudal rule over the rebellious islanders. For more than four centuries, Crete was the jewel in the crown of imperial Venice. As the island's capital, Candia was a flourishing port on the galley routes to the Levant and an export center for Cretan produce – timber, sweet wines, cheese and even table grapes. One medieval traveler, Canon Pietro Casola, who stopped off in Candia in 1494 wrote: "Candia is a very large, strongly walled city situated in a plain. It has beautiful houses, although they are flat-roofed in the Eastern fashion. It has a fine port, which is somewhat dangerous at the entrance, especially for larger ships."

To face the growing threat from Ottoman Turkey, the fortifications were rebuilt in the sixteenth century, enclosing a wide expanse of gardens and orchards within the city. Every citizen was expected to contribute both funds and labor. When the Turks eventually attacked Crete in 1648, they quickly overran the island but were stopped short by the massive defences of Candia. A twenty-one-year siege followed, one of the longest in history, before General Francesco Morosini surrendered to the Ottoman Grand

Vizier in September 1699 and sailed back to Venice with the remnants of the defending force and the city archives. Under Turkish rule, Iraklion was governed by a pasha and known as Megalo Kastro (the Great Fortress). When Crete won autonomy in 1898 with the help of the Great Powers – Britain, France, Russia and Italy – Candia became Iraklion and quickly developed into the island's most important commercial port.

Getting Around

The best starting point for exploring Iraklion is officially called **Plateia Venizelou** but is known to residents as Ta Leontaria (the Lions), after the marble lions decorating the seventeenth-century **Morosini Fountain**, one of the city's

Above: The Church of Agios Markos, often the site of art exhibits. Right: Winter rains and the sea's swell hammer at the walls of Koules fortress.

main landmarks. Fed by an aqueduct that carried water from the springs on Mount Iouhtas, 15 km away, it was originally topped by a larger-than-lifesize Roman statue of Neptune, the sea-god. The square is filled with cafes, newspaper stands, bookstalls and souvenir shops. This is the place to pick up a map, guidebooks, a copy of *Zorba the Greek* (available in sereral languages) and cassettes of Cretan music. It also boasts a renowned *bougatsa* shop where you can try a creamy custard- or cheese-filled pie, served warm from the oven.

Sitting at one of the cafes beside the fountain, you look across to the church of **Agios Markos**, built by the Venetians in the thirteenth century and named for the Serenissima's patron saint. It is used now for staging concerts and art shows. The 50-room **palace** of the Duke of Crete, a bureaucrat sent from Venice to govern the island for a two-year period, survived into Ottoman times, but all that can be seen of it now are the vaulted ceilings of the shops opposite the fountain. The

Vikelas library, the biggest in Greece outside Athens, replaces another set of Venetian administrative buildings to the south of the square. The recently restored **Loggia**, a kind of colonial clubhouse for the Venetian nobility on the island, designed in elegant near-Palladian style by the architect Francesco Basilicata in the early seventeenth century, stands just around the corner on August 25th street. From its balcony the Duke of Crete issued proclamations and presided over festivals and processions. Adjoining the Loggia is the former Venetian Armory, now the **City Hall**. The battered statue of a woman set in its north wall is thought to be a personification of Crete.

To the left, heading down to the harbor, is **El Greco park**, with a post-office caravan conveniently positioned at one side. On the far side of the park is the **"OTE"** or **"PTT"** telephone office. On the right, set back from the street, stands the church of **Agios Titos**, the patron saint of Crete, who is credited with converting the islanders to Christianity in the first century AD following the instructions of St. Paul.

The church has been rebuilt several times since its foundation soon after Nikiforos Fokas recaptured the island. It was the seat of the Orthodox archbishop of Crete, then of the Roman Catholic archbishop during the Venetian period. After the siege, the Grand Vizier ordered its conversion into a mosque. It was rededicated to St. Titus after the Turkish minority finally left the island in 1923, and the minaret was replaced by a belfry. It was not until 1966 that the mitreshaped reliquary containing the skull of St. Titus was returned from Venice, where it had been taken by General Morosini. It can now be seen in a chapel to the left of the entrance. A patch of cranium is just visible, surrounded by silver and gilt, and a steady stream of Irakliots passes in and out to say a prayer and kiss the glass case that protects it.

Continuing down the street past shipping offices, car rental and travel agencies, you reach the **inner harbor** where

123

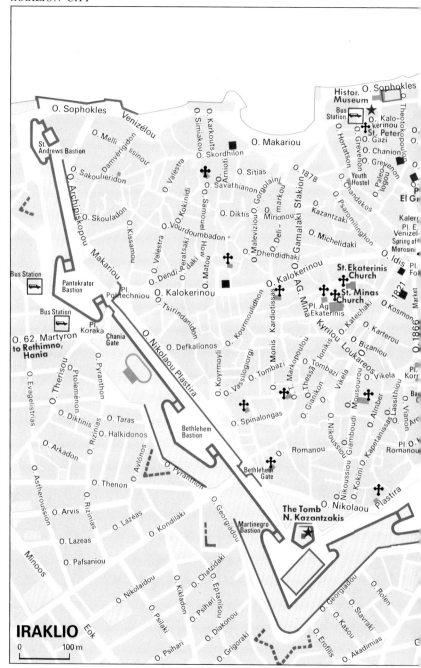

IRAKLIO

0   100 m

124

yachts moor, the fishing boats land their catch. and fishing nets are repaired.

One of the favorite meeting places of the youth of Iraklion is the **Café Marina** where you should try to take a break, enjoy a Greek coffee or a delightful, cool frappée (whipped and frozen Nescafé) and admire the fishing boats bobbing at berth and the nets spread on the wall. Looking out toward the city you will see the great vaults of the **Venetian magazine**. A series of high, vaulted tunnels are all that remains of the Venetian arsenal, once a busy shipyard where galleys were repaired and re-equipped. Each was designed to hold one vessel.

The squat miniature fortress standing guard over the inner harbor was built by the Venetians but is known now by its Turkish name, **Koules**. Now restored, it is a remarkable piece of sixteenth-century military architecture, with more than twenty thick-walled chambers and a store-room still filled with cannonballs. A ramp leads up to the battlements.

The roof terrace offers a good panoramic view of the city stretched out at the foot of the Ida range, with its wild labyrinth of modern housing, toward the left the new port where the big ferries come to anchor, and also a good view of the coastline on either side of the city. The pointed mountain on the western horizon is known locally as Stromboli. The fort's upper level is used as an open-air stage for plays and concerts in summer. (Franco Zeffirelli's version of Verdi's *Othello*, starring Placido Domingo, was filmed here rather than in Cyprus). The exterior walls carry three carved reliefs of the lion of St. Mark, the symbol of Venetian power emblazoned on monuments throughout the eastern Mediterranean.

From the fortress, you can walk along the inside of the modern harbor wall, which encloses an increasingly busy port handling passengers and containers bound for Cyprus, North Africa and the

125

western Mediterranean. The low-lying island in the distance is **Dia**, uninhabited now and a sanctuary for the *agrimi*, the long-horned Cretan wild goat.

Back at the roundabout, a right turn takes you past the skeleton of the medieval church of **St. Peter**, badly damaged in the 1941 bombing of Iraklion which preceded the German airborne invasion of the island, and past the bus station for Rethimnon and Hania.

History Comes Alive

Opposite is the **Historical and Ethnographical Museum**, housed in an imposing neo-classical mansion dating from the early 1900s. It is a pleasantly cool place to linger on hot afternoons.

The garden contains relics of war: Venetian cannons and a pile of cannonballs as well as several unexploded

Above: Entrance to the Historical and Ethnographical Museum. Right: Even in the hectic city there are sometimes peaceful spots.

bombs from World War II. Inside, a varied collection ranges from early Christian and Byzantine stonework in the basement (**Room 1**) to a handsome display of handwoven Cretan textiles in **Room 11** on the top floor.

Rooms 2 and 2a contain Venetian sculptures, including a rebuilt fountain dating from around 1600 and a handsome lion of St. Mark from the Agios Dimitrios fortress outside the city walls, with a Latin inscription saying: "I protect the Kingdom of Crete." There are stone reliefs from the Franciscan monastery which stood on the site of the Archaeological Museum and was destroyed in the Turkish siege.

Room 3 holds inscriptions from the Venetian period. **Room 4** has Ottoman sculptures, among them some elegant tombstones of Turkish officials, decorated with stone turbans, as well as attractive eighteenth century tiles taken from a mosque. In the corridor are wallpaintings from a Turkish house, showing Iraklion in a romanticized Cretan landscape.

126

On the ground floor to the right of the entrance, **Room 5** contains early Christian and Byzantine ecclesiastical items, as well as Byzantine and Venetian jewelry and a collection of gold and bronze coins. There are impressive icons from the Savvathiana monastery above the village of Fodhele and the church of Panagia Gouverniotissa on the way to the Lassithi Plain, together with richly embroidered vestments from the Asomatos monastery in the Amari valley in western Crete and a carved wooden lectern from the Valsamonero monastery on the slopes of Mount Ida. Off the hall, a partly rebuilt Byzantine chapel displays thirteenth- and fourteenth-century frescoes.

To the left of the entrance, **Room 7** holds the historical collection, dominated by items from the island's bloody revolutionary struggle for independence from the Turks and memorabilia of the independent Cretan state of 1898-1913, administered by Prince George of Greece and, from 1906, by Alexandros Zaimis. There are portraits of Cretan warrior chieftains, a fine array of their weapons, historic photographs and a flag of the independent Cretan state. Just in front of the staircase is a banner proclaiming *Eleftheria i Thanatos* (Freedom or Death), the Cretan rebels' rallying cry. It belonged to a chieftain from the Argiroupolis district of Rethimnon. On the first floor landing are more photographs dating from the days of independence, and another series illustrating the 1941 Battle of Crete.

On the left is **Room 9**, which reproduces the study of the Cretan writer Nikos Kazantzakis, (1883-1957), author of *Zorba the Greek* and *The Odyssey: A Modern Sequel*. The desk, book collection and other memorabilia come from his house on the island of Aegina. Another room on the same floor commemorates the Cretan-born statesman Eleftherios Venizelos, who dominated Greek political life for twenty years after the island was united with Greece, and another Cretan-born prime minister of Greece, Emmanuel Tsouderos. He took

127

office as the Germans invaded northern Greece in April 1941, and later escaped to Egypt.

The **second-floor rooms** contain a spectacular collection of textiles, many in the brilliant scarlet that characterizes much Cretan handwork. Embroidered motifs on silk, linen and cotton include dragons, mermaids and elaborate floral designs, while the woven blankets are sometimes decorated with lively historical scenes. **Room 10**, containing the ethnographic collection, is fitted out as a well-appointed domestic interior from the turn of the century.

Back at Ta Leontaria, the narrow pedestrian way across the street, **Odos Daidalos**, follows the outline of the city's first fortification wall and emerges close to the Archaeological Museum. Besides souvenir shops, jewelers, bookshops and newsvendors the Daidalos Street is also

Above: Wines, fresh and dried fruits, nuts: all products of Crete. Right: Peddler and pope in Iraklion – a bargain for redemption.

peppered with a slew of restaurants offering typical Greek fare.

Alternatively, a right turn beside the fountain takes you up to the traffic lights and across **Odos Kalokairinou**, the corso or main thoroughfare of Venetian days, into the crowded market street, **Odos 1866**. Butchers'shops jostle groceries filled with Cretan produce, cheeses, honey, wines, olives in brine, and pungent herbs, along with old-fashioned barber shops, and stores selling leather goods and the distinctive Cretan knives. Smells of roasting meat drift out from the covered alley filled with tavernas which opens off the east side of the street. At the top of the street, on **Plateia Cornarou**, is the **Bembo Fountain**, put together from fragments of ancient marble, including a headless Roman statue which its architect, Zuane Bembo, hauled all the way from Ierapetra on the southeast coast. The polygonal stone kiosk in front of it is a Turkish fountain house.

The main road to the right, **Odos Kyrillou Loukareos**, leads round to the

128

huge nineteenth century cathedral, **Agios Minas**. In its shadow stands the church of **Agia Aikaterini of Sinai**, an appealing mixture of Byzantine and Venetian architecture which dates from 1555. It contains a magnificent collection of Cretan icons. After the fall of Constantinople to the Turks in 1453, the Agia Aikaterini college in Iraklion, a dependency of the monastery of the same name in the Sinai desert in Egypt, became a renowned centre of learning and artistic life as dispossessed Byzantine intellectuals arrived in Crete on their way to a new life spreading classical thought and literature across western Europe.

Cretan icon painting was especially important at this period, with painters traveling to and from Venice, where they came under Italian Renaissance influence. The church contains six icons by Michalis Damaskinos, a sixteenth century painter who could work in both Byzantine and Western styles, which used to hang in the Vrondisi monastery in the foothills of Mount Ida. From the ticket desk, on the western wall of the church, they are paintings number 2, 5, 8, 9, 12 and 15.

Walking due south from the cathedral square through a maze of narrow streets, you quickly reach the **Martinengo Bastion** where Nikos Kazantzakis is buried. An alternative route is to head back to Plateia Cornarou, go up Odos Evans and turn right onto Odos Nikos Plastiras, which follows the line of the Venetian walls from the Jesus bastion. The Martinengo Bastion is the next one along. **Kazantzakis' grave** is a stone slab, marked by a tall wooden cross. An inscription from his writings reflects the spirit of his admired friend, Zorba: "I fear nothing. I hope for nothing. I am free."

The **fortifications**, designed by the Venetian military engineer Michael Sanmicheli, enclose the inner city in an angular semi-circle cut by seven heart-shaped bastions and four gates. Two of them, the Hania Gate to the west and the Jesus Gate to the south, survive. You can walk along the western and southern ramparts, which

are as much as 40 m thick in places. The moat now contains a soccer pitch and two outdoor theaters where performances are staged during the city's annual summer arts festival. Behind the children's playground outside the **Vituri Bastion**, at the southeast corner of the fortifications beside Leoforos Dimokratias, you can inspect an *agrimi* at close quarters: there are several of them living in an enclosure at the base of the ramparts.

The Archaeological Museum

Built on the side of the medieval Catholic monastery of St. Francis, a prominent landmark in wood-cut illustrations of Iraklion in Venetian times, the Archaeological Museum is situated just off **Eleftheria** ("Freedom") **Square**. Across from the museum is the **tourist**

Above: The camera of this photographer on Eleftheria Square might also land in a museum. Right: The discus of Phaestos (ca. 1650 BC).

information office. "Freedom Square" is the largest in Iraklion and a favorite spot for rendezvous on Sundays and summer evenings, with its numerous tables and chairs under the shade of planes. People often meet here for a walk in the dusk (known as a *volta*) or to go to one of the movies lining the square. The many photographers with their old-fashioned equipment are one of the square's curiosities. Various events also take place here, from concerts to demonstrations and political speeches.

In summer, it is best to visit the museum early in the morning, since the galleries quickly get overcrowded. As scarcely any Cretan antiquities are to be found in museums abroad, the Bronze Age collections provide a unique guide to Minoan art and lifestyles.

Gallery I: The finds from the Neolithic and early Minoan period (5000-2000 BC), before the great palaces were built (and before the potter's wheel arrived) illustrate the highly developed skills of early Cretan craftsmen in metal-

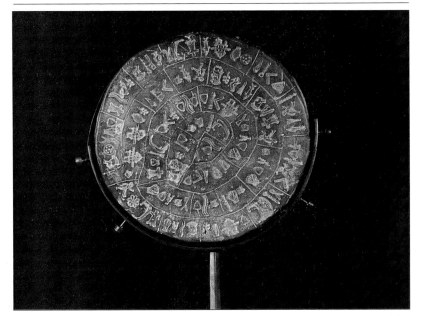

work, pottery-making and in carving stone vases and sealstones. Case 7 contains fine stone vases from an early cemetery at Mohlos, an islet off the nothern coast, in use from about 2600-2100 BC. Their shapes are designed to set off the striped limestone and marble. A *pyxis*, or small box, in soft serpentine has a lid with its handle carved in the shape of a reclining dog. Case 10 has a four-wheeled cart dating from around 2000 BC, the earliest evidence for wheeled transport on Crete, and a flat-bottomed boat, both from Palaikastro on the eastern coast. Case 16 contains a sealstone which is carved in the shape of a crouching monkey. Case 14 includes early mould-cast daggers in copper bronze and occasionally silver. Cases 17 and 18a contain fine jewelry from Arkhanes in gold, rock crystal, carnelian, ivory and faience, a kind of glass paste.

Gallery II: Finds from the early palaces (dated to 1900-1700 BC, the Old Palace or Protopalatian period), include the Town Mosaic from Knossos, a collection of faience plaques showing miniature house façades in varied architectural styles. The same case holds tablets in hieroglyphic script (not yet fully deciphered) and a bronze dagger from Malia with a gold hilt in a latticework design.

Gallery III: Distinctive pottery from the Kamares Cave, high on Mount Ida and overlooking the palace of Phaestos, comes in an amazing array of colors and designs. Delicate cups in what is known as "eggshell ware" are perhaps the most attractive, with some angular in style, imitating metal shapes. Larger vases from Phaestos, like the fruitstand with its toothed rim, or the punchbowl with appliqué flowers are spectacular creations with a hint of the rococo exaggeration that Minoan artists sometimes indulged in when they moved away from the miniature scale which seems to have suited them best.

The Phaestos disk in Case 41, made of clay with characters stamped in spiral bands on both sides, has not yet been deciphered, although it has been sug-

gested that it records an early hymn. It was found in a context dated to around 1700 BC.

Gallery IV: The finds of the period of the later palaces (1700- 1450 BC) include some of the most remarkable Minoan artworks known. Case 49 contains a jug decorated with a delicate pattern of waving grass and a rhyton, or vessel pierced for pouring libations to a god, decorated with underwater motifs in the naturalistic marine style developed by potters at Knossos in the final years of the Minoan palace civilization. Case 51 holds the famous bull's head rhyton, made of dark serpentine with eyes inlaid in red jasper and clear rock crystal. Its horns – now restored – were of gilded wood. A double axe is incised on its forehead. It was found in the Little Palace at Knossos. In Case 59 is the Lioness Head rhyton, made of white limestone and found in the Central Treasury at Knossos. Case 56 contains an ivory acrobat with arms outstretched, perhaps a bull-leaper. Long ceremonial bronze swords from the palace at Malia are displayed in Case 53, including one with an ivory hilt and rock crystal pommel.

The two bare-breasted snake goddesses wearing elaborate flounced skirts in Case 50 are made of faience. They were found, like many of the treasures in this gallery, in two stone-lined pits beneath a floor in a Knossos palace shrine, known as the Temple Repositories. Case 55 contains reliefs in faience from the same find, among them a realistic cow suckling her calf. The richly decorated Gaming Board in Case 57 has an ivory frame inlaid with gold and silver leaf, lapis lazuli, rock crystal and faience, and four accompanying ivory gaming pieces. It comes from a corridor in the palace and is dated to around 1600 BC.

Left: The snake-goddess suggests how people were clothed back then.

Gallery V: The exhibits mostly come from Knossos in the last palatial period (1450-1380 BC), when it apparently was ruled by Mycenaeans from mainland Greece. Case 62 contains tall stone lamps made from reddish marble, imported from southern Greece, and some Egyptian objects found at Knossos, including the bottom half of a thirteenth-century BC statuette of an Egyptian named User, perhaps an envoy to Crete. In Case 69 are rectangular clay tablets from several sites inscribed in Linear A, the Minoan script, which still remains undeciphered. The long narrow tablets from Knossos are in Linear B, an early form of Greek, and record stores and farm production from year to year during the period of Mycenaean influence. They survived accidental baking in the fierce fires which destroyed these sites. Case 66 contains stone vases from Knossos, including the huge, flat alabastrons made of gypsum which were found in the Throne Room and may have been used in a last-minute religious ritual intended to avert destruction of the palace. The appealing clay house model in Case 70, found at Arkhanes, illustrates several features of Minoan architecture: small windows to keep out both heat and cold, more light provided by an interior courtyard, columns tapering downwards, and an upper-floor terrace.

Gallery VI: The finds come from graves of the later palace and post-palatial periods and include some spectacular jewelry and weaponry. The Royal Tomb at Isopata contained a series of striking Egyptian alabaster vases displayed in Case 72. An unusual horse-burial from Arkhanes is on show in Case 75a: the animal was sacrificed and ritually dismembered. Case 84 contains bronze weapons belonging to the Mycenaean warriors, buried in graves north of Knossos, among them spearheads used for thrusting and short swords designed for fighting at close quarters. Case 85 holds a bronze

helmet with large cheek-pieces. A reconstructed helmet made of pieces of boars' tusk, once sewn on to a leather skull-cap, is displayed in Case 78. This kind of helmet is discribed in Homer's *Iliad* as part of a warrior's equipment. It is also illustrated on an amphora from Knossos in Case 82.

Superb goldwork is displayed in Cases 86, 87, and 88, notably the large gold ring from Isopata showing a ritual dance with a goddess and worshippers in a flower-filled meadow and a pair of earrings in an abstracted bull's-head design. Each gold granule was applied separately in a highly skilled technique.

A circular bronze mirror from Arkhanes has an ivory handle. In Case 79a is an elaborately carved ivory pyxis showing a bull-catching scene. Three huge bronze cauldrons from Tylissos stand

Above: Stucco of a bull's head from the north entrance of the palace in Knossos. Right: Religious idols of the Minoans, a clay image of a bull.

against one wall, each big enough to stew a whole sheep at a feast or celebration.

Gallery VII: Finds from villas of the later palace period and from sacred caves are dominated by the giant double axes, an important Minoan religious symbol. They come from the coastal villa at Nirou Hani and are displayed on restored poles. Case 89 holds bronze figurines of men worshipping, their right hands pressed to their foreheads in a kind of salute. One realistic, larger piece shows an older man with a protruding stomach in the worshipper stance. Case 93 contains material from the villa at Agia Triada, including several fine marine-style vases, as well as vessels containing carbonized barley, millet, beans and figs from fire-destruction levels at Phaestos and Palaikastro in eastern Crete.

Cases 97 and 98 display bronze swords and small gold double axes left as offerings in the Arkhalohori cave in central Crete. In Case 101 is one of the great masterpieces of Minoan goldwork: a pendant of two bees apparently storing a

drop of honey in a honeycomb. It comes from the Chrysolakkos cemetery at Malia and is dated to around 1550 BC.

Three other masterpieces, stone vases in serpentine carved with lively relief scenes, are shown in separate cases. All were found at Agia Triada. The heavily restored Boxer Rhyton features scenes from boxing and wrestling matches, with the fighters wearing what look like leather helmets, as well as bull-leaping acrobats. On the Chieftain Cup, a Minoan official is seen receiving a consignment of animal hides. All three vases are thought to have been made in a Knossos workshop around 1550 BC.

Case 99 contains copper ingots from Agia Triada in the shape of oxhides, each weighing around 40 kg. They were hauled by their protruding corners.

Gallery VIII: The items on display are all from the late palace-period and sur-rounding town at Zakros in eastern Crete. Case 109 contains an outstanding find: a rock crystal rhyton, with its handle made from rock-crystal beads which have turned green along with the bronze wire on which they are threaded. It was re-stored from more than three hundred fragments.

The pottery from Zakros is of high quality: Case 110 contains a rhyton in marine style decorated with starfish and shells against a background of seaweed and rocks. In Case 112 is another carved stone rhyton, made of chlorite, showing a mountain sanctuary complete with wild goats and flowers. It was originally covered with gold leaf.

Case 113 contains bronze ingots and a whole elephant tusk found in the palace store-rooms, discolored by the fire which destroyed the settlement at Zakros around 1450 BC. In Cases 114 and 118 are an extraordinary collection of stone vases, including tall rhytons in Egyptian alabaster, cups made from colorful striped limestones and several imported vases from Egypt. A bull's head rhyton in chlorite is displayed in Case 116, smaller than the one from Knossos, but just as finely crafted.

Gallery IX: Among the finds from a variety of neo-palatial-period sites in eastern Crete are a magnificent collection of sealstones in semi-precious stone displayed in Case 128, along with impressions and detailed drawings that reveal the Minoan miniaturists' lively imagination and ingenuity.

Cases 126 and 127 hold objects from the fishing town of Gournia on the northern coast, among them bronze tools and large limestone lamps. Case 122 contains pottery as well as stone lamps and vases from the island of Psira off the northeastern coast, including a striking vase in clay in a shopping-bag shape, decorated with double-axes. Case 123 contains clay figurines of people and animals, including some horned beetles which were dedicated at a sanctuary at Piskokephalo south of Sitia. A real-life example, also on show, illustrates the accuracy of the Minoan potters' study of nature.

Left: A small circular Temple with a goddess.
Right: An Agia Triada sacrophagus detail.

Gallery X: The decline of Minoan civilization is reflected in the finds from the post-palace period (1350-1150 BC), mostly from houses built in the ruins of the Knossos palace and tombs elsewhere on the island. Case 133 contains several large clay "goddesses" from a shrine at Gazi on the western outskirts of Iraklion, one with three poppy pods in her headdress, suggesting that opium was not unknown to the Minoans. Another terracotta group in Case 132, from Palaikastro, shows three woman dancing, while a fourth, in the center, plays the lyre. The comparative poverty of the period is illustrated by the jewelry in Case 139: necklaces are made of beads of glass-paste and semi-precious stones, rather than gold. In Case 143 are idols from a sanctuary at Agia Triada, including a figure on a swing.

Gallery XI: Life in Crete changed markedly from 1100 BC to 800 BC, as bronze tools and weapons were gradually replaced with iron – though bronze was still used for ceremonial objects. In the Sub-Minoan, Proto-geometric and Geometric periods, new pottery shapes and styles of decoration come into use, and burial customs changed: cremation became the rule and ashes were buried in large clay vases. Case 155 contains a burial urn found at Knossos, decorated with a scene of two lions tearing a man apart. Case 148 displays a curious rhyton in the shape of an ox-drawn chariot, and clay goddesses with arms upraised from a shrine at Karphi above the Lassithi plain. Case 149 contains finds from a cave sanctuary of Eileithyia, the goddess of childbirth, at Inatos on the south coast. Among them are clay figurines of heavily pregnant women, some giving birth in a squatting position.

Gallery XII: Items from the eighth and seventh centuries BC, the Late Geometric and Orientalizing period, reveal a new artistic liveliness, indicating that Crete was again in touch with both

mainland Greece and other regions of the southeast Mediterranean. Case 159 contains cremation vases from Fortetsa near Knossos with brightly colored designs as well as gifts for the dead. In Case 169 are some impressive bronze finds from the cave sanctuary of Zeus high on Mount Ida. Fragments from a tripod cauldron depict an oared ship with two standing figures aboard. It may represent the abduction of Ariadne from Crete by Theseus. A bronze quiver, bronze greaves and two semi-circular bronze mitrae worn below the breastplate to protect the stomach illustrate Cretan armorers' skills.

Case 170 contains a unique collection of ninth-century BC jewelry, mostly from the re-used Bronze Age tomb at Teke close to Knossos. It was found in two vases buried beside the tomb doorway, prompting suggestions that it may have been the family vault of a group of Knossos metalworkers with Near East origins. The hoard includes a gold pendant inlaid with crystal on a plaited gold chain, another crescent-shaped pendant, a necklace of rock crystal beads and a gold strip with impressed decoration of warriors fighting lions.

Gallery XIII contains a collection of decorated clay burial chests and bathtubs, which were also used as coffins by the Minoans. The chest-shaped type probably imitates a wooden original.

Gallery XIV is upstairs and displays Minoan frescoes, many of them discolored by fire and greatly restored more than forty years ago. But they still convey the Minoans' interest in elaborate religious ceremonial and their enthusiasm for nature as well as their exceptional artistic abilities. The frescoes were painted on wet plaster, sometimes molded in low relief to create a three-dimensional effect. They date from the later palace period, although some from Knossos belong to the period of Mycenaean influence.

At the top of the east flight of stairs is a wooden scale reconstruction of the palace at Knossos which gives an idea of its labyrinthine quality. Frescoes Numbers 2-5 are fragments from a religious procession of large figures and come from the Corridor of the Procession leading to the great entrance to the palace at Knossos.

The best preserved is the Cup-bearer, carrying a deep conical rhyton, who wears a sealstone on his wrist. Number 6 shows a griffin, a mythological combination of eagle and lion, discolored by fire. It comes from the Throne Room. The Figure-of-Eight-Shields in Number 7 were a popular motif also used on pottery and in ivory-carving: they are modelled on tall shields made of animal hides which Mycenaean warriors carried.

The Lily Prince, Number 9, wears an elaborate headdress of lilies and feathers and has been identified as the priest-king of Knossos, though some scholars believe he may be a boxer. The bull's head in low relief, Number 9, is thought to be all that remains of a bull-capturing scene from the north entrance to the Knossos palace. The Royal Ladies in Blue, Number 10, come from the east wing of the palace and the Dolphins, Number 11, from the Queen's apartments there.

The colored spirals, Numbers 12-13, also come from Knossos, while the Partridge Frescoe, Number 14, was found in a small building south of the palace, which the excavators named the Caravanserai.

The Bull-leapers, Number 15, is one of the liveliest frescoes found, with a young man turning a backwards somersault over a dappled bull, while two young women act as catchers. The Lily frescoes, Numbers 16 and 17, are elegant still lives from a villa at Amnisos, on the nothern coast just east of Iraklion. A series of paintings from the villa at Agia Triada, nextdoor to Phaestos, is blackened by fire: Numbers 18, 19 and 20 are all from the same room and show a kneeling woman, another woman at a shrine and a wild cat. Two procession fragments, Numbers 21 and 22, are next to a painted floor from Agia

Triada with a design of dolphins, octopus and fish.

In the center of the gallery is a painted stone sarcophagus, also from Agia Triada, which dates from around 1400 BC. It is covered with plaster painted with scenes from a funeral ritual on one long side and, on the other, a bull-sacrifice. One short side shows a procession and the other two chariots pulled by griffins and driven by women.

Gallery XV: Both La Parisienne, the haughty, long-necked priestess who seems to represent a Minoan ideal of beauty, and the fascinating miniature fresco of crowds of spectators, segregated by sex, watching an open-air ceremony, are displayed here. The restored Camp Stool fresco, to which "La Parisienne" possibly belongs, shows seated priestesses and priests holding goblets and chalices.

Gallery XVI: The Saffron Gatherer fresco was originally restored showing a boy collecting saffron: in fact it was a blue monkey. The Captain of the Blacks is a fragment from a scene showing a running white warrior followed by a group of black, perhaps Nubian, mercenaries. Three fragments from a Knossos town house show a bluebird among flowers, and scenes of monkeys in a garden. There are three small fragments, too, of olive trees in relief, painted in delicate pinks and grays.

Galleries XVII and **XVIII**, containing the Giamalakis collection, are normally closed. Back on the ground floor **Galleries XIX** and **XX** are sometimes open: they contain stone and bronze sculpture from the archaic and Graeco-Roman periods. In **Gallery XIX** are three bronze figures from Dreros in eastern Crete, made of bronze hammered onto a wooden core and secured with pins. They show Apollo, Artemis and Leto.

Right: A copy of the "The Captain of the Blacks" from Knossos.

KNOSSOS

The road to the Minoan palace of Knossos, 5 km from Iraklion, is sign-posted from Plateia Eleftheria: bear left at the cemetery and again at the turning for the coastal highway. (The No. 2 bus for Knossos leaves every 15 minutes or so from a stop next to the Morosini Fountain.) At the 3.5 km mark, a side-road forks right to the village of **Fortetsa**, from where the Grand Vizier's artillery bombarded the city during the great siege. To the left is the University of Crete science faculty, built on the site of an ancient cemetery, where more than three hundred tombs were unearthed with burials covering more than a millenium, from the SubMinoan to the early Christian periods. Curiously, no major cemetery from the period of the Minoan palaces has yet been discovered around Knossos, which prompted a heretical

Above: Northern side of the central court-yard. Right: The room of the Tall Pithos.

theory that the palace complex was simply a vast funerary monument. However, a stroll around its buildings, which still evoke an atmosphere of domestic luxury, is likely to dispel such notions. The road passes through the Roman city of Knossos, of which there is virtually nothing to see, and drops down towards the Kairatos valley.

To the right, a driveway leads to the **Villa Ariadne**, the house built by Sir Arthur Evans, the British archaeologist, who bought the site of the palace at the turn of the century and dug there for the next 30 years, though the bulk of the excavation was completed between 1900 and 1906.

A Cretan excavator, Minos Kalokairinos, was the first to dig on the Kefala hill in 1878, unearthing some of the store-rooms and a dozen *pithoi* or tall storage jars. He immediately identified the building as the palace of his name-sake King Minos, the legendary king of Crete mentioned in Homer's *Iliad*. Later, an American journalist, William Stillman, broached the idea that the building might have inspired the origins of the labyrinth myth in Greek legend. Evans arrived on Crete in 1894, but it was not until after the island became independent under Greek suzerainty and an archaeological law was drafted that he was able to purchase the entire site. While the excavations were in progress, Evans also had substantial sections of the palace reconstructed in reinforced concrete, in order to preserve the architecture, notably of the living quarters on the east side of the complex. The restorations have been sharply criticized, both by professional archaeologists and aesthetic purists, but without them it would be next to impossible to gain an impression of the size and scale of the palace. A few hundred meters further on, a left turn leads to the village of **Makritichos**, straggling down the hill to the Kairatos stream, which for years has provided skilled excavators to work at Knossos.

In mythology, Knossos was known as the home of King Minos and the prison of the Minotaur, the hybrid monster born of Queen Pasiphae's love for a white bull. Tribute owed to Minos by Athens came regularly in the form of seven maidens and seven young men, who were devoured by the Minotaur. Then Theseus, the Athenian king's son, arrived among a group of sacrificial victims and killed the monster with the help of Ariadne, Minos' daughter. She gave him a sword and a ball of thread to help him find his way back through the labyrinth. It had been designed by the Athenian craftsman Daedalus who later escaped from Crete with his son Icarus on wings crafted from wax and feathers. Ariadne eloped with Theseus, but he abandoned her on the Aegean island of Naxos and went home to Athens.

The site of Knossos, a low hill, was occupied in Neolithic times from at least 6000 BC. In the Early Minoan period the settlement grew steadily before the hill-

top was leveled off around 1900 BC to construct the Old Palace. After it was destroyed in a major earthquake around 1700 BC, the New Palace was constructed: most of the restorations are of buildings from this period. The half-dozen imposing town-houses excavated around the palace, and the **Little Palace** next to the Villa Ariadne, were built around 1600 BC following another earthquake which damaged parts of the palace. At the same time, country houses and city mansions were built all over Crete, marking the peak of Minoan wealth and artistic achievement. Knossos was at its most densely populated, with town houses built close to the palace and many other buildings scattered over the surrounding hillsides. There is no evidence for a fortification wall. Estimates of the Late Bronze Age population of Knossos vary, but it is unlikely to have exceeded 20,000.

About 1450 BC, a major disaster overtook the island: palaces and villas were destroyed in fierce fires. Invasion is considered the most likely reason for the wholesale destruction, perhaps by Mycenaean armies from mainland Greece. Only at Knosssos did occupation continue without a break, although there was some damage to the palace. Seventy years later, however, the palace and its dependent buildings were razed in a fire which baked the Linear B clay tablets recording the palace accounts in an early form of Greek. The presence of the tablets, together with pottery in Mycenaean styles, suggests that in its final years, Knossos was the Mycenaean administrative center for the island. Parts of the palace appear to have been reoccupied around 1200 BC but it was abandoned by the end of the Bronze Age and the site appears to have become a sanctuary. The Geometric period town was situated to the north and west.

In later centuries, Knossos became a city state contesting power with Gortyna in the south. But after the Roman conquest of 67 AD, Gortyna became the capital of the province of Crete and Cyrenaica – the area around Benghazi on the Libyan coast. Fine mansions decorated with statues and mosaic floors were built at Knossos during the Roman period: one, the **Villa Dionysos**, has been excavated but is not open to the public. In the early Christian period, Knossos was the seat of a bishop, and two basilicas, dating from the fifth and sixth centuries AD, have been excavated north of the Roman city. By the time of the Arab conquest in 824, Knossos had declined in importance. Iraklion, named El Khandak by the Arabs became the island's capital.

The approach to the palace is from the west, past a bust of Evans, into a paved courtyard with raised walkways. To the left are three deep circular walled pits which may have served as granaries. During rebuilding at the end of the Old Palace period, they were stuffed with rubbish, including fine pottery fragments, and then paved over. Looking down into

the central pit, you can see a staircase from an earlier house, dated to 2000 BC.

The courtyard is overlooked by the remains of the west façade, whose huge masonry blocks were once faced with gypsum, quarried just south of the palace. In the southern corner is the **west entrance** and porch, which led through heavy wooden doors – the sockets for the doorposts survive – into the **Corridor of the "Procession Fresco"**. Paved with gypsum flagstones, it turned left and left again around the southwest corner of the palace complex to enter the **Central Court**. Part of the corridor has disappeared through erosion of the hillside, so you have to enter through a reconstructed doorway.

Passing a downwards-tapering column you reach the **South Propylaia**, an imposing roofed gateway, supported on four impressive columns, which has been partially restored. (Minoan columns were made of wood, but no satisfactory explanation has been given of why they taper in reverse.) The fresco reproduction is a detail from the Procession Fresco displayed in the Iraklion Archaeological Museum. A pair of stone horns of consecration on a wall to the right once decorated the top of the south façade of the palace. The large *pithoi*, looking rather out of place in such a grand entranceway, date from the period of resettlement in the ruins of the palace around 1200 BC.

Climbing a monumental staircase you reach the **Upper Propylaia** leading on to the **Piano Nobile** as Evans called the floor where the state reception halls were probably located, borrowing the term from the Italian Renaissance. This floor was restored on the evidence of architectural remains which collapsed onto the floor below when the palace was destroyed. The lobby, Evans's Porticoed Vestibule, leads into a large hall with a small room to one side which held a large number of **stone rhytons**, including the Lioness Head rhyton in the Iraklion

1 West Porch
2 Processional Corridor
3 Central Court
4 South Propylaeum
5 Staircase to Piano Nobile
6 Throne Room
7 Pillar Crypt
8 Room of the tall Pithos
9 Grand Staircase
10 Hall of Double Axes
11 Hall of Colonnades
12 King's Megaron

13 Queen's Megaron
14 Bathroom
15 Queen's Toilet
16 East Portico
17 Court of the Stone Spout
18 Magazine of the Great Pithoi
19 Stores
20 East Bastion
21 Magazine of the Medallion Pithoi
22 North Entrance
23 Pillar Hall
24 North-East Magazines

25 Lustral Area
26 Theatre Area
27 West Court
28 Walled pits
29 Altar
30 Lower Corridor
31 Lower Magazines
32 Old Keep
33 North-East House
34 South-East House
35 House of the Chancel Screen
36 South House

KNOSSOS

0   10   20   30   40m

Archaeological Museum. A long upper corridor on a north-south axis had rooms opening off both sides, but a gap was left in the reconstruction so that you look down into the **Corridor of the Magazines** immediately below and the long, narrow store-rooms opening off it. Originally there were 23, some with additional storage space in stone chests beneath the floor, some of them lined with lead. Poles topped with double axes would have stood in the pyramid-shaped stone blocks left in the corridor, like those from the Nirou Hani villa on display in the museum. The huge *pithoi* in the magazines held oil, wine and grain: according to one estimate there was room for at least 400 jars with a total capacity of more than 75,000 liters of oil or wine. To the left of the **upper corridor** are two large inter-connecting rooms which Evans

Above: Life as it might have been in the room with the Dolphin fresco. Right: The room with the Dolphin fresco reconstructed in modern Knossos.

partially restored. Across the corridor are smaller rooms, one of which contains copies of several frescoes now in the museum, among them the Bull-leaper, the Captain of the Blacks and two panels of the Miniature Fresco. One shows a tripartite shrine of the kind found in the palace. Five columns surround a light-well, the main source of light and ventilation for the inner rooms of the palace.

To the left, a small staircase leads down to the **central court** near the Throne Room complex. A rounded corner at the bottom of the stairs is a left-over from the Old Palace. The court, about 50 m long and 25 m wide, was once paved and is aligned northeast and southwest like those at Phaestos and Malia. Scholars are divided over whether it was used for bull-leaping games: Evans believed they were more likely to have been held outside the east wing of the palace, beside the Kairatos stream. An antechamber, equipped with a replica stone seat and a purple stone basin which was found in a nearby passageway, leads

to the **Throne Room**. It is now fenced off, but from the doorway you can inspect the original throne, made of gypsum with a tall wavy back, and flanked by twin stone benches. The fresco of heraldic griffins in a field of lilies, dating from the period of Mycenaean influence, adds formality to the small room. Evans found overturned jars and large stone alabastrons on the floor, which he interpreted as part of a last-minute ritual to avert the disaster that led to the palace's destruction. Opposite the throne, steps lead down into a lustral basin, one of the small gypsum-paneled spaces that still baffle archaeologists. They are generally thought to have been used for religious rituals. Off the Throne Room was a small shrine.

Just south of the Throne Room, past a staircase leading to the Piano Nobile, is a **Tripartite Shrine**, similar to the one pictured in the Miniature Frescoes, where the sanctuary lies behind a façade of twin columns standing on either side of a central section supported by a single column.

Beside the shrine is the Lobby of the Stone Seat, from which you can peer into one of two dark **Pillar crypts**, thought to have been used for religious rituals, perhaps involving sacrifices. Troughs sunk into the floor at the base of the pillar may have been used as receptacles for liquid offerings.

The Lobby leads into the **Room of the Tall Pithos** and the Temple Repositories, named for the two large chest-shaped pits in the floor, which originally had lids. A smaller one between them was inserted at a later date. The outer chest contained the faience figures of the snake goddesses and other shrine equipment now displayed in Gallery IV of the Iraklion Archaeological Museum. The other large chest was robbed: Evans found only a few fragments of gold leaf. Heading back to the south end of the Court, you find a copy of the Priest-King figure from the Procession Fresco, looking out towards the open space.

Crossing to the right-hand side of the Court, you go down the elegant **Grand**

145

Staircase leading to the Domestic Quarter, originally built into the side of the hill. Four flights of shallow gypsum steps survive and there may have been a fifth. They are lit by a deep lightwell. This part of the palace shows off Minoan architecture at its best: rooms are divided by pier-and-door partitions to ensure warmth and privacy when closed, or an airy coolness in summer. Three smaller staircases linking the different storeys and a succession of corridors between the rooms contribute to the labyrinth atmosphere.

The reproduction of the **Shield Fresco**, of animal hides stretched on a frame into a figure-of-eight shape, may have decorated the Hall of the Double Axes below, just along the corridor from the Hall of the Colonnades. It is named for the double-axe masons' marks on the blocks of the adjoining lightwell, but is also known as the **King's Megaron**. The room was divided by double doors and had a sheltered L-shaped portico at one end.

A passage leads southwest into the **Queen's Megaron**, decorated with copies of the lively **Dolphin Fresco** and colorful rosettes, and furnished with stone benches. An Old Palace floor with irregular paving is visible below the later floor level. Beside the Queen's Megaron is a **bathroom** fitted with a clay tub. Beyond, a narrow corridor leads to a **toilet** with a drainage system to allow for flushing. Grooves in the wall and floor suggest that a wooden seat was fixed above the drain. An eleborate drainage system channeled waste water down to the Kairatos. The **Court of the Distaffs**, also named after the mason's marks found on its wall, provides light for this area. Back in the Queen's Megaron, you leave the Domestic Quarter from the Queen's verandah and turn left, past the terrace next to the Hall of the Double Axes and on to

the **East Portico**. This is the area of the palace workshops. A parallel corridor leads past a narrow store-room containing pieces of lapis lacedaimonios, a speckled green stone found only in the southern Peloponnese region of mainland Greece and used for making stone vases and seals. It appears to have been a carver's workshop and some of the lumps show traces of work in progress. To the north is a room with a stone bench, which may have been a potter's workshop. Continuing north, you arrive at the Court of the Stone Spout, which can be seen high up on the west wall and apparently channeled rain water to a cistern outside the court. Ahead are the **Magazines of the Giant Pithoi**, part of a store-room complex of the Old Palace: the huge vases date from around 1800 BC. Further north are the **Royal Pottery Stores**, also a survival from the earlier palace, where fine Kamaresware pottery was found.

A staircase leads down to the **East Bastion**, marking the east entrance to the palace, above the Kairatos. Beside the steps is a stone water channel, descending in a series of parabolic curves interspersed with settling basins – the Minoan equivalent of a storm drainage system. Climbing again, you pass the Giant Pithoi and arrive in the **Corridor of the Draught-Board**, where the richly decorated gaming board in Gallery IV of the Iraklion Archaeological Museum was found. A line of tapering clay pipes, part of the drainage system, can be seen beneath the Corridor, before you reach the **Magazine of the Medallion Pithoi**. From here, you can return to the Grand Staircase by way of the Corridor of the Beys, or go back to the Central Court up a staircase to the right.

From Central Court, you head right for the **North Entrance Passage**. To the left was a series of rooms where the Saffron Gatherer and miniature frescoes were found. Beneath them were deep, stone-lined pits from the Old Palace period,

Right: Relief of a bull and rebuilt Minoan columns.

which may have been granaries, or, as Evans suggested, dungeons. The entrance itself is guarded by a copy of a relief fresco of a charging bull in an olive grove, perhaps a scene from a bull-capture. Evans thought that this fresco may have remained in situ above the ruins for a long period after the destruction of the palace. If so, it must have helped embed the legend of the Minotaur in popular memory. The entrance was narrowed when the later palace was built and the North Pillar Hall was added, with a double row of gypsum pillars. According to one theory, the palace banqueting hall was located above the pillar hall. Domestic utensils, sorted by type, were found in the neighboring Northeast Magazines. To the left, past the North Portico, is the **North Lustral Basin**, the biggest of the lustral basins at Knossos. Evans thought, visitors to the palace underwent a ritual cleansing and anointing before being admitted.

Outside the palace, to the northwest, is the paved **Theatral Area**, overlooking a shallow flight of steps leading down to the Royal Road to the west. This may have been a reception area for official visitors. The road continued west into the Minoan town and branched north to the Little Palace. It was lined with houses: in one of them Evans found fresco fragments from around 1600 BC that were pieced together to reconstruct the Bluebird scene. On the opposite side of the road was a building that was identified as an armory.

Of the surrounding sites, the South House, the House of the Sacrificed Oxen and the House of the Fallen Blocks, where a pile of tumbled masonry from the south façade of the palace illustrates the force of the earthquake that destroyed the Old Palace, are most accessible, lying just south of the main complex. Further on down the valley is the **Caravanserai** (now closed to the public) where visitors from the south stopped before crossing a viaduct across the Vlychia stream and approaching the southwest entrance to the palace.

The **Little Palace**, where the bull's head rhyton, displayed in the Archaeological Museum, was found and the unexplored Mansion (which was eventually excavated in the 1970s), lie on the other side of the road from Iraklion, but are also closed to visitors. To the west, further excavations in the Minoan town revealed a house of the New Palace period which apparently was used as a cult center. In a basement room, the bones of at least three children were found: ten per cent of them were marked with cuts from a knife indicating that the flesh had been deliberately removed. The find, which stirred considerable controversy among archaeologists, has been interpreted as an isolated instance of ritual cannibalism in Minoan religion, but it does raise doubts about Evans's picture of life at ancient Knossos as orderly, peaceful and relatively carefree.

Arkhanes and Mount Iouhtas

Leaving Iraklion by the Knossos Road, you pass the palace and Spilia to take the right-hand fork for Arkhanes at 9.5 km. One km further on is a sharp bend, where in April 1944 two British officers, Patrick Leigh-Fermor and Stanley Moss, with a group of Cretan resistance fighters captured General Kreipe, commander of the German forces on the island, while he was driving from his headquarters in Arkhanes to his quarters at the Villa Ariadne at Knossos. Kreipe was sent to Egypt aboard a Royal Navy submarine after an arduous eighteen-day trek through the mountains to the south coast, hiding in caves to avoid pursuit.

A flourishing village, **Arkhanes** is famed for its wine and lamb chops, both available in the local tavernas. Its wealth goes back to Minoan times. Sir Arthur

Right: From the summit of Mount Iouhtas you can see all the way to Iraklion and the northern shore.

Evans excavated a reservoir which may have supplied Knossos with water, while Dr. Yannis Sakellarakis and his wife have excavated three important sites around the village. There are remains of a palace-style building to be seen in the Tourkogeitonia area of Arkhanes. It produced pieces of miniature fresco and ivory statuette fragments of similar quality to the Knossos bull-leaper figure. At **Fourni,** a hilltop to the northwest of the village, a **Minoan cemetery** was found, including an ossuary, dated to the Early Minoan period of around 2500 BC, and an unplundered royal tomb – the first unearthed in Crete. It contained the body of a young woman, accompanied by more than a hundred pieces of gold and jewelry, dated to around 1400 BC.

On the north slope of Mount Iouhtas, 3 km northwest of the village, a **Minoan shrine** was unearthed. A dirt track, the first turning to the right after passing the church on the way into the village, leads up past the local rubbish dump and on to the site. Of the three rooms, the central one contained a pair of lifesize clay feet, probably belonging to a wooden idol. The west room held evidence of a ritual sacrifice, interrupted when the building collapsed in the great earthquake of 1700 BC that destroyed the old palaces. But the bones found on an altar, along with a bronze knife, were those of a young man, indicating that in moments of crisis, the Minoans were prepared to carry out human sacrifice.

South from Arkhanes, the road leads on to the **Minoan villa of Vathypetro**, destroyed around 1450 BC. It contained evidence of weaving and pottery making as well as wine and olive presses. Heading back towards Arkhanes a left turn onto a dirt track takes you up **Mount Iouhtas**, with a magnificent view over the north coast of the island. A Minoan peak sanctuary has been excavated beside the telecommunications relay station on the north tip of the peak.

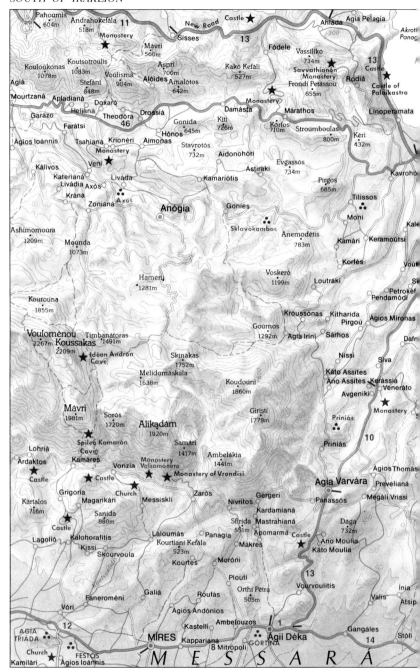

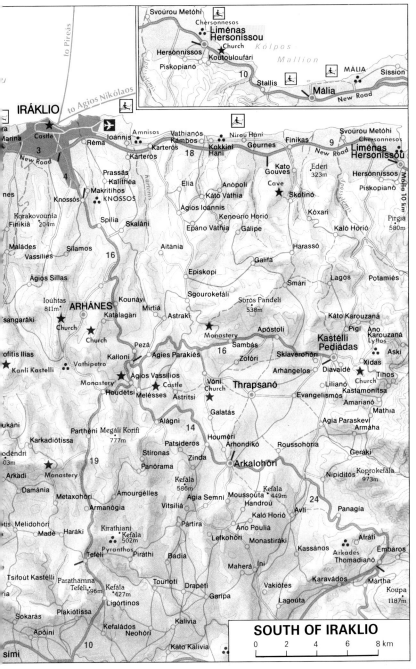

Svoúrou Metóhi

Chersónnesos
● Liménas
Hersonissou
Hersónnissos ★ Church
Koutouloufári
Piskopianó
10
Stallis
Kólpos

Mallion

MÁLIA
Síssion

Mália
New Road

to Pireás

IRÁKLIO
to Agios Nikólaos

Marina
Castle
New Road
4
3

Ioánnis
Réma
Amnisos
Karterós
Kárteros

Vathianós
Kámbos
18

Niroú Háni
Kokkíni
Háni

Gournes

Finikas

Svoúrou Metóhi
Chersónnesos
Liménas
Hersonissóu
New Road
9

Mália 10 km

Prassás
Kalíthéa
Makritíhos
Knossós
KNOSSÓS

Kato
Gouves
Ederi
323m

Hersónnissos
Piskopianó

Korakovoúnia
Finikiá
204m
Spília
Skaláni

Eliá
Anópoli
Cave

Ágios Ioánnis
Káto Váthia

Kenoúrio Horió
Epáno Váthia
Gálipe

Skotinó
★

Kóxari

Kaló Horió
Pirgiá
580m

Maládes
Vassílies
Sílamos
16

Aitánia

Harassó

Ágios Síllas

Episkopí

Galífa

Smári

Lagós
Potamiés

Ioúhtas
811m
ARHÁNES
Kounávi
Katalagári
Mirtiá

Sgourokefáli
Sorós Pandéli
538m

Káto Karouzaná

sangaráki
Church
Church
Pezá

Astráki
★ Monastery
Apóstoli
Sambás

Kastélli
Pediádas
Pigi
Áno
Karouzaná
Lyttos
Aski

ofítis Ilías
★
Kanlí Kastélli
Vathípetro
Kallóni
Ágies Parakiès
16
Zofóri
Sklaverohóri
Diavaidé
Xidas
Tíhos

Monastery
Houdétsi
Melésses
Ágios Vassílios
Castle
Astrítsi

Vóni
Church
Arhángelos

Thrapsanó

Liliano
Evangelismós
Church
Kastamonítsa

Amarianó
Mathía

Galatás

Agia Paraskeví
Armáha

ukáni
Karkadiótissa
Parthéni Megáli Korifí
777m
Alágni
14
Patsíderos
Stíronas
Zínda
Panórama
Houméri
Arhondikó
Roussohória

Geráki

odéndri
03m
Arkádi
19
Monastery
Kefála
586m

Arkalohóri

Nipiditós
Koprokefála
973m

Damánia
Metaxohóri
Armanógia
Amourgélles
Vitsiliá
Agia Semni
Moussoúta
Handroú
Kefála
449m

Avli

24

Panagia

tis Melidohóri
Madé
Haráki
Kirathianí
Kefála
502m
Pyranthos
Teféli
Piráthi

Pártira
Lefkohóri
Áno Pouliá
Monastiráki
Kaló Horió

Kássanos
Arkades
Thomadianó

Afráti

Émbaros

Maherá
Ini

Tsifoút Kastélli
Paráthamna
Teféli
596m
Kefála
427m
Ligórtinos

Badla

Toúrloti
Drapéti
Garipa
Vakiótes
Lagoúta

Karavádos

Mártha
Koúpa
1187m

Sokarás
Plakiótissa

Apóini
Kefáládos
Neohóri
10
Kalívia

Káto Kalívia

sími

SOUTH OF IRAKLIO
0   2   4   6   8 km

From Iraklion to Kanli Kastelli

Leaving Iraklion by the Hania Gate, you turn left at the first traffic light outside the walls. The road passes through vineyards and along a river valley before climbing to Tsangaraki and the village of **Profitis Elias**, 19 km away. It used to be known as Kanli Kastelli, the Turkish for "bloody castle" after a 1647 battle in which the Venetians severely defeated the Turks. On the rocky hill above the village is the castle of **Temenos**, built by Nikiforos Fokas after he had driven the Saracens off the island in 961. He intended to make it the center of a new capital inland, to protect the Cretans from pirate raids. But few islanders were willing to move away from Iraklion and Fokas was called back to Constantinople without building more than the castle.

Above: A vineyard in spring – the tender leaves are used to make dolmades. Right: Grapes are dried to raisins on strips of paper.

The fortifications were restored in the fourteenth century and in the sixteenth century, when Muslim pirates again threatened Crete. From the top of the village, a path leads up to the fortress along the north side of the hill. The main north entrance is guarded by overlapping curtain walls. There are few visible remains on the summit of the twin-peaked hill, but the view is impressive. The road continues to Venerato on the Phaestos road, 6 km further, or you can go back to Tsangaraki and turn right 2 km further on to Agios Syllas and Fortetsa and down to the Knossos road, with a left turn bringing you back into the city center.

Tylissos

Leaving Iraklion by the Hania Gate, take the Old Road for Rethimnon, turning off for **Tylissos** after 10 km. The road climbs another 3 km to reach the village, passing through the vineyards of the Malevisi district, famed in medieval times for its sweet grapes which pro-

duced the wine known in western Europe as Malmsey. In Minoan times, Tylissos straddled the route from Knossos to western Crete through the foothills of Mount Ida. Even its name is thought to be a survival from the Bronze Age: on Linear B tablets it appears as Tu-ri-so.

The complex of three Minoan villas, built at the same time as the later palace at Knossos, lies on the outskirts of the village. It was first excavated early this century after the three huge bronze cauldrons displayed in the Archaeological Museum were discovered by chance. House A, in the center, consists of two blocks linked by an open courtyard. It has all the architectural features of a wealthy two-storey Minoan house, including storerooms still containing tall storage jars. House B is built on a rectangular plan with few recognizable architectural features. House C has well-preserved walls standing remarkably high and a circular cistern built when the site was re-occupied in the post-palace period. A paved Minoan road runs along the length of its west side.

Beyond Tylissos, the road climbs through more mountainous country. 6 km further on it cuts across another Minoan site, this time a large country house with walls built of roughly hewn fieldstone rather than fine masonry. It overlooks the **Sklavokampos valley**, named after Slavs resettled there by the Byzantine Emperor Nikiforos Fokas in the tenth century. The road continues past the village of Gonies to reach Anoghia, 32 km from Iraklion.

From Iraklion to Fodhele

Leaving Iraklion by the Hania Gate, take the New Road west, which climbs above the broad sweep of the coastal plain. At 10 km, look right for the **castle of Palaikastro** which was captured by the Venetians from the Genoese and later rebuilt about 1573 as part of a massive programme of fortification against the Turks. A stone lion of St. Mark in relief still looks out from the ramparts. 3 km further on, a dirt road leads right to **Ligaria bay**, a good place for a swim after a

153

morning's sightseeing. Beyond lies **Agia Pelagia**, where a hotel complex is built over Minoan and classical remains.

A turning left leads up to the village of **Rodia** with a spectacular view over the Iraklion bay. Some medieval houses survive, and 5 km beyond is the superbly sited **convent of Savathiani**. The turning for Fodhele comes at the 22-km mark, where the road winds through orange groves into a narrow valley. The beach opposite was the landing place in 1668 of an Ottoman army under the Grand Vizier Mehmet Koprulu, which finally forced the Venetian defenders of Iraklion to surrender the following year.

Fodhele is traditionally the birthplace of the painter Domenico Theotocopoulos (1541-1616), better known as El Greco, although recent research indicates he was probably born in Iraklion. El Greco, who made his way to Toledo in Spain after first emigrating to Venice, like many other ambitious young Cretans in the Renaissance, is commemorated with a bust and an inscription in Greek and Spanish on a stone quarried in Toledo. It was erected in 1934 by students and faculty of the University of Valladolid.

From the center of the village, a track leading down and across the stream takes you on a pleasant stroll up the opposite side of the valley to a fresco-decorated Byzantine church of the Panagia, built among the ruins of an eighth-century Christian basilica.

SOUTHEAST OF IRAKLION

From Iraklion to the Kazantzakis Museum and to Kastelli Pediadas

Heading out of Iraklion, you take the Knossos road, passing the palace on your left and climbing up the hill past the early nineteenth-century aqueduct at the top of

Right: The potters of Thrapsano still practice their traditional art.

Kairatos valley. At the 10 km mark, you branch left for the village of **Skalani**. A right turn just before the village, signposted for the Nikos Kazantzakis Museum, puts you on the road for **Mirtia**, the modern name for Varvari, the village where the novelist's father, a prosperous Iraklion merchant, was born. (Kazantzakis senior appears, thinly disguised as the fervent drinker and patriot Captain Michalis, in the novel *Freedom or Death*). From there the road continues south through rolling hills carpeted with vineyards. There are spectacular views across to the foothills of **Mount Ida** rising on the right and of **Mount Dikti** on the left. After 10 km, the road branches right into the village.

The **Nikos Kazantzakis Museum** is housed in a carefully restored mansion overlooking the village square. It contains an interesting collection of photographs and memorabilia illustrating Kazantzakis' literary career, travels and political involvement, starting with his childhood in Crete, when the family fled the island more than once to escape Turkish reprisals after a rebellion. After law school in Athens and philosophical studies in France, Germany and Italy, he divided his time between Athens and a house on the island of Aegina. He served briefly as minister of education in 1945 before leaving Greece and settling in Antibes in the South of France. One room is devoted to Zorba, his partner in a lignite-mining venture in the southern Peleponnese, who inspired his best-known novel *Zorba the Greek*. An upstairs section holds theatrical memorabilia, from productions of his own plays as well as adaptations of the novels as plays, musicals and films.

Beyond Mirtia, the road continues to **Agia Paraskeves** where you take a left turn. Continue for 6 km before taking a right to **Voni**. Bearing left just outside the village, then right a kilometer further on, you head for the village of **Thrapsano**,

famed for its pottery-making tradition. The workshops are on view as you approach the village. They specialize in large storage jars known as *pithoi:* each can take almost a week to make. (At some shops you can pay by credit card and have your *pithos* shipped home by air.) 3 km beyond Thrapsano on the road to Kastelli lies the village of **Evangelismos**, where the domed cruciform church of the same name has some rare fourteenth century fresco scenes from the Old Testament, including the Garden of Eden and the Creation of Adam and Eve. Ask for the key to the church, which is kept by Kyria Katerina at the cafe across the street. Continuing towards Kastelli, you pass through **Arhangelos** before reaching **Sklavohori**, where the church of Eisodia Theotokon (known to villagers as the Panagia) also contains some good quality frescoes, dating from the fifteenth century. They include a lively scene of St. George slaying a dragon and rescuing a princess. **Kastelli**, the center of the **Pediada district**, is named after a Venetian

castle which no longer exists. You follow the signs for Iraklion through the town, but when the road swings left, keep straight on for the village of **Xidas**, 3.5 km further on. There are few remains to be seen, but the view over the Pediada district and up towards Lassithi is well worth the short climb up to the two churches that mark the site.

The simplest route back to Iraklion is to return to Kastelli and follow the signs for Iraklion. For **Agios Panteleismon**, a unique church with interesting frescoes of the thirteenth-fourteenth century, turn right down a dirt track just under 1 km from the town. After 2 km you reach the church, which is flanked by two oak trees and a pleasant taverna, where the key is kept. (If it's closed, the key can be found at the village of **Pigi**, another kilometer down the track.) The church incorporates many fragments of ancient masonry and inscriptions. From Pigi, you head for the Lassithi road, 8 km away, and then turn left for the drive back to the coastal highway and Iraklion.

155

THE SOUTH

Leaving Iraklion by the Hania Gate, you turn left to Mires and Phaestos at the 2.5 km mark. A right turn 5 km further on is signposted for Agios Miron. This is an alternative route, which is slower but has much less traffic. The road climbs past the new University of Crete hospital buildings, rising incongruously from the vineyards, and the view opens out: you look back to Iraklion and the sea, and to left and right over valleys chequered with vineyards and olive groves.

At 13.5 km, you reach **Agios Miron**, an attractive village complete with a statue of a local revolutionary hero, Yiannis Makrakis, and a thirteenth-century church dedicated to Agios Miron himself, a third-century Bishop of Knossos, who suffered a martyr's death. In local legend,

Above: Autumn has settled in the vineyards around the village of Agios Miron. Right: The Odeon of Gortyna where the first Code of Laws was found.

he was famed for killing a dragon that was devouring the faithful. On the way out of the village, you pass his hermitage on the left-hand side of the road, a grotto with icons and censers hung against a background of dripping rock. Agios Miron is the capital of the Malevisi district, renowned in Venetian times for growing the grapes which produced the sweet Malmsey wine.

At 19 km you reach **Kato Asites**. From here, a side road ascends to the Gorgolaini convent, 2 km away, with a magnificent view across much of central Crete. The road continues into the foothills of Mount Ida to Sarhos and Kroussonas, 8 km away, a noted weaving center, from which you can return to Iraklion through Korfos and Keramoutsi.

Continuing south, you pass **Ano Asites** to reach a flat promontory overlooking the main road to southern Crete, with a white chapel of **Agios Panteleimon** built on its tip. This was the acropolis of the ancient city of Rhizenia. At 23.5 km, a path leads off to the site. Italian archaeol-

ogists excavating here found a Late Minoan refuge site, dating from the end of the Bronze Age, with a sanctuary that remained in use into the seventh century BC. The main foundations of two seventh-century BC temples were also unearthed and the ruins of a Hellenistic fortress can be seen. The road passes through the village of **Prinias** and then joins the main Phaestos route at the village of **Agia Varvara**, said to lie at the exact center of the island.

The Messara Plain

The Messara Plain, the rich agricultural heartland of Crete, comes into view as you continue south, filled with olive groves interspersed with hundreds of plastic-covered greenhouses where cucumbers and tomatoes are grown. Temperatures are noticeably warmer here than in the north of the island. The plain runs parallel to the south coast, but is separated from it by the arid **Asteroussia Mountains**. In Early Minoan times, this region was already extensively settled before Phaestos became the center of economic activity from around 2000 BC.

At 44 km, the village of **Agii Deka** is named after ten early Christian martyrs who died, like Agios Miron, in the persecutions of the Roman Emperor Decius in the third century AD. A signpost leads around the village to the thirteenth-century church named after them, partly constructed – like many other buildings in the village – of re-used masonry from the Roman city of **Gortyna**.

The sprawling site of Gortyna, the capital of Crete in the Roman imperial period, lies 2 km further on, among the olive groves to the left of the road. To the right is the Basilica of **Agios Titos**, the island's patron saint. The well-preserved basilica, dating from the sixth century AD, is supposed to be the burial place of the saint, who was asked by St. Paul in 67 AD to convert the Cretans to Christianity. To the north lies the **Odeion**, a small first century BC amphitheater rebuilt in the second century AD. Behind is a brick

157

shelter where the **Gortyn Law Code**, the earliest in Europe, is displayed, inscribed on stone blocks. It dates from the first half of the fifth century BC and is written in a Doric dialect and inscribed in boustrophedon style, in the way an ox ploughs a field: the lines read alternately from left to right and then from right to left. It is six hundred lines long and contains detailed laws on marriage, divorce, assault and rape, inheritance, property and the position of slaves. The code is said to have inspired the lawgivers of ancient Athens and Sparta, Solon and Lycurgos, and was also much admired by Plato.

A **Venetian watermill** stands on the river bank just beyond the Odeion: some of the law code blocks were found in the stream nearby. From the Odeion, a path climbs to the **acropolis** of Gortyna, the heart of the city in classical Greek times, when it vied with Knossos for su-

Above: Sun reflecting on the hot-houses in the Messara Plain.

158

premacy. Much of the Roman city is still unexcavated, but Italian archaeologists, who have worked here since the 1880s, recently completed a full topographical survey, and a detailed plan is displayed at several points on the footpaths sign-posted around the site. The remains include several temples, a well-preserved small theater and public baths. Gortyna was destroyed in the seventh century by Arab raiders and never rebuilt.

Phaestos

Continuing through **Mires**, the market town of the Messara Plain, you reach the left turn for **Phaestos** and Agia Triada at 59.5 km. Cross the Geropotamos river and climb the hill to the **Minoan palace**. It is magnificently situated with a panoramic view across the plain to the south and up to the twin peaks of Mount Ida, also known as Psiloritis. The site was occupied in the Neolithic and the Early Minoan times before the Old Palace was built around 1900 BC. Like Knossos, the

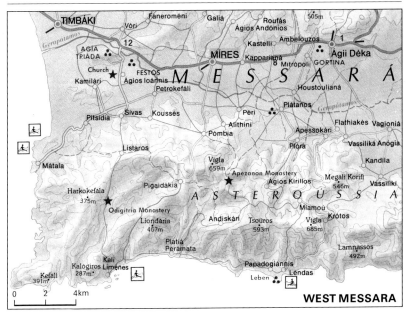

WEST MESSARA

palace was destroyed in a devastating earthquake around 1700 BC and immediately rebuilt on a grander scale. The later palace was razed around 1450 BC in the great wave of destruction that spread across the island. Phaestos was reoccupied at the end of the Bronze Age and went on to became a flourishing Greek city until it was wiped out by Gortyna in the second century BC.

Phaestos has been excavated by Italian archaeologists since Frederico Halbherr started digging in 1900. Its plan echoes Knossos in many respects, with an imposing entrance from the west leading into the central court, shrines and store-rooms side by side, reception rooms to the north, workshops in the northeast quarter and town houses built close alongside. But the monumental **Grand Staircase**, with shallow steps leading up to the **Propylon**, is a unique feature. You enter down a flight of stairs leading into the west court, where the façade of the Old Palace has been exposed. Above it, the later palace façade is set 10 m back.

Climbing the grand staircase you pass through the Propylon porch into a light-well and then take a narrow staircase down to the **central court**. Large *pithoi* are still in place in the Old Palace store-rooms to the right. In front of the double row of Later Palace store-rooms was a square hall looking out to the court. Further right, the southern section of the palace has been eroded away, as has much of its eastern area. Along both long sides of the central court stone bases can be seen for wooden columns that supported a portico. The north side of the court is cut by an elaborate doorway flanked by wooden pillars and recesses where a guard may have stood. Their walls are painted with a simple diamond pattern in red on a white ground. Double doors opened onto another passageway, similarly painted, that led up to the reception rooms on the upper floor.

The passage leads to the **north court** and then to the **Private Quarters** which have been roofed and fenced off. Looking in, you see a room with pier-and-door

159

partitions, similar to the King's Megaron at Knossos, with a portico to the east and a verandah to the north with a view of Mount Ida. A dark smudge beneath the right-hand peak marks the **Kamares Cave**, where the delicate multi-colored pottery displayed in Gallery III of the Iraklion Archaeological Museum was first found. To the south, a smaller room with a gypsum bench and four columns resembles the Queen's Megaron at Knossos. West of the larger megaron is a **lustral basin**, lined with fresh gypsum slabs, and a toilet connected to a drain in a separate complex of rooms. In the westernmost is a series of chests made of mudbrick: in one of them the Phaestos Disk was found in 1903. Returning by the stairs leading south you pass the **workshop area** along one side of the east court. A metalworking furnace is fenced off in its center. To the south are the rooms known as the east wing, including

Above: The monastery of Valsamonero on the south slope of Mount Ida.

a main hall, a peristyle court, a bathtub and a colonnaded court that offers a stunning wiew across the landscape to the Asteroussia Mountains.

Agia Triada

The road to Agia Triada takes you past a church which once belonged to the Agios Georgios monastery and winds around the western edge of the ridge. (A footpath is signposted which takes you through orange groves to the site in about 30 minutes). The site has a spectacular view over the **Gulf of Messara**, with the **Paximadia Islets** at its center. **Agia Triada**, dating from the Later Palace period, was once thought to be a summer residence for the rulers of Phaestos, but recently scholars have argued that it consists of two separate but related villas, like those at Tylissos. The site was reoccupied after the 1450 BC destruction and the area of the lower town with its row of shops was constructed around 1200 BC. On the upper level, the court was over-

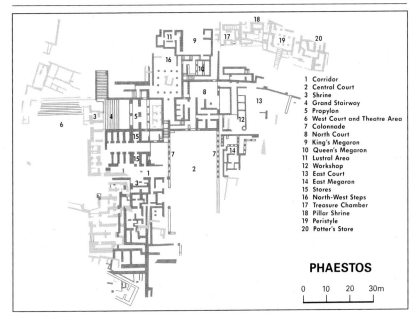

1 Corridor
2 Central Court
3 Shrine
4 Grand Stairway
5 Propylon
6 West Court and Theatre Area
7 Colonnade
8 North Court
9 King's Megaron
10 Queen's Megaron
11 Lustral Area
12 Workshop
13 East Court
14 East Megaron
15 Stores
16 North-West Steps
17 Treasure Chamber
18 Pillar Shrine
19 Peristyle
20 Potter's Store

PHAESTOS

0   10   20   30m

looked by Later Palace-era buildings laid out in an L-shape. The eastern wing had an elaborate drainage system and rooms decorated with gypsum slabs. A staircase leads down to the Lower Court, enclosed to the east by a five-columned portico and to the north by a thick-walled building which may have been a warehouse. A Minoan road leading to the sea starts from the upper court courtyard, passing along the north side of the L-shaped complex. To the left are the storerooms, some still containing huge pithoi. A gypsum staircase was totally blackened by the fierce fire that destroyed the building. The rooms in the western wing had a fine view of the sea. A hall with pier and door partitions led into two successive columned porticoes, then to the lightwell and a small inner room with gypsum benches around the walls. The gypsum slab in the center may have been a base for a bed. One of the adjoining set of rooms to the north was decorated with the frescoes of a woman in a garden and a cat hunting a pheasant that are now in the Iraklion Archaeological Museum. The famous stone vases fell from upper rooms in the west wing, while the bronze ingots were found in a narrow treasury on the lower floor north of the porticoed hall.

Back in the lower court, you take the stairway down to the town, which mostly dates from the fourteenth and thirteenth centuries BC, although some buildings are constructed over houses of the Later Palace period. Opposite, on the right, is a line of shops, the only ones known from the Cretan Bronze Age. On the way out, the final building to the east is a fourteenth-century BC shrine which had a frescoed floor with marine motifs, now in the Iraklion Archaeological Museum.

Vori, Valsamonero and Vrondisi

Returning to the main road after visiting Phaestos and Agia Triada, you turn left in the direction of **Timbaki**, an agricultural village being transformed into a wealthy market town thanks to the income from growing early vegetables in

161

greenhouses. A right turning is sign-posted for **Vori**, 1 km away, where a beautifully arranged folk museum in a restored village house illustrates Cretan rural life and customs. Weaving, basket-making and smithing are all represented, and there also are informative labels in English.

Heading back towards Iraklion along the main road, turn left for Zaros just before reaching Agii Deka. The road climbs gradually through the foothills of the Ida massif. At **Zaros**, a large village with springs that once supplied water, carried by aqueduct, to ancient Gortyna, take the road for Vorizia and Kamares. At the 6 km mark, the **Monastery of Vrondisi** is signposted to the right, 2 km away.

A fifteenth-century Venetian fountain stands outside the monastery, decorated with battered figures of Adam and Eve.

Above: Mountain goats are curious but they keep their distance. Right: View of the snow-capped White Mountains from the Psiloritis (Mt. Ida).

The twin-aisled church contains fine fourteenth-century frescoes, with a striking Last Supper painted in the apse of the southern aisle.

3 km further on, you reach **Vorizia**, where a left turning at the end of the village is signposted for **Valsamonero**. The *fylakas* will open the church of **Agios Fanourios** in the mornings: his house is down the hill on the way to the church, opposite a cafeneion. The oddly-shaped church is all that remains of the Valsamonero monastery. It has twin aisles and a third at right angles across the west end, decorated with outstanding fourteenth- and fifteenth-century frescoes. The drive back from Zaros to Agia Varvara through Nivritos and Gergeri offers a series of splendid views.

Hike to the Summit of Psiloritis

The **Psiloritis**, also known as Ida, 2456 m, is Crete's highest mountain. It is said that every Cretan should stand at least once in his or her life on the mountain's

summit, but few ever fulfil the pledge. It is also said that only goats and sheep can ever make it to the top.

The important role attributed to the Psiloritis by Cretans is obvious from the chapel that has been erected on the range's highest summit, Timios Stavros. The mountains already had mythological significance before the Christian era. The **Kamares cave** on the southern slopes of the range served as a religious and sacrificial place for the early inhabitants of the island. The ceramics found there gave an entire epoch its name and are exhibited in the Archaeological Museum in Iraklion. And anyone who casts a glance from the entrance of the cave down onto the land and sea stretching below will suddenly understand the godly quality of this place.

The second major excavation site is the **Ida cave** in the eastern wall of the mountain above the Nidha plateau. That is where the infant Zeus grew up, protected from death at the hands of his cannibal father, Cronos, by the ancient Curetes.

Several different roads lead to the summit of the Psiloritis, from the Arkadi Monastery, for example, from Kouroutes in the Amari basin, from Anoghia and from Kamares.

The shortest route, one that can be managed in a single day, is the climb beginning at the **Nidha Plateau** (1370 m). The most beautiful path up to the summit is the Kamares climb because of the fascinating view of the Messara Plain and the southern coast below. It is however almost impossible to do the climb in a single day and one should plan for a night's stay in the **Kollita refuge** on the way up or down. Hiking in the upper regions requires considerable endurance and several things will be needed: good hiking boots, sun protection, a large bottle of water, a sleeping bag or even a tent, flash lights, food for two days and seasonal clothes and/or a raincoat.

The trek begins at the eastern border of the village of Kamares by a supermarket where a gutter crosses the street. Climb the winding road and after a short while

163

you will see another gutter made of cement that will be seen often on the way up. The trail is the mainstay of a number of travel agents and has therefore been given red markings. The higher you get the more fascinating becomes the view over the densely packed houses of the village of Kamares to the rolling hills in the background.

It is worth starting the climb in the early morning but even then one soon begins to sweat and you will require frequent halts. The road leads by the edge of one gully and later to another. Then there is the gutter again which you follow for a while. After about one and three-quarter hours you arrive at a watering place and a sheep enclosure (**Mandra Kalamafka**). The road divides here: the left path leads to the Kamares cave. The way north leads to the summit of the

Above: The south coast at Pitsidia not far from Matala. Right: The artificial caves of Matala are a particularly interesting attraction.

Psiloritis. The road to the Kamares cave follows a water-pipe and leads to a reservoir known as the partridge reservoir *(perdhikonero)*. A steep slope leads to the cave. The distance between Mandra Kalamafka and the Kamares cave is about one and three-quarter hours' walk.

The trek to the Psiloritis from Mandra Kalamafka winds through some of Crete's wildest mountain landscapes. If you are lucky you may even spot some lammergeyers that have become quite a rarity. The path goes steeply alongside a deep gully. After about one and a half hours one arrives at the **Vulture Source** (Skaronero) at an elevation of 1650 m. Unfortunately too many of these birds of prey became the target of trophy hunters. You are more likely to find them shot, stuffed and covered in dust decorating the insides of taverns and kafenions in spite of legal protection from nature conservationists. The **Kollita refuge** is about a three-quarter hour walk upward from the Vulture Source. You can spend the night in the modest little shepherd's hut if you

would rather not sleep in a tent or simply outdoors. The summit is two and a half hours from the refuge.

The path leads in a northerly direction and soon meets up with the eastern trail (from the Nidha plain). A one and a half hour walk in an northwesterly direction up a long cleft takes you to a crater-like gully that can be circumvented on the right. Continue in the same direction but on a saddleback offering a splendid view of the northern coast with Iraklion in the distance. From here trek westward on the eastern ridge all the way to the summit and chapel.

A word of warning: in spring areas covered in snow and ice can be quite dangerous to cross. Should your equipment be inadequate we would advise leaving out the climb to the summit.

On a clear day the view from the top is fantastic. The sea sprawls at one's feet on two sides, and the view in the east and west is crowned by the high mountains of the Dikti range and the Lefka Ori. In the south the greenhouses of the Messara Plain glitter in the sun. The little stone hut in the southwest belongs to the mountain climbers' club of Rethimnon. If you don't wish to take the same way back to Kamares take the southwesterly trail. It leads to **Kouroutes** or **Fourfouras** in the Amari basin. A good sense of direction and an accurate map are both necessary.

Matala

Returning towards Phaestos, turn right to take the lower road past the monastery church, which leads to Matala. A kilometer further on you pass the church of **Agios Pavlos**, set among cypresses and surrounded by a wall. It is said to be the oldest church in Crete, and was originally just a copula supported on four massive pillars. The nave was added later and the outer narthex dates from the Venetian period. After another 2 km you reach the main road from Mires to Matala and turn right for the village of **Pitsidia**. One kilometer further on, a track to the right leads down to one of the best sandy

165

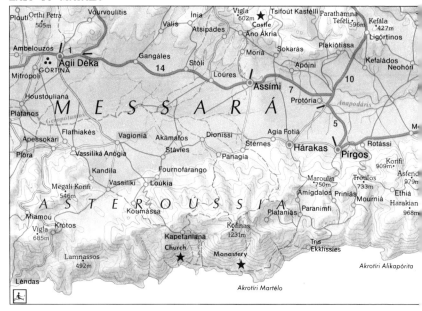

beaches on the southern coast. It is over-looked by the Minoan site of **Kommos**, which Evans thought was an important harbor and customs post. A large administrative building dates from the later palace period. Subsequently a series of Greek temples were constructed over it: the first dates from the tenth century BC and is thought to be the earliest in Greece.

Back on the main road, you pass a series of hotels and rooms for rent to reach **Matala**, now a flourishing resort. The second-century AD Roman tombs cut in the soft sandstone of the cliffs enclosing the cove, once the only accommodation in the village, are now fenced off. But there is a campsite above the beach for the "hippies", as backpackers are still known in Crete.

The significance of Matala Bay goes far back into the mythological past. This is where Zeus, in the guise of a bull, reached the coast of Crete carrying the beautiful princess Europa on his back. It is also where a part of Menelaus' flotilla drifted on its return from the Trojan war.

His men narrowly escaped death when the waves smashed his ships onto the cliffs (*Odyssey* 3, 291). Matala first became significant as a harbor under the Romans. The caves in the cliffs served as burial grounds in the early Christian era.

An excursion in a fishing boat around **Cape Lithinon**, Crete's southernmost point, to the little fishing village of Kali Limenes is possible in calm weather. You can also reach it on foot via the monastery of Odigitrias. It is far less tiring to go by car, but beware – the road is in very poor condition.

East of Matala

Returning towards Phaestos, a right turning at the 2-km mark is signposted for **Sivas**, a pleasant village from which a dirt road leads to the Odigitria Monastery and the harbor of Kali Limenes (Fair Havens), mentioned by St. Paul (Acts 27, 12). At 4 km you reach the village of **Listaros**. Beyond it, the landscape grows drier and wilder until you find the walled

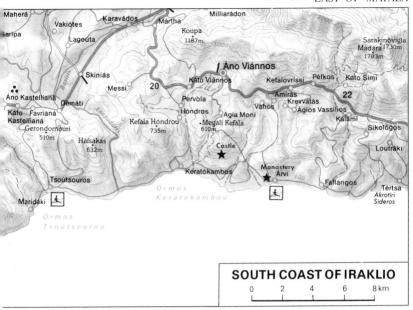

SOUTH COAST OF IRAKLIO

0   2   4   6   8 km

monastery compound at the 8 km mark. **Odigitrias** is the westernmost monastery complex in the Asteroussia mountains. The austere, burnt, hilly landscape runs along the southern edge of the Plain of Messara and offers a natural defense against the redoutable winds that blow from North Africa. The highest peak is the **Kofinas** (1231 m). The starkness of the Asteroussia Mountains reminded the early Christians on Crete of Mount Athos and so it is no small wonder that one should find several remote monasteries here. The church contains fine icons, including one of Christ with the twelve Apostles in a branching vine, signed by the fifteenth-century painter Angelos. The door to the square tower is opened with huge iron key. In the nineteenth century, a Cretan rebel, an ex-priest, reportedly held off Turkish attackers by hurling beehives down from its top, but was eventually killed together with his family. Other rooms in the compound room contain an old-fashioned grinder for olives and a press for extracting the oil. The track continues for another 4 km to reach Kali Limenes, with a fine beach on the Libyan Sea and pleasant on tavernas. A better road leads there from Mires via Pombia and Pigaidakia (23 km). There is also a daily bus in the late afternoon. **Kali Limenes** (Fair Havens) was mentioned in the Bible (Act 27,8) as the place where the apostle Paul stopped on his way from Cesarea to Rome. The former beauty of the bay has been rather spoiled by the huge oil tanks that stand on the islet of Agios Pavlos outside the bay. There is a chapel dedicated to the memory of Paul stands to the west of the village.

Another dirt track leads east along the coast from Kali Limenes to the site of **Lendas**, 10 km away, but it is easier to reach from the main Phaestos road. A left turning just before the Basilica of Agios Titos takes you through **Mitropoli** and across the Messara Plain to **Platanos** and **Plora**, where a right fork leads to the isolated **Monastery of Apezanon**, 10 km away. The church of the monastery has

167

been consecrated to St. Antonios Agio-farangitis. During the Turkish occupation of the island the monastery was a place of learning. As well as a library, it also possesses holy relics.

If you bear to the left you reach **Apesokari**, where domed graves from pre-palatial days were uncovered. At this point one turns right toward **Miamou**, a small mountain village that lies at an altitude of 480 m. Around 1900 the Italian School of Archeology conducted excavations in the region that turned up grave sites from the Neolithic age. Now the road climbs up into the **Asteroussia Mountains**. There are spectacular views on the descent to the sea. At 29 km you reach **Lendas**, the site of ancient Lebena and a famous sanctuary of Asklepios, the ancient Greek god of healing. In all probability the ancient name Lebena or Levin

Above: The Kofinas is the most prominent elevation in the Asterousia mountains.
Right: Banking the coals in an ancient stove as it has been done for centuries.

stems from a Phoenician-Semitic word for lion and refers in this case to the promontory that looks like some predatory animal about to jump into the sea. It reached its historical high point in the fifth and sixth centuries when it served as Gortyna's harbor and became a mecca for pilgrims who came to take its healing waters. The excavations on Lendas were carried out by the Italians. Only 100 m from the beach, between the foothills of Lendas and Psamidomouri, they discovered the remains of the holy shrine of Asklepios. Only two of the sixteen columns still stand. Under a mosaic floor in the nortwestern corner of the temple is an underground chamber that probably contained the precious objects given as offerings by the citizens of Gortyna. This treasure was probably plundered during the Roman or Byzantine era. The pebble mosaic floor dating from the third century BC shows a seahorse framed by waves. Healing springs at the site were credited with curing sciatica among other ailments, and the buildings included a

hostel where the pilgrims stayed. The sanctuary was in use from the fourth century BC until Roman times, according to archaeologists. People today still place a great deal of faith in the healing powers of the water. It is suppose to cure ulcers and wounds of all sorts and the ill come regularly from Athens and other points on the mainland to be cured.

The Asteroussia Mountains drop steeply into the sea east of Lendas. Surrounded by the sea, the **Koudoumas monastery** stands here, beneath the jagged peak of Kofinas (1231 m). To reach it you must follow the road from Agii Deka through Vagonia to the hamlet of **Loukia** (the terminus of the Agii Deka bus line). The dirt road at the southern end of the village winds its way for about 8 km through the arid landscape to the village of **Kapetaniana**, lying in a green hollow. From here the Koudoumas monastery is another 6 km over a very poor, very winding road. Nevertheless its unique and remote location makes it very much worth a detour if you have time.

There are no roads running along the coast in the southern foothills of the Asteroussia Mountains. In order to continue the drive to the eastern part of the district of Iraklion, you must turn back to the southern section of the national road which has been under construction for years. 14 km after Agii Deka, the road leads to the town of **Assimi** and 12 km later to Pirgos. Another 15 km takes you to **Kato Kastelliana**, a little village on the eastern edge of the Messara Plain. A dirt road leads from here in a southerly direction to **Tsoutsouros Beach**, renowned for its fine sand. Alongside it is a valley that drops down gently toward the coast. A permanent stream runs through here and crabs of all sorts and sizes live in the dense oleanders growing on its banks. In Tsoutsouros there is a hotel as well as self-catering accommodation kafenions and tavernas.

Another dirt road takes you from Tsoutsouros along the southern coast eastward to **Keratokambos**, another quiet resort with a beautiful beach, pri-

169

vate lodgings and taverns. A road leads steeply from Keratokambos up to **Ano Viannos** (550 m) between the impressive rocky crags of Kefala Hondrou and Megali Kefala. Ano Viannos is the capital of a district bearing the same name. Its white houses are arranged as in an amphitheater on the southwestern foothills of the Dikti chain. The luxuriant vegetation and the many fountains are quite remarkable. The little village nestled amongst olive groves stands on the remains of the ancient city of Viannos, that once upon a time possessed minting rights. In 1954 excavations in **Galana Charakia** uncovered two large graves containing 30 burying *pithoi* and clay figures from the early and middle Minoan ages. A further late Minoan settlement was unearthed in **Kefala Hondrou** between 1956 and 1959.

Above: Sorting out the grain requires a woman's patience. Right: Sitting on the shaded terrace of the cafenion, a job requiring man's patience.

Today Viannos has several medieval churches containing beautiful frescos. The frescoes in the Agia Pelagia date to the fourteenth century; those in the Agios Georgios to the thirteenth century. About 7 km east of Ano Viannos, in the village of **Amiras**, a road leads down to the beautiful beach of **Arvi** (14.5 km). Dozens of thick, black plastic pipes carry water from springs on the southern slopes of the Dikti Mountains down to the greenhouses and banana plantations on the beach. There is also a monastery. Selfcatering accommodation and taverns make Arvi a favorite destination.

The most beautiful part of the trip begins east of Amiras. The elevated road offers a splendid view of the varying landscape. You leave the district of Iraklion just before the resort of **Mirtos** from where a good road takes you to Ierapetra.

THE EAST

Start your trip from Iraklion by taking the old road that leaves from Plateia

Eleftheria near the Archaeological Museum. At 7 km you will pass the beach at **Karteros** and then after the riding center at 8 km you reach **Amnisos**, another port of Minoan Crete. This is where the Lilies fresco – now in the Iraklion Archaeological Museum – was found. The site has now been reexamined by a team from Heidelberg University.

13 km east of Iraklion one reaches **Hani tou Kokkini**, the site of a Minoan villa covering an impressive 100-sq-m area.

The villa, dating from 1500 BC, was discovered in 1918 and resembles the architecture of Knossos with some 40 chambers, two corridors and two courtyards being dug out. The complex is so huge that some archaeologists argue it is a Minoan palace, probably a seaside resort for the leaders of Knossos.

2 km east of Hani tou Kokkini you reach the seaside village of **Gournes**, where a huge US communications airbase has been built. The installation is the site of frequent anti-American demon-

strations, but Gournes has adapted to the needs of the servicemen.

Further east, 26 km from Iraklion, one comes to **Limenas Hersonnissou**, a highly acclaimed sea resort with an excellent beach and a favorite spot for windsurfing. A number of bars, taverns and hotels accommodate the traveler although a room in the summer high season must be booked well in advance.

Limenas Hersonnissou was an ancient Minoan port, housing the huge temple of Brytomartis (a deity in ancient Crete called sweet maiden) which has disappeared through the years. The area also served as a port for the Romans and traces of fountains and harbor works from that era can still be seen.

Malia

Malia is situated 34 km east of Iraklion, halfway to Agios Nikolaos. The village has one of the best beaches in Crete, but has lately lost some of its charm as huge new hotels overshadow the natural

171

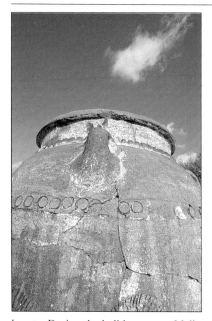

beauty. During the holiday season Malia never sleeps as tourists drink and dance the night away in bars and discos.

4 km east of town a narrow side-street leads to Malia's archaeological sites. Ancient Malia provides the best of the natural environment, situated between sea and mountain and engulfed by olive groves and fruit trees.

The Malia **Minoan palace** dates to 1900 BC and was built at about the same period as the palaces of Knossos and Phaestos. It was first discovered by Greek archaeologist Joseph Hatzithakis in 1915, but a systematic study of the ruins was begun in 1922 by the French School of Archaeology.

The first palace of Malia was ruined in 1650 BC. What is seen today are the remains of the second palace which survived until 1450 when it was destroyed by the major earthquake which also leveled Knossos and Phaestos.

Above: A storage jar from Malia. Right: Just another village conversation.

A labyrinth of paved but narrow roads, starting from the palace's northern end, lead to the **central court**, a huge open area measuring 48 m from north to south and 22 m from east to west. In the middle of the court a pit served as a sacrificial site to the gods and the slaughtered animals were then roasted in a ceremony attended by the high priest. The sacrificial pit is a unique feature of the Malia palace not found in any other Minoan palaces on the island. The central court was also used for bull-fights evidenced by a series of holes and columns on its perimeter to protect the spectators, among them the king himself who watched the events from the second floor of a building at the court's west side. The ground floor communicated with the palace's upper level via a main staircase at the court's northern side, where the main kitchen was situated. The rooms on the south side of the court were used as **workshops** while the whole east side is covered by a series of long and narrow chambers that served as granaries. The **royal apartments** were

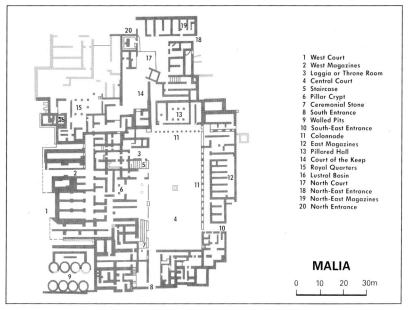

1 West Court
2 West Magazines
3 Loggia or Throne Room
4 Central Court
5 Staircase
6 Pillar Crypt
7 Ceremonial Stone
8 South Entrance
9 Walled Pits
10 South-East Entrance
11 Colonnade
12 East Magazines
13 Pillared Hall
14 Court of the Keep
15 Royal Quarters
16 Lustral Basin
17 North Court
18 North-East Entrance
19 North-East Magazines
20 North Entrance

MALIA

0   10   20   30m

situated on the palace's northwest corner and resemble typical Minoan architecture – separate rooms for the king and the queen, but a common bathroom. The Malia palace housed a total of about 350 chambers and is the third largest in Crete after the ones in Knossos and Phaestos. A complete tour of this magnificent complex takes more than an hour to go through numerous corridors, storage magazines and various other rooms used for religious purposes.

Excavations in the 1960s around the palace have revealed a number of structures (houses, benches, tombs, roads) indicating the existence of a large Minoan town. The most important find is 500m east of the palace, close to the sea shore. Here a huge tomb, 40m long and 30m wide, served as the burial site for the royal family. The place is called Chrysolakkos (pit of gold) and brought to light a number of gold treasures, the most famous being a gold honeybee pendant now housed at Iraklion Archaeological Museum.

Offbeat Beaches

The steep slopes west of Iraklion hardly offer any opportunity to swim. A few kilometers beyond city limits lie the beaches of **Linoperamata** and **Ammoudara**. 21 km along the national highway, shortly beyond Rethimnon is the fork leading to the bay of **Agia Pelagia**. Another swimming hole is a few kilometers further near the fork off to Fodhele.

East of Iraklion are several beautiful beaches: **Amnisos**, **Nirou Hani**, **Herssonissos** and **Malia**. Unfortunately tourism has made heavy inroads here which might not be to everyone's taste.

For idyllic coves and beaches with modest lodgings, a few taverns and kafenions, head for **Pitsidia** and **Matala** on the southern coast of the district of Iraklion. Mass tourism has also spared the beaches of **Kali Limenes**, **Lendas**, **Tsoutsouros** and **Arvi**. The beaches located on the Libyen Sea are sunny and warm even in the winter months and attract many globetrotters all year round.

173

IRAKLION
Accommodation

LUXURY: **Galaxi**, 67 Demokratias Avenue, Tel: 081/238 812. **Xenia**, 2 Sofocles Venizelou Street, Tel: 081/284 000. **Astoria**, Platia Elefthenias, Tel: 081/285 025. **Knossos Beach**, Kokkini Hani, Tel: 081/280 381, (mostly bungalows). **Creta Beach**, Tel: 081/252 302.

MODERATE: **Atrion**, 9 Palaiologou Street, Tel: 081/229 225. **Castro**, 20 Theotokopoulou Street, Tel: 081/285 020. **Ammoudara Beach**, Tel: 081/254 312.

BUDGET: **Kronos**, 15 Epimenidou St, Tel: 081/282 240. **Daedalos**, 081/224 391. **Olympic**, Kornarou Square, Tel: 081/288 861. **Tsangarakis Beach**, Ammoudara, Tel: 081/251 768. Staying in town is more convient, given the traffic jams around Iraklion, but can be stifling hot in July and August. Few moderately priced hotels are fully air-conditioned (the Atrion is a welcome exception). The beach hotels lying a few kilometers west or east of the city and are not always prepared for the individual traveller (half-board is the rule), but are cool and well-equipped for water sports.

Hospitals

Apollonion General Hospital, Alber and Markou Moussourou Streets, Tel: 081/229 713, 287 411. **Venizeleion Hospital**, Knossos Road, Tel: 081/231 931, 237 502.

Museums & Sites

Iraklion Archaeological Museum, off Plateia Eleftherias (Tel.: 081/226092). Timings: 11.00-17.00 hrs Mondays, 8.00-19.00 hrs (October through April 8.00 - 17.00) Tuesday through Friday, 8.30-15.00 hrs Saturdays and Sundays. **Historical and Ethnographical Museum**, Sophocles Venizelos Street, opposite Xenia Hotel. Timing: 9.00-13.00 and 15.00-17.30 hrs. Closed Sundays and public holidays. **Agia Aikaterini Icon Collection**, next to Agios Minas Cathedral. Timing: 9.30-13.00 hrs, Mondays through Saturdays, 17.00-19.00 hrs (winter 16.00-18.00) on Tuesdays, Thursdays and Fridays. Closed Sundays and public holidays. **Iraklion Harbor Venetian Fortress** (Koules). Timing: 8.30-1500 hrs. Closed Mondays. **Knossos Archaeological Site**. Timing: 8.00-19.00 hrs (17.00 hrs October through April) daily.

Post / Telegraph / Telephone

Iraklion: Area code 081.
Main office: Plateia Daskaloyianni. Timings: 8.00- 200 hrs, Monday through Friday. Main Telegraph office, OTE, El Greco Park.

Restaurants

Hotel restaurants in Crete generally serve bland meals: eating out is almost always a better alternaive.

Kyriakos, Dimokratias Avenue, close to the Galaxy Hotel. A sophisticated Cretan taverna which features good meat dishes and some of the island's best wines. **Ippocambos**, Mitsotakis Street. An ouzerie, or informal eating place where places of hot snacks, or mezedes, accompany ouzo, wine or beer. (There are other ouzeries worth trying in the pedestrian zone off August 25th Street, near the Agios Dimitrios church). **Yakomis** is the best of the tavernas in meat alley, the arcade off Evans Street near the butchers'shops. Nea Ionia, a traditional lunching place on Evans Street has good baked dishes, especially vegetables.

Tourist Information

National Tourist organization (EOT) office: I Xanthoudides Street, opposite the Archaeoiogical Museum. Tel: (081) 225-636. Timings: 8.00-18.00 hrs (weekends and winter 14.00 hrs). **Information desk at Iraklion Airport** (4 km east of the city). Timings: 9.00-21.00. **Tourist Agency**: Solmar: Bufort 8, 227702.

Rent a Car

Avis, 25 August St. **Hertz**, 25 August St. **Hellas Cars**, 25 August St. **Vallilakis**, Airport. **Byron**, A. Titos St.10. **Yiatromanolakis**, 4 Ikaros St. **Kretcar**, 25 August St. **Ida**, 62 Martyron St.144. **Interrent**, 62 Martyron St.117.

Shopping

The traditional Cretan red woven blankets, shoulder-bags and embroidered tablecoths and pillowcases have becomme antiques, but can still be found in a few shops in August 25th Street and around the Museum. Contemporary versions are easily found. Woolen floor rugs come in varied designs. Silverwork is good quality: a stroll down Daidalos Street given an idea of what is available. Cretan knives are good value, whether ornamental daggers or plain kitchenware. A pair of blanck leather kneeboots made to measure will last for years. You can also find heavy sweeters made from wool that still contains natural oils.

Local Festivals

In July and August, the outdor theaters in the Venetian moat feature plays and concerts, usually with an emphasis on Cretan music and theatre, though foreign performing arts groups often combine appearances at the Athens Festival with a show in Crete. St. Mark's in Lion Square offers art and photography exhibitions almost year-round. Cretan "lyra" players perform at some tavernas - there are several on the Knossos road, which are also good places to see unselfconcious Cretan dancing.

Access & Local Transport

Frequent flights to Athens from Iraklion Airport on Olympic Airways. Terminal: Plateia Eleftherias, Tel: (081) 282- 285. Ferry boats to Piraeus daily from the East Quay, operated by Minoan Lines(central ticket office 78, August 25th Street, opposite Agios Titos church, Tel:(081) 229-602 and ANEK (central ticket office) 33 August 25th Street, Tel: (081) 222-481. One-day cruises to the islands of Santorini and Ios in the Cyclades are available in summer. Further afield, there are regular sailings from Iraklion to Alexandria, Egypt, Dubrovnik, Yugoslavia and Venice with the Adriatica Line (Tel: Athens (01) 322-3693), for Limassol, Cyprus with the Stability Line and for Kusadasi, Turkey with Marlines, Tel: (081) 226-697, Arabatzoglou Travel Agency, 54 August 25th Street.

Most car-rental agencies are in August 25th Street. The long-distance bus station for east Crete is just east of the traffic circle at the bottom of Doukas Bofor Avenue, Tel: (081) 282-637. The bus station for Phaestos, Gortyna and southwest Crete (also Tylissos and Anoghia, and Fodhele) is outside the Hania Gate to the right, Tel: (081) 283-287. The Station for Hania and Rethimnon is opposite the Historical Museum, Tel: (081) 221-765. The bus station for Thrapsano, Varvari and other villages in central Crete is outside the Venetian walls close to the New Gate.

CENTRAL CRETE

Accommodation at:

LIMENAS HERSONISSOU (area code 0897):
LUXURY: **Creta Maris**, Tel. 22115, on the beach, airconditioned, heated swimming pool, bowling, open air cinema, children's playground, sauna, shopping area, health center. **Cretan Village**, Tel. 22996, on the beach, beach bar, tennis bar, disco, two swimming pools, four tennis courts, mini golf, shopping arcade, baby-sitting on request.
MODERATE: **Belvedere**, Tel. 22371, 250 meters from the sea, swimming pool, disco, several sports. **Grecotel Cretan Sun**, hotel and bungalows, Tel.41103, on the beach of Gouves, all rooms with private refrigerator, four tennis courts, three swimming pools. **King Minos Palace**, Tel. 22881, two swimming pools, two tennis courts, mini golf. **Marina**, Tel. 41361, on the beach of Gouves. **Chrissi Ammoudia**, Tel. 22971, 300 meters from the beach. **Hersonissos**, Tel. 22501, 50 meters from sea, swimming pool, sauna.

MALIA (area code 0897):
LUXURY: **Ikaros Village**, Tel. 31267, on the beach, swimming pool, sauna, three tennis courts,bazaar. **Kernos Beach**, Tel. 31421, on the beach, two tennis courts, two swimming pools, sport facilities, hairdresser. **Sirens Beach**, Tel. 31321, on the beach, two swimming pools, tennis court.
MODERATE: **Alcionides**, Tel. 31558, on the beach, two swimming pools. **Alexander Beach Hotel**, Tel. 31038, on the beach, swimming pool, heated pool, surfing and tennis school. **Anastasia Hotel Bungalows**, Tel. 31180, 300 m from the beach, all rooms with view of sea. **Ariadne**, Tel.31680, on the beach.
BUDGET: **Minoa**, Tel. 31456. **Sofokles Beach**, Tel. 31348.

Restaurants

There are few restaurants to be found in the villages of central Crete. But simple dishes are often available at cafenions: salad, omelettes, beans, and fruit, along with lokal cheese and wine, or raki, the Cretan firewater. In the evenings, spit-roast meat and grill can be found at local "kentra" on the outskirts of most villages.

Museums & Sites

Kazantzakis Museum, Varvari village. Timings: 9.00-13.00 and 16.00-20.00 hrs on Monday, Wednesday, Saturday and Sunday. Mornings only on Tuesday and Friday. From November through February, mornings only. In winter, Sunday mornings only. **Tylissos Archaeological Site**. Timings: 8.30-15.00 hrs daily. Closed on Sundays. **Gortyna Archaeological Site**. Timings: 8.00-19.00 hrs (17.00 in winter), Monday through Friday, 8.30- 15.00 hrs Saturday and Sunday. **Phaestos Archaeological Site**. Timings: 8.00- 19.00 hrs daily (17.00 hrs in winter) daily . **Agia Triada Archaeological Site**. Timings: 8.00-19.00 (17.00 hrs in winter) daily. **Vori Folk Museum**: 10.00-18.00 hrs daily.
The siesta hours (14.30-17.00 hrs) should be avoided, even in winter, when looking for the keys to locked Byzantine churches, or visiting monasteries.

Camping

Caravan Camping, Limenas Hersonissou (0897) 22025, persons 108, tents 36. **Creta Camping**, Gouves (0897) 41400, persons 270, tents 90. **Iraklion Camping**, Ammouda (081) 250986-8, persons 858, tents 283. **Pitsidia-Matala Comm. Camping**, Matala (0892) 42340, persons 300, tents 100.

LASSITHI

LASSITHI PLAIN
AGIOS NIKOLAOS
ELOUNDA / SPINALONGA
KRITSA / LATO
GOURNIA / IERAPETRA
VAI / KATO ZAKROS
VALLEY OF THE DEAD

The Lassithi *nome* occupies the eastern part of Crete. It covers an area of 1818 sq km, and it has a population of about 85,000.

Lassithi is engulfed by two mountain ranges – Dikti (2148 m) to the west and the Sitian mountains (1476 m) to the east. The Cretan Sea forms the wonderful Gulf of Mirabello on the northern coast, and the Libyan Sea to the south washes Ierapetra, Greece's southernmost town.

Despite its relatively poor archaelogical finds, Lassithi endured domination by all the peoples who invaded the island. The area flourished during Minoan times and successively passed to Roman, Byzantine, Venetian, Turkish, German, Italian and Greek hands.

Up until the 1960s Lassithi was largely unknown to foreigners and its first regular visitors were hippies enjoying beautiful sites, sandy beaches, cheap accommodation and Cretan hospitality. But the area which is now described as the "Riviera of Greece" was destined to become one of the most visited parts of the country. In the summer months Lassithi's population more than triples and some 80 percent of the locals are occupied with

Preceding pages: Windmills above Lassithi Plain. Left: Safe from the sun in the shadow of one's home.

tourist services. Where rocks once stood, luxury hotels have been erected and all major credit cards are accepted in an area where not so long ago mules were the main means of transportation.

But progress came with a cost. Lassithi and mainly its capital town Agios Nikolaos have lost their calm charm as disco music, noisy motorbikes and empty beer bottles dominate in the high summer season. Still, Lassithi is relatively untouched in comparsion with other parts of Crete. The Gulf of Mirabello and the entire area close to Ierapetra provide beautiful sandy beaches, exceptional views of the sea and fine dining in traditional tavernas, offering local specialities and fine retsina wine. Far east, the Carpathian Sea washes Europe's unique palm tree forest of Vai.

The Lassithi Plain, overlooked by Mount Dikti, is one of Crete's most fertile areas producing top quality fruit and vegetables for export around the world. The plateau is irrigated by thousands of windmills pumping water without a stop for almost two centuries. Lassithi farmers were the first in Europe to built an extensive network of hothouses which with the aid of the mild climate give a variety of agricultural products all year round.

Temperatures in Lassithi range in the winter between 12 - 26 degrees Celsius while in the summer they can go up to 42 degrees with the southern "sirocco" wind blowing from the Sahara in June and July. The northern "meltemia" wind, on the other hand, brings cooler temperatures in late August.

Agios Nikolaos provides the best of Cretan culture in the summer months with festivities of various kinds taking place around the town's bottomless pool where according to legend an ancient goddess used to bathe.

Here you can enjoy fresh fish in the tavernas, admire the view of the Gulf of Mirabello and buy fine leather goods as a memento of your stay in eastern Crete.

From Malia to Neapoli

After passing Hersonissos and Malia on the National Road from Iraklion to Agios Nikolaos you arrive at a a wild ravine featuring the exceptionally beautiful monastery of **Agios Georgios Selinaris** (43 km east of Iraklion).

Built into the mountain rock the monastery, which has now been turned into an old-folks home, is the most frequent stopover for travelers bound for Agios Nikolaos. Enjoy lunch in one of the many cafes and restaurants offering a variety of Greek cuisine but mostly the traditional souvlaki and spring water straight from the rock. The monastery attracts a huge crowd on April 23, the name-day of Agios Georgios (St. George).

If you choose to stay on the new road, nothing now stands between yourself and Agios Nikolaos to the east. But if there is time spare, the old road from Selinari leads to some other archaeological sites worth a short visit.

On the old road 49 km east of Iraklion, turn left to **Milatos**, a small village that took its name from the Doric city of Miletos which reached its peak in 1400 BC. Miletos is associated with Sarpedon, brother of King Minos, and is mentioned in Homer's *Iliad* as one of the seven

WEST OF LASSITHI

0   2   4   6   8 km

Cretan cities which sent troops to Troy to aid King Agamemnon. The ruins of the Doric establishment can still be seen but nothing important has been found.

Sarpedon fled to Asia Minor from Miletos after he was defeated by Minos in a series of wars. There, he built a new city also named Miletos which later became the greatest commercial center in Asia Minor.

Coming back on the new road you wind down to **Neapoli** 52 km east of Iraklion. The town was until 1904 the capital of the Lassithi Nome, now administrated from Agios Nikolaos. Neapoli is one of the most advanced towns in Crete with a fine **Technical School of Domestic Science** and other educational institutions. In 1340 a boy by the name of Petros Philargos was born in Neapoli. An orphan with no money he was raised by Venetian monks in the area. Philargos

Above: View over the fertile Lassithi Plain.
Right: Windmills are used in thousands to pump water from deep wells.

grew up to become Pope Alexander V in Rome. A road from the town's main square leads to **Kremasta Monastery** after 3 km. The complex housing some 170 monks was built in the late 1600s and achieved fame during the Ottoman occupation when it served as the residence of the Turkish governor of Lassithi, Kosstis Pasha, who in 1868 named Neapoli the capital of Mirabello and constructed a number of roads and public buildings.

A left turn from Neapoli leads to the ancient city of **Dreros**. The site was an archaic settlement with an acropolis and a small temple dedicated to the god Apollo Delphinios, dating to the seventh century BC. Here Apollo resembled a dolphin that led Greek sailors in their quest to establish new colonies. Apollo Delphinios is also linked, according to Plutarch, with the Ionian city of Miletos in Asia Minor (mentioned earlier) which leads to the conclusion that the people of Dreros played an important role in the establishment of this Cretan colony. The temple also revealed three bronze fig-

urines known as the **Triad of Dreros** showing Leto and her two children Apollo and Artemis. Dreros is also representative of the classical period with a temple which was later turned into a Catholic chapel by the Venetians. The town remained strong up to the Hellenistic period and was then destroyed at about 220 BC in a series of wars with nearby cities. Finally, digging revealed two bilingual Eteocretan-Greek inscriptions which could prove crucial in the eventual decipherment of the Eteocretan language, one of the oldest in the world.

Lassithi Plain

Before proceeding on the main highway to Agios Nikolaos a right turn from Neapoli leads through a group of villages to the flat farmland of **Lassithi Plain**.

Many tourist buses head for Lassithi Plain so that their passengers can glimpse the picturesque "Valley of the Windmills". Yet few tourists actually explore the area on foot. Those that do find it easy to traverse, pleasantly unspoiled and incredibly fertile. Its natural flora is quite lovely and the borders of the fields and orchards are carpeted with wild flowers later in the spring than lower-lying areas. The Lassithi Plain sits at a height of about 866 m and is surrounded by the greenish peaks of Mount Dikti, making it blissfully cool during the scorching heat of midsummer.

Measuring 8 km long and 6 km wide, the plain is one of Crete's most fertile areas producing grain, potatoes, apples and rare wild orchids. But what makes the plain a spectacular site today are some 10,000 windmills used for decades to pump water for irrigation. These days, unfortunately, many windmills are out of use as petrol-driven pumps are preferred by the locals.

A number of villages lie on the road ringing the Lassithi Plain and from them one can hike to monasteries, peaks and caves. On the eastern side is the village of **Tzermiado** and just east of it is the **Cave of Trapeza**, largely interesting because it was declared the earliest settlement on the Lassithi Plain by Sir Arthur Evans and John Pendlebury. Its tombs had remains dating to the Neolithic Period but nothing much is left today.

Marmaketo, a little further along the road, was the birthplace of Manolis Kazanis, a hero of the Greek resistance against the Turks. The house where he was born is one of the buildings of the ethnological museum, showing a charming recreation of life in former years on the plain.

The **Kroustellenia Monastery**, that can be reached in a two-hour walk on a side road near **Mesa Lassithi** and **Mesa Lassithaki**, soars high above the southeastern side of the plateau. It was founded in 1543 by two sisters who were part of a group of refugees escaping the Turks in the Peloponnese.

In a two-hour walk from the monastery, one reaches the **Katharo Plateau**, scattered with a few villages inhabited only in the summer. The plateau is situated at a height of 1100 m and surrounded by the peaks of **Mount Dikti** (2148 m) and **Mount Lazaros** (2085 m). In a four-hour walk you can reach the village of **Kritsa** which is linked by a dirt road with Katharo Plateau. For more isolation, walk for one more hour to the **Horeftes**, an idyllic retreat with the romantic name Neraidokolyvio or "The Swimming Pool of the Nereids".

The most popular stopover in the area is the small village of **Psyhro**, situated at the plain's southern end. Psyhro was founded in the fifteenth century, taking its name from an icy spring nearby (*psyhro* means cold). Every one of the village's inhabitants at some point will tell you the sad story of the Papadakis brothers. The two boys, Manolis and Antonis, fled to Egypt in 1823 when Turkish General Hasan Pasha devastated Lassithi.

Manolis later enrolled in the Egyptian army and after becoming an officer, he was sent back to Lassithi in 1867 to aid the Turkish governor Omer Pasha to suppress the Greek revolution against the Ottoman Empire. During one of the battles he was killed. In the meantime Antonis had left Egypt, found fame and fortune in Russia, and provided arms to the Cretan revolutionaries. When he heard of Manolis' death, he was deeply shocked and exclaimed: "My brother was killed by one of my weapons!"

Psyhro is situated next to the mountain Dikti (2,148 m) and is a base for visiting **Dikteon Cave**, traditionally known as the legendary "birthplace of Zeus". A twenty-minute climb from Psyhro brings you to the cave's entrance. But do not go alone or without a flashlight, good clothing, and steady shoes as it is cool, slippery and dark inside. At the end of the descent a huge stalactite cavern opens to the left. Its floor is covered by water and you will be overwhelmed by the breathtaking view of hundreds of bizarre stalactites and stalagmites.

Myth has it that the ancient god of gods, Zeus, was born in the cave where his mother Rhea found refuge after escaping the wrath of her husband Cronus. Cronus, the master-god of the earth, ate the rest of his children, being afraid that they would steal his glory. In modern times the cave was excavated by British archaeologists in 1900 and revealed a number of offerings to Zeus including bronze double-axes and statuettes. The cave is furnished with a number of stalagmites and stalactites giving it spectacular natural beauty. Adventurers who want to ascend Mount Dikti can do so in about eight hours from Psyhro. For the breathtaking walk you should take water with you. Rooms are available en route in village houses in **Limnahoro**.

If you choose you can spent the night at Psyhro or go back to Neapoli and continue east to Agios Nikolaos.

Right: The slopes of the Dikti massif rise up in the south of Lassithi Plain.

Agios Nikolaos

With a population of only 6000 people, Agios Nikolaos has become more of an international tourist attraction than any other Cretan town. Its hospitable people, mild climate and crystal-clean beaches make it one of Greece's top vacation sites.

Situated 67 km east of Iraklion, the town overlooks the spectacular Gulf of Mirabello, which includes Crete's best known sandy beach. Here, apart from swimming and water sports, one can enjoy fresh fish in a number of traditional tavernas with a view of sea and mountains and exciting night life in discos and bars lasting until the early morning hours.

Agios Nikolaos takes its name from the small Byzantine chapel of St. Nicholas, on the port's nothern side. The village was founded in the year 1870 by settlers from Kritsa and Sphakia. During

Above: A narrow channel connects Lake Voulismeni with the sea.

Venetian times the site was called Porto di San Nicolo, the saint of sea travelers. The chapel becomes the center of activity every December 6, when the saint's feast day is celebrated.

The port itself was linked in 1870 through a man-made channel with the small inland freshwater **Lake Voulismeni**. The lake is 60 m in diameter and 64 m deep although legend has it as the "bottomless pond" where goddess Athene bathed 3000 years ago. During the summer months the lake becomes a center of cultural festivities sponsored by town authorities. Travel agencies often organize Cretan nights with local food specialities, dances and songs. The municipality organizes annual festivities nicknamed "Lato" which include folk dances from around the country and abroad, film presentations, exhibitions of art, Cretan handicrafts and swimming competitions.

On even years (1990, 92 etc.) the town lights up with spectacular fireworks over the harbor to celebrate the Greek Naval

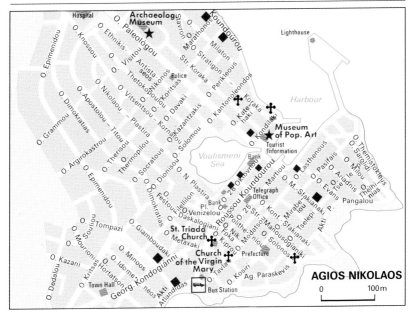

Week which also includes waterskiing, swimming and windsurfing races. During Easter week, on the eve of the Resurrection, a puppet in the likeness of Judas is burnt on a platform in the middle of the lake. The event dates to the eighteenth century and becomes even more exciting as spectators light up candles to brighten the night. On New Year's Eve decorated fishing boats enter the harbor to symbolize the arrival of the new year and when the clock chimes twelve, the sky lights up with hundreds of colorful fireworks. Festivities or not, a walk *(volta)* around the lake and on the port's periphery is highly recommended for the natural beauty it offers.

In ancient times the town was named *Lato pros Kamara* after an important archway *(kamara)* in the area. Lato was fortunate as it suffered little from continuous wars among other Cretan cities during the Minoan period and a single dispute with nearby Elounda over the temple of Aris (God of War), situated between them, was settled after the inter-

vention of Knossos which ruled that the temple should be shared.

Little is known about the city's fate under Roman, Byzantine and Arab rule. It then became a Venetian colony with the rest of Crete in the thirteenth century. The Venetians named the gulf Mirabello (lovely view) as well as the spectacular castle on the port (very few ruins to be seen today) which was erected in 1206 by architect Enrico Pescatore of Genoa. The **Mirabello castle** was one of fourteen which Pescatore built or reconstructed in Crete. The castle was probably ruined in an earthquake and never reconstructed.

Agios Nikolaos, as seen today, was mostly built in the mid-1800s by local immigrants and has little to offer for the archaeologically inclined visitor.

The **town's museum**, situated a few blocks away from the lake, has a collection of Minoan and post-Minoan artifacts up to the Middle Ages. The most important collection includes findings from some 250 Minoan graves at Agia Fotia dating back to 3 000 BC. In the gold sec-

187

tion is a splendid Minoan diadem, decorated with the figures of three *kri-kri*, the Cretan long-horned goat. The piece was discovered on the islet of Mohlos in the Gulf of Mirabello along with a hairpin shaped like a daisy, a lily-shaped bead and various other jewelry used by Minoan maidens. The museum has an important pottery collection of some 700 vases from the early Minoan period, used for storing oil and other goods.

The museum also features three "daedalic" statuettes dedicated to Daedalus, the legendary craftsman, who worked for King Minos in the seventh century BC. Finally, there is a big collection of Mycenaean pottery and ivory objects from the Bronze Age.

Shopping around in our times, Agios Nikolaos offers good leather buys and handmade pottery by local craftsmen.

Elounda and Spinalonga

Your next drive to eastern Crete must be to **Elounda**. Situated 11 km north of Agios Nikolaos, this small fishing village has become the most visited beach resort on the island. Originally called *Olous*, it was a Minoan town which flourished commercially. In post-Minoan times it was conquered by Romans, Venetians, Turks, English and during World War II by Italians and Germans. In 1937 the French School of Archaeology unearthed an early Christian church decorated with spectacular mosaics which can still be seen.

Elounda was one of few Minoan settlements which minted its own coins, indicating the independence of the city. The coins featured on one side the head of the goddess Artemis and on the other the head of Zeus with the word *Olontion* (Elounda). Nowdays Elounda is occupied by tourists and has lost most of its calm

Left: The bungalows on Elounda beach.
Right: Conversation with ancient rocks.

and charm. But the beach is furnished with some of the most acclaimed hotels in southern Europe which are luxurious in class, offering every possible accommodation, and of course luxurious in price (see hotel section).

At the entrance to the bay of Elounda lies the islet of **Spinalonga**. The name of the islet, separated from the mainland by a narrow isthmus, was given by the Venetians whose presence is still felt in the ruins of a magnificent **fortress** built in 1579 by Venetian governor Jacobo Foscarini. Spinalonga went on to be conquered by the Ottoman Turks in 1715 who used the castle to protect their ships in the harbor and a Turkish village was built. In 1823 Turkish general Mohamed Berbantis slaughtered about 1,500 Greek revolutionaries who were captured in the Milatos cave where they sought refuge from Turkish troops. In 1903 the Cretan authorities ruled that Spinalonga should be turned into a leper colony until its abolition in 1957. The suffering of this period is illustrated in an inscription:

"Every hope is lost to those who enter this place".

Don't worry, there is no risk of getting leprosy today. Enjoy instead a fine view of Elounda across the isthmus and return to the mainland via a number of *kaikis* (fishing boats) at your service. A final word on Spinalonga is that the Greek shipping tycoon Aristoteles Onassis once planned to turn the island into a casino.

Kritsa and Lato

Another popular excursion from Agios Nikolaos is to **Kritsa**. To approach the village, exit Agios Nikolaos via the road leading out to Sitia and Ierapetra and 1 km out of town follow the sign to Kritsa, 12 km from Agios Nikolaos. Just before entering the village you come across the whitewashed chapel of **Panagia i Kera**,

Above: The Byzantine Panagia i Kera Church dating from the 13th century. Right: Popes in the village of Kritsa, waiting for Godot perhaps...

the best example of Byzantine art in Crete, built in the middle of a charming olive grove.

The church, which dates to the thirteenth century, consists of three naves, with corresponding semicircular apses. Buttresses and tambour were added at later dates.

Adorning the church's interior are superb frescoes from the fourteenth and fifteenth centuries which are considered major ensembles of Byzantine paintings during the Paleologus era. The central nave is dedicated to the Assumption of the Virgin Mary with restored paintings from the life of Jesus Christ, his birth, the beheading of John the Baptist, the last supper and the crucifixion. The south nave honors St. Anne, the mother of the Virgin Mary with paintings from their lives as told in the bible. The north nave is dedicated to St. Anthony and portrays the Second Coming of Christ, paradise and the weighing of the souls. A number of saints and martyrs complete the magnificent interior. The church can be vis-

ited every day until 3 p.m. except on Tuesdays and Wednesdays.

2 km further on, the main road leads to **Kritsa**. The village, clinging to a mountain side, was the site where the film version of Kazantzakis' *Christ Recrucified* was made with the participation of local inhabitants in minor roles next to the French and Greek actors chosen by American director Jules Dassin who later directed the film *Never on Sunday*. Kritsa is also known for its traditional textile handicrafts which can be bought at bargain prices.

Just before entering Kritsa, a signposted dirt road to the right brings you to **Lato**, an ancient Doric city founded in the post-Minoan era which flourished around the fifth century BC. Lato was excavated by the French School of Archaeology in 1900 and brought to light remains of a prosperous city with an amphitheater, a market place *(agora)*, fortifications, houses, roads, two acropolises and a temple, dedicated to the God of Light, Apollo. A walk to the north

acropolis gives a fantastic view of the Gulf of Mirabello.

Gournia and Ierapetra

Your next tour from Agios Nikolaos is 19 km south towards Ierapetra at the village of **Gournia**. The site is especially appealing for its archaeological treasures, presenting a unique Minoan town complete with remains of streets, houses and of course an ancient palace.

Gournia was excavated in the early 1900s and the findings indicate that the city flourished in about 1600 BC before being destroyed by the same earthquake that hit Knossos. The ancient town resembles a typical large Cretan village today with narrow streets and small crowded houses. The town's main street extended from north to south and was the site of intense commercial activity evidenced by the huge number of artifacts, tools and other items unearthed. Gournia was never inhabited after the Bronze Age and was completely forgotten. The town,

whose Minoan name is not known, takes its present name from the stone washing basins *(gournes)* found outside every house during the excavations.

Most travelers continue from Gournia further south to **Ierapetra** via Pahia Ammos, Vasiliki and Episkopi villages. Ierapetra, 38 km from Agios Nikolaos, was until 1960 a place offering little more than a spectacular view of the Libyan Sea, good local wine and golden beaches. But in the last twenty years this town has flourished. Local farmers were some of the first in Europe to introduce hot-houses to raise their crops, produced year-round for markets abroad. Earlier, Ierapetra was discovered by the hippies who made it one of their main sites with its cheap accommodation, mild climate and welcoming people. In the 1970s a Minoan discovery in nearby Mirtos brought in more traditional visitors forcing the area's rapid growth.

Above: This fisherman in Ierapetra is fixing tears in his nets.

Ierapetra, the fourth largest town in Crete, took its name from the ancient port of Ierapytna which served as a junction between the island and Africa in Minoan and post- Minoan times. Ierapytna dominated southeastern Crete about 145 BC. It fell into Roman hands in 67 BC but continued its growth in the Byzantine period and the Venetian occupation when it was renamed Ierapetra. During Roman rule the city had an impressive population of 120,000 and magnificent buildings which included a theater, public baths, and an aqueduct which stood until 1000 AD. The Romans also used the city as a military port for their attacks against Egypt. The **Venetian castle** guarding the port was built in 1630 and is 50 m long from east to west and 25 m from south to north. It was armed with five large cannons and some 200 smaller guns. Ierapetra was conquered by the Turks in 1650 and from then on it fell from grace. The town's voyage through time can be seen at the local **museum** with a small collection of finds from each period.

These days, Ierapetra is occupied by discos, tavernas and hotels on excellent sandy beaches nearby. But avoid a visit during the middle of summer. Don't forget that you are only 300 km from the African coast and temperatures can get pretty high. Ierapetra was the place where Napoleon stayed overnight on his way to and from Egypt. The ruins of the house where he slept can still be seen in **Kato Mera**. A caique trip 13 km to the south brings you to **Gaidoronissi**. The islet is deserted but the sea around it is excellent for scuba diving.

A short drive west from Ierapetra (15 km) lies the small village of **Mirtos** where British archaeologists brought to light a Minoan settlement dating to 2200 BC. The remains of a villa, built around 1600 BC, which served as the residence of the local Minoan governor, can still be seen and its architecture is a miniature copy of the Knossos palace. The villa was destroyed around 1450 BC probably by the volcanic explosion on Santorini and the earthquake that followed. About ninety rooms have been uncovered, containing a multitude of vases, seal stones, bronze utensils and tools.

From Ierapetra to Sitia

From Ierapetra east through the mainland you will eventually reach Sitia. It is better, however, to avoid the route through the mountains and drive instead back north to **Pahia Ammos** (a small village next to Gournia) and then east on the coast road. The stretch you now enter, from the village of **Kavoussi** to Sitia, is one of the most enjoyable Cretan rides through olive groves, orchards and villages overlooking the sea below. Locals call the area the "Cretan Riviera" which also includes the villages of Lastros, Sfaka, Tourloti, Mouliana (famous for its red wine), Khamezi (another Minoan and Venetian site), Skopi (known for its wedding celebrations), and eventually Sitia.

IERAPETRA

0   100m

Mohlos

Mohlos, a tiny islet between Agios Nikolaos and Sitia on the stretch of coastline known as the "Cretan Riviera", was once connected to the cape on the eastern side of Mirabello Gulf.

Mohlos has recently attracted notice because of finds excavated by an archaeological team led by Nikolaos Platon. Mohlos is close to the larger islet of **Psira** and both can be reached by boat on excursions organized in Agios Nikolaos or by private caique from the mainland beach town of Mohlos, which has hotels and pensions.

Both Psira and Mohlos were ports trading with Egypt and other Middle Eastern countries during Minoan times. Traces of the harbor have been found in shallow water off the islet under what would have been the sandy spit connecting it to the mainland. Late Minoan houses are on the south side of the islet and can be seen from passing boats. Others are submerged in the sea.

Dragonáda

Gianissáda

to Ródos
Akrotíri Síderos

Órmos
Ténda

195m
Mouros

Itanos
Erimoúpoli

Vái
Órmos

Grándes

Akrotíri Faneroméni

Monastery

Toploú (Monastery)
Grándes

Seteia (Castle)
Sitia
Órmos
Sitías
18
Mertidia
Angáthia
Palékastro
Petras
Lídia

Agia Fotiá
Módi
539m
Ágios Nikólaos
Roussolákkos

7
Roússa Ekklissia
Pétsofas
215m

Kímouriótis
Káto Episkopi
Skopí
Piskokéfalo
Xirolimni
17
Langáda
Órmos
áspóri
Ahládia
Arnikó
Stavroménos
Karoúbes

9
Krionéri
Mitáto
Káto Dris
Hohlakiés

Zoú
Hónos
Vrissidi
Priniás
803m
Kellária

Maronia
Stakia
Karidi
Azokéramos

Epáno Episkopí
Adravásti
Traóstalos
515m

Kriá
Ágios Geórgios
Sandáli
Katsidóni
Sitanos
Klissidi

Néa Pressós
Praisos
Kalamáfki
Zákros

Sikiá
Sklávi
Katelónas
KÁTO ZÁKROS

Papaguiana
Ágios Spiridonas
Vigla-Zákrou
711m
Órmos
Zákrou

Vori
14
Lamnóni
Akrotíri Avláki

Handrás

Etiá
Ziros

hines
Arméni

Etiani Kefala
715m
Plágia
819m
Hamétoulo

Apidi
Xerókambos

Pezoúlas
Epáno Perivolákia
Perivolákia
Kaló Horió
Agridomoúri
628m
Agía Iríni

Agía Triáda

eró
Kapsa Monastery
Sárgou Kefala
539m

Goúdouras

Ather nolákós

Akrotíri Goúdouras

EAST OF LASSITHI

0   2   4   6 km

The most significant artifacts in Mohlos were found in the tombs built up against the cliff. A rich cache of stone vases and jars, sealstones and gold jewelry are now on display in museums in Agios Nikolaos and Iraklion.

Excavations in the early part of the twentieth century by American Richard Seager turned up a settlement on Psira similar to Gournia and also flourishing during the Early and Late Minoan periods. Scant remains in the town, including a well, are reached via a long street with steps leading from what was the harbor. Two painted reliefs from houses on Psira are now in the Iraklion Archaeological Museum.

Sitia

Sitia (72 km from Agios Nikolaos), is the largest town in eastern Crete which is still mostly untouched by the tourist storm which transformed Agios Nikolaos and Ierapetra. The town's name in the Minoan era was *Itia* and it was known as the birthplace of Myson, one of the seven sages of ancient Greece. Sitia flourished through the Roman and Byzantine times and took its present name after being occupied by the Venetians. In fact Sitia provided the name for the Lassithi nome. "Lassithi" derives from "La Sitia", the name the Venetians gave to the region in the fifteenth century.

It was during that period that the town was devastated a number of times by earthquakes and attacks from the Ottoman Turks. In 1651 the Venetians deliberately destroyed the town so that it would not fall to the Turks, who eventually made Sitia their provincial capital in 1870. The ruins of the Venetian fortress, overlooking the port, are worth a visit before lunch or dinner in one of the many tavernas serving fresh fish and local vegetables. A new museum has some notable pieces from the area's history and an airport will soon be built.

Above: The tightly-knit houses of Sitia.

Sitia is famous for its *soultanina*, a sweet local raisin, which attracts huge crowds every August 30 to the "raisin festival", when producers celebrate the gathering of the year's crop with folk dances and Cretan music.

Sitia is a stopover for ships that pass weekly between Rhodes, Santorini, and Piraeus. The town's inhabitants are considered the most hospitable in Crete.

Toplou and Palaikastro

Before proceeding to Palaikastro and Vai make a stopover 7 km to the east at the village of **Agia Fotia** where a Minoan necropolis was discovered in 1971 thus providing the museum in Agios Nikolaos with its most important archaeological collection.

Continuing on the beach road east of Sitia you arrive after 15 km at the Christian Orthodox **Toplou Monastery** which dates back to the fifteenth century. Today's building replaces an older church which was destroyed by an earthquake in 1612. The church was originally dedicated to Agios Isidoros but the name Toplou was given by the Turks in 1460. Toplou derives from the word top and the building has the look of a fortress which was repeatedly used as a refuge by Greek resistence fighters against the Turks or the Germans in World War II.

The present monastery was built by the famous Kornaros family of Sitia. Vicenzo Kornaros is the author of the Cretan epic poem *Erotokritos*,while Yannis Kornaros painted, in 1770, the *Greatness of God*, an icon still considered to be a masterpiece of the island's renaissance. The icon, filled with figures and scenes from the bible, still adorns the monastery and is worshiped by locals as a miracle healer. Toplou Monastery is one of the richest in Greece as it owns most of the surrounding land.

A short drive (15 km) further east brings you to **Palaikastro**. The village

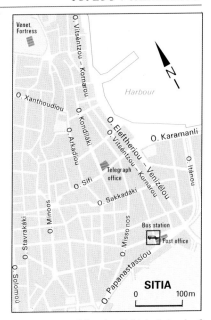

was excavated by the British School of Archaeology at the beginning of the century, unearthing a Minoan port town, perhaps as important as the one found in Gournia. It includes a palace with many rooms used by the local prince and a central street lined with remains of houses and shops. The site has the usual acropolis of Minoan settlements and must have played an important role as a commercial port in late Minoan times as it was one of few places on the island to be rebuilt after the great catastrophe in 1450 BC. Remains of more recent periods include an Archaic-Hellenic temple where a column (now kept in the Iraklion Archaeological Museum) is inscribed with a prayer to Zeus, many bronze and ivory items and a number of vases.

Vai and Kato Zakros

Palaikastro gives you the choice to head north to Vai and Itanos or south to Kato Zakros. **Vai** (9 km from Palaikastro) is the only **palm forest** in Europe, which

197

ends at a lovely sandy beach on the Carpathian Sea. The site is heavily crowded by hordes of tourists in the summer, who often camp in the palm grove despite a police warning against it. Campers or not – the forest is magical; during a full moon it resembles a tropical lagoon on a South Sea island. According to legend, Egyptian warriors created the forest in ancient times to honor a Pharaoh who believed that palm trees were the source of wisdom.

2 km north of Vai lie the ruins of ancient **Itanos** near to the easternmost part of Crete. Herodotus mentions the site in his *Histories*, explaining how a fisherman from the area guided a group of colonists from the island of Santorini to the African coast in about 650 BC. The colonists went on to build the city of Cyrene whose ruins can still be seen in Libya. It is said

Above: The unique palm beach of Vai is a nature conservation area. Right: This is all that remains of the great palace of the Minoan period in Kato Zakros.

that Itanos was originally founded by the Phoenicians but disco- veries in the region indicate that the Minoans were there first creating yet another port which survived through Hellenic and Roman times but was destroyed in the ninth century AD by pirates, and never rebuilt.

The south route from Palaikastro leads through a group of villages to **Ano and Kato Zakros**, two of the loveliest villages in eastern Crete, overlooking the Carpathian Sea. The two villages are 7 km apart with Kato Zakros attracting more attention due to its impressive Minoan finds.

The village was first excavated in the late 1800s and revealed some 15 houses of the late Minoan period and finds from the Myceanaean age. In 1961 new digging took place after ancient objects were found in the area by local habitants and these excavations revealed a major Minoan harbor-town and a palace smaller only than the ones of Knossos, Phaestos and Malia. Archaeologists, who are still on the site, now say that the settlement

was a commercial center of Minoan civilization bringing in trade from Egypt and other countries in northern Africa and the Middle East.

The area was first inhabited about 2500 BC, evidenced by grave sites found at the north end of the village. The settlers built two Minoan palaces, the first in 2000 BC and the second in 1600 BC. The new palace was badly damaged by earthquakes in 1500 BC, but was immediately repaired only to be totally destroyed 50 years later by the same catastrophic quake which ruined Knossos and Phaestos. The palace, covering an impressive 6500 sq m, was a labyrinth of 300 rooms, similar in design to the ones in Knossos. The huge central court is engulfed by a number of appartments, storage halls, stairways and other structures while the area around the royal quarters was a well-planned harbor-town with large buildings and paved roads.

Recent findings indicate Kato Zakros had strong commercial ties with nearby countries. It brought copper from Cyprus,

ivory from Syria and gold from Egypt. Its exports were oil, honey, wood, wine and various agricultural products.

Kato Zakros is the only Minoan settlement where, despite its destruction, so many finds were discovered in such good condition. Thousands of vases, metal and ivory tools, along with 35 giant containers, would be enough to fill up a small museum. Indeed, Kato Zakros has its own special place in the Iraklion Archaeological Museum, where the finds are exhibited.

Back in the palace, the royal appartments were placed on the eastern side with the king and the queen having different rooms. The biggest rooms of the complex lie to the west and communicate via a staircase to the upper floor where a huge chamber known as the **Hall of Ceremonies** is found. It was here that the king held meetings with his associates or presided over cultural and religious ceremonies. At the palace's northern side an equally huge room surrounded by a maze of smaller ones served as the kitchen. Fi-

nally, in a separate area north of the palace where excavations still take place, blocks of small houses served as living quarters for lower-class people probably employed at the harbor or the families of sailors.

Hike through the Valley of the Dead

We shall begin this hike in the middle of Zakros. From the main square you turn into the street "Odos 25 Martiou", where a church stands. Take the path leading downward on the right of the church and go under the aqueduct, along a water canal until you reach the southwest end of the village. After about fifteen minutes the cement road gives way to a gravel covering which you must follow for about another 50 meter. At the fork you head left over the stream. Proceed amidst fields and vegetable gardens, up a cement

Above: A plunging view into Crete's version of Death Valley from the old road to Kato Zakros.

road, on a path alongside a water pipe in the direction of the valley.

Go through a gate and straight through a plot of land. After passing the fence the road forks again. Do not go right down toward the stream, but left up a gentle slope leading above the tree-tops of the planes and oleanders lining the stream. About half an hour later you get a first glimpse of the opening to the gorge.

The path then leads in part along the stream in the shade of the plane trees. Another valley joins laterally from the left. At this point you can cross over to the stream's right bank and walk along an irrigation canal. The cliff above is dotted with little niches and caves. Some served as burial grounds for the dead in the pre-Christian era which is why the gorge has been called the **Valley of the Dead**.

About 500 meter further the path leads back to the stream which you can once again cross. You are now standing in a giant stone cauldron surrounded on all sides by cliffs. The path is in good shape; light shoes such as sneakers suffice. De-

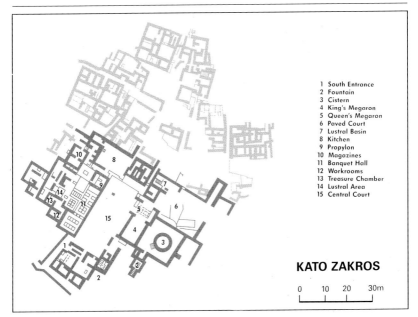

1 South Entrance
2 Fountain
3 Cistern
4 King's Megaron
5 Queen's Megaron
6 Paved Court
7 Lustral Basin
8 Kitchen
9 Propylon
10 Magazines
11 Banquet Hall
12 Workrooms
13 Treasure Chamber
14 Lustral Area
15 Central Court

KATO ZAKROS

0   10   20   30m

pending on the season the stream might be dry, in which case the splashing and murmuring of the water is supplanted by a deathly silence in the almost 200 m high cliff walls.

Finally the stream bed widens, the path becomes stony, oleanders join the shrubby blue summer lilac and out of nowhere the little stream re-emerges. The reddish walls of the gorge appear ragged and hollow before disappearing altogether. (A banana plantation has been sited here.)

Now a normal road crosses the stream bed. This is the old road to Zakros, which you can take to get back to your starting point, and once again it offers a spectacular view of the gorge. First, however, make a quick excursion to the sea. The path to the left leads by the excavation site of the Minoan palace of Kato Zakros. The taverns along the beach are very inviting, and the bay can be an idyllic spot to bathe and sunbathe provided no tourist buses have stopped here. If you are tired of walking, try catching a ride back to

Zakros, or use the old road leading upwards on the right of the gorge's exit.

South of Sitia

Sitia offers a base for a southern excursion towards the Libyan Sea through a purely Cretan territory of rigid cliffs with little cultivation, that has remained largely unchanged for thousands of years. A short drive (3 km) brings you to the village of **Piskokefalo**, founded in the fifteenth century during the Venetian occupation. In the surrounding area two minor Minoan sites dating to 1600 BC have brought to light a Minoan villa and a farming village with houses, storerooms, stables and a sanctuary.

7 km further south you reach **Nea Pressos**, built next to the ruins of ancient Pressos. The city which is spread across three acropolises was a major center for Eteocretans, a post-Minoan culture that flourished for a millenium after the collapse of Knossos and other Minoan centers. Four Eteocretan inscriptions dating

to 600 BC were discovered in 1884 along with the remains of a Minoan villa and a Hellenistic necropolis. Pressos was destroyed in 144 BC following long wars with Ierapetra.

Your next stop further south is the mountain village of **Ziros** dating back to Venetian times. The local church of **Agia Paraskevi** is lavishly decorated with frescoes of the Cretan renaissance.

From Ziros a secondary southern route leads to **Kapsa monastery**, dedicated to St. John the Forerunner. Built in the fourteenth century by a group of monks, the original monastery was ruined by the Turks in 1471, but was rebuilt by the Venetians. A monk called Gerontoyannis (Old John), made news in the nineteenth century with his miraculous healings. His reputation attracted huge crowds from other villages who still come every August 29 when Kapsa celebrates the feast day of St. John. The monastery offers a unique view of the Libyan Sea and the nearby village of **Kalo Nero** (Good Water) has a wonderful beach.

Koufonissi, about 4 km off the southern shore of Crete near Atherinolakos, is the largest island in the archipelago, once known in antiquity as the *Leucae*, the White Islands. Evidence has been found of a settlement from the Early Bronze Age. The largest remains, however, including part of a stone-built theater, are from a prosperous Roman town. Excavations under the Greek Archaeological Service which were begun in 1976, continue each summer.

The cultivation of a form of brilliant crimson dye obtained from a gland in the shell of a spiny seasnail, began in Minoan times. It was responsible for Koufonissi's prominant position in the Mediterranean

Right: Hotel owner Spyros Kokotos wants more comfort for tourists. Following pages: Seasonal fruits. A woman's hands at rest. A Cretan speciality: snails in olive oil, onions, tomatoes and spices.

textile industry, known as the "purple trade", which especially flourished during the Roman era.

An exhibit in the Sitia Museum illustrates the methods of harvesting the shells and obtaining the scant drops of the precious dye so highly prized by the Phoenicians, Greeks and Romans.

Offbeat Beaches

West of Ierapetra, the beach at **Arvi** is long enough to handle the crowds that gather. The main virtue of the area is the fertile land around the beach on which fruit is grown. Take a stroll around the banana plantations.

Mirtos is a small village with some rooms for rent and a few tavernas and also good opportunities for swimming. During the last two decades an increasing number of big hotels have expanded throughout the area around **Ierapetra**. 24 km further on, just before the road branches off to inland Sita, you will reach the village of **Makrigialos** which has a beautiful beach. Along the coastline, to the east, at **Kalo Nero**, **Goudouras**, and near **Kapsa monastery** there are more rewarding beaches .

The beaches of **Kato Zakros** and **Palaikastro** on the east coast of Crete are renowned for their tranquility, some friendly tavernas and rooms to rent. Undoubtedly the most scenic beach on the eastern coast, however, is the palm beach of Vai which is a protected area today where camping is prohibited.

The Istron Beach Hotel in **Istron** is on a cliff above a lovely beach, much nicer than the one at Kalo Horio. It is the best beach outside Agios Nikolaos.

Mohlos is a friendly village and a good place for diving.

The posh hotels outside **Agios Nikolaos** have attractive beaches restricted to guests. At **Elounda**, people swim off the flat rocks at Olous or at the large pebble beach at **Plaka**.

SPYROS KOKOTOS, LUXURY HOTEL OWNER IN ELOUNDA

Spyros Kokotos, the architect who designed the Elounda Beach and Astir Palace Hotels, and who owns and designed the Elounda Mare and the newly constructed Porto Elounda Hotel, is a successful innovator in the tricky hotel industry on Crete.

Instead of taking a predictable path and building a traditional high-rise hotel in his home town of Iraklion, he chose to construct small, low-slung deluxe hotels and adjacent bungalows with private swimming pools, on the ruggedly beautiful coast outside Elounda.

The six-year-old Elounda Mare Hotel, his spacious "magnum opus", caters to upscale clients who crave privacy and "want to be pampered". While striving to achieve this goal, Kokotos discovered that the main weakness of Greek hotels, according to complaints of guests, is the low quality of service.

This is evident, he feels, in both an in-adequate number of personnel and the negative attitude of the workers. "Where are the smiles? What happened to the joy?" he asks ruefully. "The traditional Cretan hospitality is vanishing."

Kokotos and his wife Eliana, daughter of a prominent Cretan hotelier and educated in hotel management at Cornell University, feel this can be corrected by proper education.

The carefully selected 135 employees who cater to the maximum 190 guests, get training through an introductory course, supplemented by mini-work-shops given two or three times a week by supervisors in each department. The kitchen personnel are sent to France for training in a luxury hotel.

This policy has had outstanding re-sults. Elounda Mare is the only Greek hotel to have the prestigious Ralais & Chateau approval for small family-run hotels. While tourism in Greece has been dropping in the last few years, Elounda Mare has had an increase in guests and operates at 90 percent occupancy.

AGIOS NIKOLAOS
Accommodation
LUXURY: **Istron Bay**, Tel. 61347, 61325, on the beach, sea-water swimming pool, shopping arcade, private beach, tennis court. **Minos Beach**, hotel and bungalows, Tel. 22345, on the beach of Ammoudi, swimming pool, tennis court, all bgls with refrigerator and mini bar. **Minos Palace Hotel**, Tel. 23801, swimming pool, refrigerator and mini-bar in all rooms, all bgls. with sea view and private patio. **Mirabello Village**, Tel. 28401, on the beach, two heated swimming pools, indoor swimming pool, sauna, three tennis courts, night club. **Hermes**, Tel. 28253, on the beach, swimming pool, mini-golf, beauty parlor. **St Nicholas Bay**, Tel. 25041, on the beach, swimming pool, tennis court, pool bar.
MODERATE: **Ariadni Beach**, Tel. 22741.**Coral**, Tel. 28363 **El Greco**, Tel. 28894
BUDGET: **Almyros Beach**, Tel. 22865. **Kera**, Tel. 28771.

Useful phone numbers
(Area code 0841) **Police** 2225, **Tourist police** 22321, **Harbour police** 22312, Hospital 22369.

ELOUNDA, SPINALONGA
Accommodation
LUXURY: **Astir Palace Elounda**,Tel. 41580 on the beach, swimming pool, greek taverna, cinema, disco. **Elounda Beach**, Tel. 41412,on the beach, swimming pool, tennis court, all water sports including deep sea diving. **Elounda Mare**, Tel. 41512, 50 rooms and 40 Bgls with private swimming pools, automatic dialing and mini bar refrigerators in all rooms. **Elounda Marmin**, Tel. 41535, 100m from the beach, swimming pool, tennis court.
MODERATE: **Driros Beach**,Tel 41238.
BUDGET: **Kalypso**, Tel. 41316.
(area Code 0841, Police 41348)

IERAPETRA
Accommodation
LUXURY: **Ferma Beach**, hotel and bgls Tel. 61341, on the beach of Ferma, swimming pool, tennis court, golf. **Lyktos Beach Resort Hotel And Tennis Club**, Tel. 61280, on the beach, swimming pool, tennis courts, water sports, library, cinema, card room. **Petra-mare**, Tel. 23341, on the beach, swimming pool, hairdressing.
MODERATE: **Blue Sky**, Tel. 28264. **Minoan Prince**, Tel. 25150 **Porto Belisario Hotel**, Tel. 61358.
BUDGET: **Zakros Hotel**, Tel. 24101.
(area code 0842, Tourist police 22560)

SITIA
Accommodation
LUXURY: Sitian Beach, Tel. 28821, on the beach, two swimming pools, disco. **Sunwing**, Tel. 51621, beach club, swimming pool, two tennis courts.
MODERATE: **Aldiana Club**, Tel. 94211. **Maresol Bungalows**, Tel. 28950.
(area code 0843, Tourist police 22266)

Festivals
Naval Week: Agios Nikolaos is probably the best place to be during Greek Naval Week every June. The public is invited to go aboard warships anchored in the harbor from where they can watch events connected with the sea. This include water sports, swimming competitions and varios exhibitions. A spectacular firework display is held on the final evening.
Lato-Kornaria: These are cultural activities organised in June, July and August in Agios Nikolaos, Ierapetra and Sitia. They include lectures, art exhibitions, folk and modern music festivals, track and field games and wine tasting.
Sultana Festival: The festival is held in Sitia by local raisin producers during the second fortnight in August. The event attracts many visitors who are invited to sample some 40 wine varieties and other local products. Folk music and water sports complete the festivities.

Museums at:
AGIOS NIKOLAOS: Archeological Museum (Tel.: 0841/24.943), Paläologou St. 68. Finds from the excavation in eastern Crete.
SITIA: Ethnological Museum.
IERAPETRA: Archeological Collection.
Monasteries
Selinari, Kremasta, Afetiou, Arvi, Krousteliana, Toplou, Faneromenis, Exakoustis, Kapsa.
Archeological Sites
Gournia, open daily 8:45 - 3 p.m. **Agia Fotia** (protominoan Nekropolis), **Kato Zakros** (Minoan Palace) open daily 8:45 a.m.-3:00 p.m., **Ierapetra** (archeological collection), **Mohlos** (protominoan Nekropolis), **Neapoli** (archeological collection), **Palaikastro** (Minoan settlement).
Camping
Gournia Moon, from Agios Nikolaos on the road to Sitia (0842) 93243, persons 165, tents 55. **Ierapetra Camping** (0842) 61351, persons 123, tents 41. **Koutsoumari**, Agios Ioannis (0842) 61213, persons 198, tents 66.
Beaches
Agios Nikolaos (Ammoudi), Ierapetra (east along the coast), Mirtos, Milatos, Anatoli, Lithines, Makri Gialos, Sitia, Palaikastro, Vai.

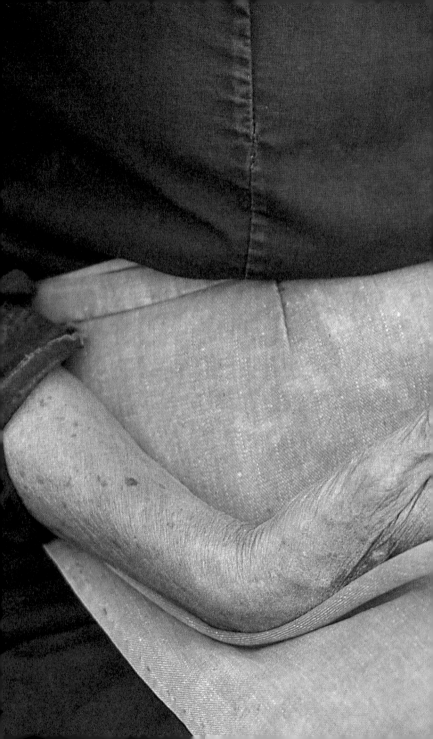

FLORA AND FAUNA

Crete has a good range of common Mediterranean bird species with a number of rare ones, either residents or visitors, seen on their migratory route.

The best time to see both is in the spring. Crete is on one of the main migratory routes for species that winter in East Africa but breed in northern Europe. The autumn migration is also a time to spot some species on their way south but the numbers of birds are greatly decreased.

Smaller songbirds are at greatest risk in Crete, often falling prey to overzealous hunters or collectors who cage them. Another hazard is the destruction of their habitat, a process that has taken place at an alarming rate in coastal areas and some of the flat interior. For this reason, the mountainous areas are home to some

Above: "Live free or die," was the motto that almost led to the eagle's extinction. Right: Cretan hunters tend to shoot on anything that moves.

of the more fascinating smaller birds and a really impressive array of birds of prey.

The Blue Rock Thrush and the Rock Nuthatch are found on mountainsides. Colonies of noisy Alpine Choughs are especially prolific near the Kamares Cave on Mount Psiloritis.

Although some unfortunate magnificent predators end up as poorly preserved stuffed specimens decorating "kafenions", many Cretan hunters are slightly more respectful towards larger birds, if not towards the laws that protect them.

Attempts have been made to restrict the indiscriminate use of pesticides sprayed from planes, or poisoned baits to exterminate unwanted animals. The use of these measures has been directly responsible for the dwindling numbers of many species.

During the warmer months, the mountains are home to long-legged buzzards, fairly languorous birds, the Golden Eagle and at lower levels Bonelli's Eagle and Bearded Vultures. This extremely rare bird, one of Europe's largest and most

majestic species, has its largest Greek population in Crete, particularly in the Samaria Gorge. In the winter, many of these birds fly down to the plains.

Most birds of prey breed in the early and mid-spring, although Eleanora's Falcon, common on the rocky islets off Crete, nests in late summer. The vultures nest in winter. The vultures are also exceptional in that the male is larger than the female. In most vultures, which mate for life, the female is bigger and stronger.

The in-flight foreplay that precedes breeding is dazzlingly fanciful and agile. The birds soar over the area they have chosen for a nest, first playing with one another, then flying with interlocked toes. One of them will dive to the ground, at the last moment rising again. The male, as a finale, offers food to the female and she accepts it while making sounds similar to the calls of her young.

The Griffon Vulture, whose most abundant numbers are in Crete, is an ominous looking creature with a long neck, fierce eyes and a huge hooked bill. Griffons are gregarious. They eat carrion and a few of them together can strip a large carcass in very short order.

The Lammergier Vulture, also a huge bird with a wing span of almost 3 meters, is distinguished from the Griffon by its narrower wings and longer, wedge-shaped tail. It is extremely rare but more common in Crete than anywhere else. Occasionally, it may be sighted gliding over the Lassithi or Omalos Plains.

Coastal lagoons, marshy river deltas and wetlands are not common in Crete but afford good bird watching where they do exist. The river bed near Agia Triada in Iraklion is frequented by herons, egrets and sandpipers. Marsh Harriers can often be seen drifting and darting over reed-beds near rivers, wings in open V-shape, looking for fish, frogs and snakes.

The marshes and reedbeds near Agia Galini have nightingales and warblers. The river bed or hillsides near the Preveli Monastery may be the place to find the Sardinian Warbler or the even rarer Ruppell's Warbler, distinguished by a black

cap and throat, red eye and white mustache. The chukar, a partridge reminiscent of those in the lovely Knossos frescoes, favors hillsides.

Adaptable kestrels and red-footed falcons, both predators, congregate in bushes or scattered trees in open areas or sometimes on telegraph wires on the edge of towns. Both are protected.

Two stunningly marked birds, the Pink, Black and White Hoopoe and the Yellow and Black Oriole, can sometimes be spotted in woodland or olive groves. Another frequent visitor to olive groves, as well as large gardens and old buildings near settlements, is the tiny insectivorous Scops Owl. Its mottled markings adapt it perfectly for daytime snoozing against tree bark and if disturbed, it will freeze and raise its protruding ear tufts. Its most distinctive characteristic and one that for many symbolizes the atmosphere of the Greek islands, is its powerful and per-

Above: Crete is a wonderful place in spring, not only for sheep.

sistant nocturnal call which sounds like "kook".

The hauntingly beautiful Barn Owl, whose shrill voice and preference for settling in old ruins has created the superstition that it is cursed, was the victim of hunting and pesticides around 1970. Its numbers were greatly reduced and consequently the rat population, part of its prey, rose significantly in Crete, illustrating the importance of birds of prey in the ecosystem.

The fauna is otherwise rather on the poor side. The cri-cri, Crete's wild goat, barely escaped extermination by being resettled on the islands off the northern coast. One still finds these stringently protected animals near the gorge of Samaria and in some of the more remote mountainous areas. On the other hand, a fair number of smaller animals live on the island, including rabbits, swamp turtles (in Lake Kournas), weasels, snakes and lizards. There is no need to fear the snakes: of the five types extant on Crete only one, the adder, is venomous, but not dangerous for humans because usually the snakes slither off at the slightest sound.

Trees and Shrubs

Crete was among the earliest of advanced civilizations in the eastern Mediterranean region. Deforestation of erstwhile dense woodlands in addition to climatic changes have resulted in the landscape as we know it today, consisting principally of lower vegetation, thorny undergrowth and hardy thickets. Man's hand, however, also played a role in importing new plants and trees from other parts of the world. Grapes and olive trees were already being cultivated during antiquity. Citrus fruits, agaves, opuntias and eucalyptus arrived on the island with the discovery of new continents.

The most common trees on Crete today are pines, cypresses, various oaks, planes, chestnuts and eucalyptus. In many places the landscape has been shaped by plantations of utility trees such as olive, orange, lemon, fig, almond, walnut and carob. Of more recent date are subtropical fruits including avocados, kiwis and bananas.

Among the most prevalent shrubs are broom, holly, oleander, myrtle and the Macchia's panoply of hardy growths. The lower vegetation – known as phrygana – includes a large number of medicinal plants and herbs such as sage, thyme, oregano and diktamos.

Flowers

To see Crete in the early spring, blanketed in a colorful array of wild flowers and flowering shrubs, is a joyful experience for anyone, even those without a smidgeon of formal knowledge about the science of botany. For naturalists, the Cretan countryside, which boasts over 2000 species of plants, 130 endemic to the island, is paradise and

they may immerse themselves in the sighting and study of these forms, to the exclusion of everything else.

Crete is the only mountainous island to have all four of the major habitats which include the coast, cultivated land, low hillsides and mountains. In the lowlands, most plants are burnt out during the scorching heat between mid-July through late September, though the mountains still have some greenery. In the autumn, a second spring occurs, with many plants flowering between October to December.

A love of flowers goes back to the ancient times of the Minoans, whose art reflected the wide range of the flora, most of which is still blooming in Crete today. Pottery, drawings and frescoes of Minoan Crete show flowering plants such as the Barbary Nut, an iris with bright blue flowers with white centers and yellow markings, the white, pink or yellow Turban Buttercup, crocuses, lilies, pale yellow sternbergias and clusters of Sea Daffodil.

The mythical and healing associations of Cretan plants are vast. One of the most outstanding in this respect is the Madonna Lily, one meter high with a few large funnel-shaped flowers of pure white, that is the most frequent floral motif of Minoan art. It symbolizes grace and purity, and both Greeks and Romans put wreaths of lilies and corn on the heads of those being married.

In Crete, the white lily is strongly associated with Brytomartis, the "sweet virgin" who was pursued by Minos. She jumped into the sea and was saved from drowning by a fisherman drawing his nets. She later became called both Dictynna, "mother of the nets," and the Mother Goddess.

To later Greeks the lily was the flower of Hera who was the goddess of marriage and childbirth. The flower was said to have a magical power against witches and evil. The juice, or an ointment made from the bulb, is soothing for skin ail-

ments and if pulverized with honey, makes an excellent face masque to remove wrinkles. The lily can be found in Crete on dry, stony slopes from May to July. Another variation, also a motif of Minoan art, is the brilliant scarlet Chalcedonicum, found in woodland clearings on mountains from June to August.

A number of flowering plants must be eaten to release their powers. The Sea Daffodil, or Pancratium, was believed to be a cure-all, as its Greek name (*pan* – all, *cratium* – strength) implies. Dioscorides describes the edible bulb as being good for a wide range of ailments from coughs to heart disease to chapped feet. It blooms on coastal sands from July - September.

One of the weirdest of the edible flowering plants is the mandrake, steeped in myth and magic because its shape often resembled a human figure and the plant is depicted as having a human head. It is a narcotic plant that is said to utter a shriek when dug up, the sound of which is harmful to men. Therefore a dog was used to extract the root from the soil.

Besides being used in sorcery, the root was used as a painkiller during operations, and as a cure for gout, sleeplessness and as a love potion. It flowers in fields and stony places in both spring and autumn.

The white or pink-flushed peony, which blooms on stony hillsides from April, is also known to have powerful curative and magical properties. Theophrastus and Pliny suggested its root, said to cure convulsions, epilepsy and lunacy, should only be dug up at night for a person doing so during the day is in danger of losing his eyesight.

Cistus is a shrub with pink flowers that blooms from March until June in stony places. A gum, ladanum, exudes from the plant and is collected by pulling a leather-thonged flail through the plants in the hottest part of the day or it can be collected from the beards and legs of goats feeding nearby. The gum is still used in

Above: Beauty that pricks. Right: The fields are in full bloom during spring time.

214

medicinal plasters and perfumes and a tea can be made from an infusion of the leaves.

Although the cultivation and development of land on Crete has interfered with the natural habitat of wildflowers, there are still more varieties in Crete than in all of Britain. Those wanting a thorough and scientific guide to the Cretan wildflowers should consult Huxley and Taylor's *Flowers Of Crete*.

Mountainous and stony areas cannot be cultivated, so are especially rich in wildflowers. One logical way to see wildflowers is to combine looking for them with a visit to the ancient sites. The land has not usually been tampered with since ancient times, although unfortunately the use of pesticides has destroyed some flowers and harmed other sensitive species, especially the delicate orchids.

Polyrrhenia, a few kilometers south of Kastelli, is relatively unknown but has remains from Minoan to Byzantine times and, in addition, has a breathtaking panorama of the coastal plain and the sparkling sea. Above the white houses of the village on the crest of the hill, during March-June, there is a splendid profusion of the woody-stemmed shrub Tree Spurge, which has clusters of yellow flowers. In the midst of fortifications, ruined towers, and old walls are poppies, gladioli, crown daisies, Venus, Looking Glass, wild leek and feathery-leaved Pheasant's Eye.

Gournia, in mid-Crete overlooking the Bay of Mirabello, has paved floors in the ancient town that are covered in the spring with anemones, Turban Buttercups, Star of Bethlehem and Widow Iris. Outside the town walls grow impressive Giant Orchids.

At **Phaestos**, a complete cross-section of endemic Cretan spring flowers – anemones, irises and orchids, including the insect-imitating orchid Orphys cretica - are enhanced by the appearance of the exotic blue-flowered Love-in-a-Mist. From

Phaestos in the south, one can see anemones, mandrakes and orchids. Also from Phaestos, it is an easy walk to **Agia Triada,** a smaller site with a wider array of orchids, Cretan Ebony and anemones.

The originally Doric site of **Lato**, near Agios Nikolaos, has a view across vast alive and almond groves to the sea. Its floral highlights are a bright yellow form of Turban Buttercup, Rock Lettuce and Alyssoides cretica, a much branched perennial with bright golden flowers.

Near **Agia Galini**, towards the cliffs to the west that rise among typical "phrygana" or scattered scrubby bushes, growing on limestone, one might find Tassel Hyacinths, Jerusalem Sage, and Giant Fennel, over 2 m high. An orchid with the name Orphys fuciflora or the Late Spider Orchid, with a distinctive blue pattern, grows here.

On the open hillsides near the **Preveli Monastery** grow spring flowers and aromatic herbs such as sage, rosemary, lavender or the Cretan Dittany, a white woolly shrublet with pink flowers.

215

CAVES

Most visitors to Crete come in search of sun and surf but there are more and more individualists who will be happier delving into its darker depths in the form of caves. Probably the most famous "caves" at Matala are not really caves but rock-cut Roman tombs inhabited by a colony of free spirits during the 1970s.

Many Cretan caves have mythological associations, such as the **Ideon Cave** on the slopes of Mount Psiloritis, which was identified as the birthplace of Zeus in those days. The Psyhro or **Dikteon Cave**, below Mount Dikti, is considered a rival to the Ideon Cave as the birthplace of Zeus, although most scholars believe it was the sanctuary of the Minoan mother goddess. It is also believed to have been the scene of the seduction of Europa by

Above: The entrance to the Melidoni cave near Perama. Right: The Bears' Cave at the Gouvernerto Monastery on the Akrotiri peninsula.

Zeus, a union which produced Minos, the founder of the Minoan dynasty.

Kamares, a cave at the southern foot of Mount Psiloritis, is thought to have been inhabited since Neolithic times. Excavations of the cave after its discovery by a shepherd in the late nineteenth century yielded the distinctive polychrome pottery with striking geometric designs now displayed in the Iraklion Archaeological Museum. The artifacts were votive offerings from the Phaestos rulers to the goddess Elithia who was worshipped in a sanctuary in the cave. A well-paved road from Iraklion cuts through peaceful hamlets, surrounded by groves watered by abundant streams. The path to Kamares Cave begins almost opposite the cemetery in Kamares Village 56 km southwest of Iraklion. It is best to ask the friendly villagers about hiring a guide because the steep ascent up the mountain side takes at least three hours and the path is marked sporadically with orange splashes. The cave nestles below the peak of the Dhijenis, at an altitude of 1524 m.

The **Skotino Cave** is a comfortable walk of 8.5 km from the main road running between Iraklion and Agios Nikolaos. The enormous cave is considered one of the most important sanctuaries on Crete. Skotino was first investigated by Sir Arthur Evans, then by French archaeologist Paul Faure, followed by Greek excavator Davaras. Faure speculated that the grotto was used as a religious sanctuary originally dedicated to Brytomartis in the Middle Minoan period, when she was worshipped along with Artemis.

The area around **Elos**, south of Kastelli Kissamos, presents some possibilities for hiking through wooded hillsides and ravines, with several breathtaking views of the sea from the highest altitudes. Near the Koutsomatados Ravine, one of the most picturesque canyons on the island, the road enters a tunnel which leads to the **Agia Sophia Cave**. The cave has a chapel near the entrance and was inhabited in Neolithic times.

Melidoni Cave, northeast of Perama, an undistinguished town south of the Re-thimnon-Iraklion road, is known as the home of Talos, a bronze giant, notorious in mythology for hurling boulders at passing ships.

In 1824, several hundred people escaping from marauding soldiers in nearby villages, were trapped in the cave by the Turks, who blocked the entrance with brushwood and set fire to it, suffocating the villagers who all died. Melidoni is only a 5-km walk from Perama. From outside the entrance one has a lovely view across the Mylopotamos Valley up to the Psiloritis mountain range.

Milatos Cave is 6 km from the coast to the east of Malia, on a side road that leads past the village of Sission. Milatos was the site of another horrific incident during the resistance in 1823. 3700 Greek children, women, and old men were besieged in the cave by 16,000 Turkish troops, before finally surrendering to Hasan Pasha. The old men were killed and the women and children sold into slavery. A memorial service is held each year on the anniversary of this event.

217

CRETAN COOKING

Traditional Cretan cooking is, to a degree, different from that of mainland Greece. Recent culinary "arrivals" such as feta cheese, souvlaki, pastichio and doner kebab were unknown on the island until relatively recent times. In many cases basic ingredients and combinations resemble those of the mainland but tasting betrays subtle differences determined by the addition of local ingredients or favored spices and herbs that betray contacts with, or influences from, the many different peoples who have either settled on the island or lived within its shores.

Cretan cooking is a blend of Greek, Roman and Byzantine traditions interacting within a relatively isolated region for over 2000 years. In the course of these centuries Arabs, Slavs, Anatolian Greeks, Venetians and Turks have all lived for considerable lengths of time on the island. Moreover, many of their descendants continue to live there and culinary traditions whose origins are obscure. Today, people all over the world enjoy the cultural influences of other countries and poeples, and recipes travel from the land of their origin to be adapted and adopted into international cuisine. Until very recent times the diet of the Cretan people was very distinctive and many ancient Cretan recipes remain a jealously guarded secret. At least one factor that determines some of the peculiarities of Cretan cooking is the relative isolation that parts of the island enjoy due to mountains, valleys and plains. Village and urban life on the island have always been sharply poised against each other. Thus in Crete there is urban cooking, village cooking, that of the mountain areas and that more common to the plains and seacoast. Seasonal availability also plays its part in determining diet.

Above: Waiting for customers at a tavern in Rethimnon. Right: Hospitality is one of the golden rules in the mountain villages of Crete.

Cretan cheeses were famous in the Middle Ages – even in Europe. The most distinctive cheeses native to the island are *graviera, mizithra, staka, malaka* and *ladotyri*. Graviera is a more or less fresh and unripened cheese, mild and used widely. A salted and slightly aged version is *kephalotyri*. Both of these also are found in Greece. Staka is derived from the fats that accumulate while milk is being prepared for cheese making and is a great delicacy as is mizithra made from fresh sheep's milk. Ladotyri is almost always home-made and concocted from what remains after cheese making. It is preserved in oil – hence its name.

Green Vegetables

Cretans are great vegetables eaters and the island has an abundance of them in the spring and even mid-winter. Some are boiled, some are specially set aside for pies or meat dishes. The former always incorporate cheese – either graviera, mizithra or malaka. The names of these vegetables invariably differ according to the various areas – *vlatzakia, stiphanos, radika, radikia, stamnangathia, maratho, staphilinakis, kokkoraki* and *askrolimbi* are but a few.

Pies

Cretan ovens were traditionally heated to an almost incandescent heat and used during the cooling down period for the preparation of different foods. Bread went in first to be followed by meat (if used) and then pies. The latter would have been made of different kinds of dough depending on the nature of the filling. For meat pies stock and oil were incorporated. Pies made of cheese, greens etc. on occasion use doughs prepared with *tsikoudia* – a native Cretan *raki* prepared from either the distilled remains from grapes or mulberries (this is the most common). Sweet pies or doughs prepared for making desserts incorporate orange or lemon juice as well as tsikoudia.

A very famous dish used to be prepared in the Sphakia/Selinos region of Crete when ibexes were still hunted for sport and food. This was prepared with an ibex kid that was stuffed with mizithra, staka, dill, various other herbs, greens, heavily peppered and then sealed in an earthenware pot with dough crust and baked in an oven. A modern variation is sometimes prepared using a whole kid or baby lamb.

Stews are very popular and varied. Some of these, such as fricasse, incorporate lemon sauce as well as different kinds of vegetables. Celery root is used widely with meat stews and the leaves of *maidano* (Italian parsley) are cut up finely with tomatoes to prepare sauces in which fish or meat are cooked. Artichokes are found in great abundance in Crete and are cooked with meat with or

Above: The best bougatsa – a farmer's cheese specialty – you will find at Kir Kors in Iraklion. Right: An edible nature morte: bread, wine, olives, cheese, salad.

without lemon and egg sauces. It is said, that the Cretan diet is very healthy.

Meats

Traditional meats eaten by Cretans are baby lamb, kid, piglet and hares or rabbits. Chicken, while eaten, was once considered to be almost the equivalent of a poor man's meat. An especially delicious way of preparing lamb calls for marinading it with lemon juice overnight and then placing it on a bed of thyme and (or) oregano sprigs. Heavily peppered, it is baked in a slow oven. Another preparation bakes the lamb in a preparation of yoghurt, eggs and melted butter. Hare or rabbit is quite often buttered and fried. It is also incorporated in onion stews heavily flavored with orange juice (or rind), bay leaves, cinnamon and cloves. Snails are also eaten widely *(hohlous stifado)* and appear in stews concocted with tomatoes, potatoes, and onions or even baked in tomato sauce – usually laced with orange juice.

Seafood

Seafood is widely popular along the coastal areas of Crete and eaten grilled, stewed, baked or even raw. A favorite childhood pastime was sucking out periwinkles and tiny crabs while on the lookout for sea urchins that were either eaten on the spot or taken home and eaten raw there.

The great variety of fish that once inhabited the seas around Crete has diminished due to foreign poachers, dynamite fishing and pollution. There are many varieties of bream, mullet both grey as well as red, and larger fish such as sword fish. Octopus is very popular and is cooked over charcoal, or eaten in stews, as are cuttlefish. The latter are also cooked with pasta in a very distinctive Cretan dish. Kalamares are usually dipped in butter and fried. In winter *bacaljaro* often is served.

Warning: May be that you expect your seafood to be cheaper than at home. You are wrong!

Spices

Spices are greatly used in urban cooking in Crete. Hania and Rethimnon were always known for their rich and elegant dishes and these traditionally incorporated spices that were readily available in their markets. Crete, especially during Ottoman times, was a mid-way stop in the spice trade that ran from Alexandria and other North African ports to the southern shores of Crete. From here, goods were brought up to the northern coast and then made their way to Izmir and Istanbul. Cinnamon invariably appears in some meat dishes, sauces and sweets along with cloves. Hot chillis (grown on the island) are used in making the filling for small cheese pies called *skaltsounia*. They are also used in stews and salads. Cumin and coriander are used more widely than on mainland Greece and on occasion are dusted on grilled fish and used in sauces. Mint, dill, and parsley are used in a myriad preparations. Rosemary is used especially with fish.

221

ENTERTAINMENT

Tourists expect to find more than just a sun tan and antiquies. A lot of entertainment is also expected. No problem. **Hania's** bars and restaurants are far more varied than one would expect from a small town. Kytaro in the old town serves Chinese, vegetarian specialities and curries along with Greek dishes and lovely dry white wine from the Kastelli region. Oleander, in a restored Venetian mansion with tasteful antiques in the old Jewish quarter, serves fairly pricey but good international cuisine. Tamam, on Zambeliou 49, has a reasonable eclectic menu. For authentic *mezedes* (appetizers), go to Zorba's Cafe Ouzeria, serving tasty tidbits to accompany your before-dinner aperitif. For simple taverna fare,

Above: Entrance to a night club in the old town of Hania. Right: Tafli means board and is played in a variety of fashions. Following pages: The dolphin fresco in Knossos.

go to Jimmy's opposite the cathedral or Faka's, a real bargain. The owner at Faka sometimes takes down a bouzouki and strums along to haunting rembetika songs sung by the patrons.

Ideon Andron, in a lovingly restored Venetian building, pipes classical music into its charming garden café next to the *shadirvan*, or ritual fountain of the museum. Palatzo, behind the tourist mosque, is an ideal place to nibble on mezedes while watching the sunset.

Fagotto is a sophisticated club open in the summer when it plays recorded jazz interspersed with live performances. Amaryllis is a charming piano bar in a cosy restored hotel in the Jewish quarter.

Bars in Hania seem to specialize and attract particular types of customers. Le Monde, on Odos Kondilaki in the old town, is filled with tipsy American servicemen having the time of their lives. Ladies will get a lot of attention here. Ablomov on the same street attracts a more sedate hip young set, while Cuckoo's Nest is Hania's gay bar.

Those in the mood to dance might try the large Ariadne or Estelle discos. For traditional Cretan lyra music and folk dances, go to Yorgos Drakakis' taverna at the Venetian port. Larger *kentra* (nightclubs) such as Lefka Ori and Zamania operate in the summer on the outskirts of town and are the places Haniotes go to for a special night out.

Rethimnon is smaller and less developed for nightlife but has its share. It used to have an abundance of clubs with live Greek music now found only at Bar Retro. Discos include Fortezza and Disco Leski. The wine festival in late July features electrifying live music and dance troupes and is a good place to mingle with the locals.

The Knossos taverna at the Venetian harbor is run by a friendly older couple, Joseph and Anna, and is open all year. They serve reasonable local favorites – tiny olives, *paximadhi* bread and *fava*.

Iraklion is the hub of traditional Cretan music and during the summer about a dozen places feature lyra music and dancing. One of the most popular is Psiloritis on Akti Koundourou and the Glass House in the same vicinity. Iraklion also caters to foreigners and cosmopolitan Greeks in its discos such as Babylon on Doukas Bofor and the Opera.

In Jam on Dedalou you can listen to good recorded music in a large courtyard. In the same area are the Curry House and a Chinese restaurant. For more authentic and well-prepared fare, go to La Parisienne, a tastefully understated bistro run by a Belgian and his Greek wife, which adds a touch of class to a generally uninspired restaurant scene.

The Palaeokastro restaurant outside Iraklion has terrific axinous (sea urchin roe) and Balahoutis, also outside Iraklion, is a working class taverna that specializes in snails. Other resort areas have discos that are mobbed with international merrymakers during the height of the season. Some of the established ones are Cosmos and Flash in Malia, Zorba's outside Matala and the Palaeohora Club in Palaeohora.

BYZANTINE CHURCHES

It has been estimated that there are over 600 frescoed Byzantine churches in Crete. In the course of traveling through the island the search for them provides fascinating diversions and their discovery is at times quite difficult. Many of them are hidden in what are today out-of-the-way places on the edge of villages, in fields, groves of olive or plane trees and on occasion on craggy ridges.

Most of these churches have neither been cleaned nor restored. They are usually locked and keys must be searched for among the villagers. They are badly lit by small, narrow slits of windows and to make things worse, candle soot, layers of accumulated oils and resins from incense and calcification blur and in some cases, completely obscure the images. It is always a good idea to take a powerful and

Above: The Panagia i Kera Church in Kritsa.
Right: A fresco from its interior.

wide-angled flashlight when visiting one of these churches.

Architecturally the churches of Crete fall roughly into four categories. The first of these consists of large, three-aisled basilicas that show strong influences of Syro-Palestine traditions. There are the remains of over 40 of these basilicas, many of them domed and decorated with mosaic floors that date from prior to the ninth century when, in 825, the Arab Emirate was established on the island. It would appear that most of these churches were destroyed before and (or) during the Arab occupation. At Sougia, Hersonnissos, and Panormos the basilica remains date from the fifth century and have rich mosaic floors. At Gortyna, the surviving upper courses of the Basilica of St. Titus provide some idea as to the great dignity of these buildings.

The second category of churches are also basilicas, either single-, double- or triple-aisled. These are by far the most prevalent and are usually quite small, with vaulted roofs covered with tiles. A few of these are domed as at Kritsa which has a high central vault over which is set the dome resting on a blind drum. Most of these churches are painted and appear ubiquitously all over the island and all can be dated to after the tenth century when the Byzantines re-took Crete from the Arabs. An especially beautiful example that has recently been cleaned and restored can be seen in the Church of the Panagia in the village of Kournas, that has frescoes from the late eleventh or early twelfth century.

Domed cruciform churches make up the third category and are usually datable to the fourteenth century and after. These churches are roughly square in shape with three aisles over the center of which is contructed the dome.

A variant is to be found in churches that have equal-length arms over the central crossing of which a dome is built. The drums of these domes are usually

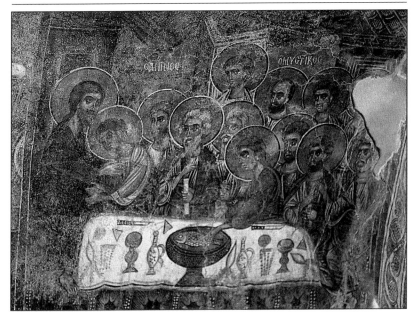

quite high and are characteristic of Byzantine architecture as it evolved in the course of the thirteenth – fourteenth centuries in Macedonia and the southern Balkans. The Panagia at Lambini (c.1350) and the Panagia Gouvernitissa at Potamies, also of the fourteenth century, are good examples.

Finally, there are the churches that have a transverse arch that is higher than the nave, giving the building a cross shape – either externally or internally. These buildings are also dated to the fourteenth century. Good examples of these can be found in Agios Nikolaos at Mouri, Agios Giorgos in the village of Anydri, Agios Nikolaos in Males and the Church of the Saviour in Stamni.

The interior decoration of Byzantine churches is determined by traditions that are faithfully maintained and consistent. Variations are determined by specific architectural forms or their absence.

The dome is the most sacred area and is always reserved for an image of Christ as the *Pantokrator*. The apse with its half

dome is reserved for an image of the Virgin as *Theotokos* or God-bearer. All vaulted areas are decorated with scenes from the *Dodekaorton* or Twelve Festivals, i.e. the cycle of events marking out the drama of the Redemption.

If a church does not have a dome then the Pantokrator image is set in the apse and the Theotokos image takes second place to it elsewhere. In the lower part of the apse are almost always portrayed images of the great saints. At least three are: St. John Chrusostom, St. Basil, and St. Gregory the Theologian. A fourth one can be St. Nikolaos. On the lower walls of a church any one of a number of saints can be depicted and (or) cycles from the lives of Christ, the Virgin or saints.

Even if your time is limited, you should try to visit at least one church that displays several schools and techniques. The Church of Kyra at Kritsa (fourteenth-fifteenth century) has recently been restored and its paintings cleaned and is one of the finest and most characteristic churches on the island.

GRAPES AND OLIVES

Only a stone's throw away from a sandy beach lined with hotels near Iraklion, the scene that greets the visitor willing to walk off the beaten track could be straight out of *Zorba the Greek* by Nikos Kazantzakis. On about August 16, after the feast day of Panagia, under a scorching sun, it is time to harvest the grapes. Whole communities go out to the vineyards where they work hard all day long, talking and laughing as they gather the fruit that will end up as table grapes, raisins or wine.

Harvest time has changed little since dried raisins were sealed inside bulky clay amphorae, loaded onto sleek sailboats and shipped around the Mediterranean. Now the raisins are sifted and packed into burlap sacks, carried off in new Japanese four-wheel drive trucks and bought by the European Community.

Above: No pits in these white grapes that lie out in the sun to dry.

Entry into the EC has literally saved the lives of farmers and their families who can now sell their Cretan quality raisins on better terms.

Growing grapes is a labor-intensive process. It begins in the fall, with the cutting of ditches and rain drains near the roots. In January when the vines are dormant, they are pruned, the dead branches cut off at the main shoots. In the spring the vineyard is sprayed against disease such as mildew and other fungi that could ruin a whole year's work. This spraying continues until the last minute when the dreaded month of August arrives. At the hight of the summer heat the harvest begins. Families gather children, grandparents and even relatives from far off cities such as Athens and workers from Poland. In ten to twenty days the grapes are cut and sent to market or laid out to dry as raisins.

Making raisins is a long process which includes dipping each grape into a potassium carbonate bath that punctures the thin waxy skin so that the juice is allowed to escape. Undipped grapes just rot in the sun. Grapes are then laid out to dry on racks several rows high or metal structures set in long lines. They dry in the wind or else they are purely sun dried on paper laid on the ground with a linen tent waiting at the end of each row for the dreaded summer rainstorms. No time is lost in gathering the grapes for even a September downpour can rot all the grapes in the vineyard and send the drying raisins down the ditches. The tourist boom in Crete is competing hard against grape production as a livelihood for the Cretans.

Olives

No one knows exactly where olives came from but it is assumed that they originated somewhere in the eastern Mediterranean. They have been cultivated in Greece for several millenia already; on Crete alone the number of olive trees has been estimated at a million. The olive tree was holy to the goddess Athena and the winners at the Olympic games were crowned with an olive branch. For Jews and Christians it was a symbol of peace. The Phoenecians traded olive oil and contributed to spreading the tree.

For Cretans the olive treee and its produce are an indispensable part of life. Virtually every family owns at least one or even several olive groves.

The oil from the fruit is used mainly in cooking. In earlier times it also fed oil lamps. Oil that has already been used is cleaned and worked into soap. Olives are also cleaned and either pickled or salted and form one of the basic foods of Cretans. Once all that appeared on the table or was carried to the fields was "bread, olives and wine." Olive wood is particularly hard and provides good firewood in winter.

Olive trees can grow for up to a thousand years and are 10 – 16 m high. Their almost grotesque, gnarled shape never

ceases to amaze. The olives ripen between December and February. During this period the olive harvest leaves villages deserted but the groves are alive with pickers. All you need is a few dozen olive trees to be busy for several months from dawn to dusk. Most of the olives serve to make oil. To reap the fruit a fine-mesh net is placed around the tree and the branches are struck with long poles. The work is arduous, especially if the trees stand on a slope and the heavy sacks have to be carried away by a donkey. Some of the less accessible trees are not even harvested for precisely that reason.

In past decades heavy machinery allowed terraces to be cut into the slopes. A new Italian hybrid has been cultivated, a smaller tree that yields after five years and is easier to harvest. To speed up the harvest on older trees someone came up with an ingenious idea: blowing the olives off the branches using compressed air.

The best olive oil comes from the first light pressing (virgin). Further pressing produces a lower quality edible oil. The "lees" and the seeds yield a low quality oil that can be used in making soap.

Young foreigners who spend their winters on Crete frequently form the rank and file of olive pickers. One either agrees on a percentage of the oil produced from the crop or on a daily rate equivalent to about 20 US dollars.

Those who have sampled fresh olives will know that their bitterness makes them impossible to eat. To make them edible they have to be placed in water for several weeks and the water has to be changed daily. To speed up the process the olives are either crushed or nicked with a sharp knife. Once the bitterness is gone they are pickled in brine. Edible olives are generally larger and produce little oil. The most famous are the Kalamata olives. In order to avoid any damage to the fruit they are hand-picked from the tree.

TOURISM IN CRETE

If you get disheartened by the charmless concrete complexes overrun by hordes of tourists on Crete's coast and you long for immersion in "authentic" Crete, head for the mountains.

Stop off at any of the numerous little hamlets tucked away on one of the mountain ranges. When you are approached by one of the smiling villagers, still wearing his traditional costume of high black boots, baggy vraches and black lacy mandilli wrapped around his head, he may remind you of Wordsworth's lines, "Thou wear'st upon thy forehead clear/The freedom of a mountaineer/A face with gladness overspread."

Traditional Cretan hospitality still abounds in these peaceful pockets cut off from time, almost as though the inhabitants are unaware that the interest in Crete sparked by Cacoyannis' film *Zorba*

Above: Hardy hikers carry their rucksacks.
Right: The less hardy go by car.

The Greek had mushroomed, bringing millions of foreigners to the island over the years.

The locals will probably try to treat you to a *tsikoudhia*, a powerful spirit, or a comforting cup of aromatic "tea of the mountain", usually sage or dittany. You may be invited to dinner, a spare room offered if there are no hotels or pensions and usually a proud ex-resident of the US will give you a guided tour of the town. Nothing is expected of you other than to enjoy yourself and to share some of your life and impressions of Crete.

Most visitors to Crete list the sun, sea and traditional hospitality as the qualities that impressed them. Spiros Kokotas, architect and owner of the Elounda Mare Hotel, rues the fact that traditional hospitality has been eroded in many areas of Crete. "When you ordered an ouzo in Crete, you were always brought a small plate of mezedes (appetizers). Now it is rare to find this." Kokotas also complains about the quality of service. "A few years back, you were greeted by a smile and a friendly hello. Now you can expect in-difference or a frown."

Crete has one of the busiest tourist trades, with over 1 million visitors in 1988 and 1989. It is one of the most popular destinations for tourists from the northern climates of Germany, Austria, England, Holland, Belgium and Sweden. The numbers of English visitors has dwindled in the last years due to restrictions on "seat-only" airline tickets.

Based on figures for 1988, revenue from tourism in Greece reached US$ 3.842 billion, making it the nation's third largest industry. Yet per person expenditure for tourists in Greece was US$ 270, among the lowest in the Mediterranean basin. France tops Greece with US$ 350, the Greek National Tourist Organization (GNTO) goal for 1989.

The GNTO is also trying to lure the Americans – typically the biggest spenders – back to Greece. It has launched an extensive three-year campaign designed to attract upmarket American tourists by emphasizing Greece's sunny climate, history and reasonable prices.

Evangelos Smaryanakis, member of the Cretan office of GNTO, commented, "The fact is that the average tourist to Crete is much younger now and therefore in a lower income bracket, so unable to spend much money."

Hoteliers are awakening to the fact that one reason for the decline in quality tourists is the level of their facilities. Of the 259 hotels built during 1984-88, only one was in the luxury class, eleven were in class A and thirty-four in class B. The majority were smaller, more cheaply built structures in the C, D, and E categories. Many tourist industry leaders feel the market needs more quality hotels such as Elounda Mare in Elounda or the Cretan Village in Hersonissos. Quality must be emphasized instead of quantity.

Besides upgrading roads and airports, other projects that should attract up-market visitors to Crete are the construc-

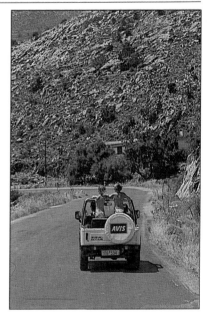

tion of five new marinas equipped for luxury yachts, and a posh new casino.

The developers in Crete followed GNTO's lead in restoring traditional houses, now rented to guests, in various places such as Mani, Santorini and Pelion. Several projects are underway or completed in Hania, Anoghia and Maoules. Some funding is from the EC, from private interests such as the Agricultural Bank, or the prefectures themselves.

The percentage of the population participating directly or indirectly in the tourism industry has increasingly grown over the past ten years. To counteract some of the negative aspects of this invasion, there is some need to guard against too great an economic boom and the development of the island in other ways should not be neglected.

Crete has over 1000 km of coast and a climate mild enough to make swimming possible all year round. A new ski resort is being built in line with GNTO's promotion of Greece as a vacation destination for any season.

ZORBA'S DANCE

"Another time when my child died, I got up and danced. The others said "Zorba's gone mad." But I knew that if I didn't dance at that moment, I would go mad."
From *Zorba The Greek*

Dancing is not considered effeminate in Crete. In fact, as Zorba demonstrated, being a good dancer is a prerequisite for being a "real man". Many Cretan dances are lively and complex, with the leader performing athletic leaps and turns.

Known since Mycenaean times, the main instrument of Cretan music is the lyra, usually carved from mulberry wood or occasionally walnut, with three metal strings. A lyra is placed on the musician's thigh and played with a bow that sometimes has *yerakokoudouna* (hawk bells) attached, instead of resting on the player's shoulder like a violin. The

Above: The lyre, Crete's folk instrument.
Right: The flutist from Phaestos.

232

strings are stopped by the edge of the fingernails rather than the finger pads.

The lyra produces a haunting primitive sound that is usually accompanied by one or two *laoutas* (lutes) which are larger and deeper in pitch. The violin used to predominate in eastern Crete but the lyra's popularity spread from Rethimnon and largely replaced it. Ironically, it is difficult to find lyra music in Rethimnon today. The *askomandoura* (goatskin bagpipe), guitar, *bouzouki* and *diouli* (small hand drum), can also accompany the lyra nowadays.

The most popular Greek film coproduction is Michalis Cacoyannis' adaptation of Nikos Kazantzakis' *Zorba the Greek* (1965), starring Anthony Quinn as a quixotic drifter who pairs up with a proper Englishman (Alan Bates), in an attempt to reopen a mine in Crete.

The movie was responsible for the influx of thousands of tourists attracted by the stunning scenery and the popularity of the "Zorba Dance". The dance however, is not Cretan but a simplified version of the fast *hasapiko*, which has its origins as a dance performed by the Butchers' Guild in Constantinople from the time of the Byzantine Empire.

Crete's three great mountain ranges divide the island into three parts and each one has developed a dance which is now pan-Cretan. From Hania comes the stately line dance syrto, from Iraklion and Sitia, the leaping pedekto, and from Rethimnon, the jig-like pentozale and the sousta, the springy couple dance.

Many of Crete's finest lyra players perform in and around Iraklion in the summer and spend the winter playing in *kentra* (night spots) in Athens. The town of Anoghia, 35 km southwest of Iraklion, is the home of some of the greatest lyra players including the famed Xylouris family. Anoghia has tavernas which offer typical Cretan music and cuisine and it holds a festival with a lyra competition during the summer.

The lyra players Antonis Peristeris and his son Manolis play in the summer at Adelphi Tziblo Stephanki in their home town of Gergeri, nestling in the mountains south of Iraklion, and at their own popular club To Kastro in Hymettos in Athens during the cooler months. Other notable lyra players such as Yiannis Sopasis, Tassoula Mamalakis and Yiorgos Papadakis play in the Athens area.

One fine musician in self-imposed exile is an Irishman, Ross Daley, a longtime resident of Hania. Daley plays a variety of instruments including the lyra, now mainly in concerts in Athens or in festival on the islands because he refuses to "plug in" and become amplified. The electrification of instruments is so popular that it is virtually impossible to hear accoustic-style music in the clubs.

To experience truly authentic Cretan traditions in music and dance, try to catch the festivities during the holidays, especially Easter, and at village weddings, baptisms and name days. Another Cretan tradition is the singing of *mandinades*,

rhymed couplets mostly about love, with similies drawn from the Cretan countryside. One can still hear mandinades, originally serenades under the window of a loved one in the early morning, at local celebrations.

Most mandinades sung today come from the vast repertoire of oral tradition, some with words in Cretan dialect that date back to Homeric times, and are often accompanied by dancers doing the Cretan version of the *sta tria,* the dignified *siganos.*

The epic romantic poem *Erotokritos*, laced with nationalistic overtones, was written by Vincent Cornaro around 1645. It has over 10,000 lines, providing inexhaustible sources for mandinades.

Unluckily, improvizational mandinades, the most exciting form, are rarely heard these days. Composed on the spot by high-spirited minstrels, usually fueled by lots of wine or raki, participants match wits as they fire off responses to one another's witty, and sometimes naughty rhymed verses.

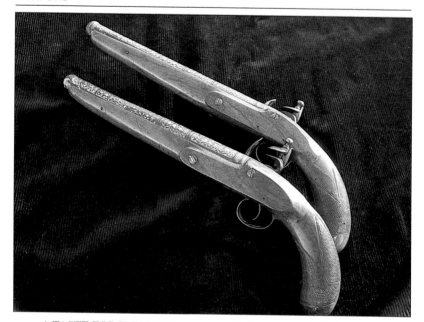

A TASTE FOR WEAPONS

"There are people who call God by prayer and tears, others by patience and resignation and others by – blaspheming. Cretans call Him with gun shots."

From *Captain Mihalis*

The Cretans are warriors and have felt to be for centuries. Maybe it is not obvious in Iraklion, Rethimnon or Hania, where the Western costume, especially among the young, tends more and more to replace the traditional clothes of the Cretan men.

But as soon as you go deep in the countryside, to small villages such as Sphakia or Agios Miron, many Cretans still wear the traditional garments: riding breeches, high Cretan boots, called *stivania*, the cummerbund, the waistcoat and the little black turban with a fringe of small black beads.

Above: These traditional hand guns are more than just a souvenir for Cretans.

Such a costume is fit for war or, these days, the hunting of *kri-kri*, the wild goat that climb up and down the Cretan mountains. The head scarf and the shirt are black, as a sign of mourning, and the large belt holds a knife.

A Silver Knife

Because they feel to be warriors the Cretans have a taste for weapons. Treated with care and love, they are passed on from one generation to another, from grandfather to father and to grandson, in the same way as the name or the dowry of girls.

After the German occupation, the Cretans were supposed to give back any gun they possessed. But most of them did not. Today there is a good gun in many Cretan houses. It is used for hunting, especially in the mountains, but it comes in handy in case of a fight against another man.

Maybe not everybody has a gun in Crete, but every man at least has a knife.

The knife is still today a prominent object in the shop windows of Rethimnon or Hania beside the steel water bottles on leather straps, the binoculars, the boots and the shotguns, everything needed to live in the mountainside.

With its handle in the shape of a goat's leg and its folding blade, the Cretan knife is an inseparable part of the manly Cretan costume. Slipped in the waist band, the handle to the right, the sheath to the left, it was a symbol of youth and virility, and useful too.

"He wore at the waist a silver knife
A knife such as that one
Nowhere will be found..." ,
　　　　　　　　says a popular song.

Such hand-made knives can be found at Bonatte Stylianos, King George VIII Street, Hania.

From Minoan times to the present day, at work, during festivals, or in the struggle for freedom, the Cretan knife was part of life. By engraving the sheath, craftsmen tried to make it a work of art. One of the best artists was Gregoris Karydakis, who died in 1958.

Pallikare et Philotimo

From the great Cretan insurrection against the Turks (1866-69) comes the tradition of *captains* and *pallikares*. The "captain" was the best fighting man, chosen by common consent by the other men in the village to guide them in combat. The *pallikare* is a hero, ready at any time to defy death in the struggle for the freedom of the island.

A lot of words in the Cretan language express the glory of the fight, explains Jacques Lacarriere, a French author and Greek specialist. *Pallikare* means beauty and courage, physical as well as moral. *Philotimo*, on the other hand, means the unrestricted fidelity of a man to his family and to his people.

Two episodes of Cretan history can testify to this. The first is the attack on the monastery of Arkadi, which the Cretan guerillas used as a stronghold against the Turkish occupation. It took two days for the Turkish army to enter the monastery, and then the besieged set fire to the powder magazine, blowing up themselves and the enemy. Another is the strange Battle of Crete, the first full-scale paratroop invasion in the history of mankind. On May 20, 1941, according to Hitler's directive 28, the seventh airborne division of German paratroopers invaded the airdrome of Maleme at precisely 7 a.m. Code-named "Mercury", it was to be the first and last of the airborne invasions by parachutists.

Max Schmeling, former world heavyweight boxing champion told Berlin Radio after landing as a paratrooper that, "The fighting was hard but if the enemy had any heavy arms we could not have beaten them".

The Vendetta

Today, Cretans are considered as the best soldiers in Greece and often chosen to be included in the élitist divisions of the Greek army.

But a more controversial aspect of this tradition of fighting, freedom and proudness is the practice of the *vendetta*, still alive today. The Cretans often do not trust social justice and want personal revenge for any crime or wrong done to a member of their family.

It is possible today to see in remote parts of the island, on the door or the walls of a house where somebody has been killed, crosses drawn with the victim's blood. Some families treasure a shirt that is stained with the blood of the dead person, and this is handed from father to son until the crime is revenged. Sometimes years go by and it seems that the vendetta is over, before the opposite side hits back.

HUMAN SACRIFICE

During the summer of 1979 two excavations with sight of each other produced the first archaeological evidence to suggest that there was a dark side to the otherwise peaceful Minoans. These were the Greek excavations directed by Yannis and Efi Sakellarakis at Anemospilia near Arkhanes and the British excavations directed by Peter Warren in the town of Knossos.

The recent excavations at Anemospilia cleared what remained of a small building placed on the northern slopes of Mount Iouhtas. The building had been destroyed by an earthquake at the end of the Old Palace period, about 1700 BC, trapping four occupants apparently engaged in a sacrificial ritual, not of a bull or goat, but a young man. The grisly

Above: Dr. Sakellarakis in Anemospilia.
Right: Is research casting a new light on Minoan cannibalism?

scene was uncovered in the westernmost of three rooms connected by a long corridor leading from the building's entrance in the east. The collapsed masonry lay over the skeletons of the three people: a woman in her late twenties, a man in his late thirties – already beyond the average life expectancy of a prehistoric Cretan –, and a young man of about eighteen. The young man had been bound and lay on a raised stone platform or altar. The excavators suggest that he had just been killed by the old man who slit his throat with a bronze hunting knife left on the spot when the building was destroyed. The woman may have been a priestess, and a fourth skeleton, found in the corridor near a fine vase decorated with a bull, may have been a temple attendant in the process of taking the victim's blood to offer it to the god. He never made it. The full force of the quake brought down the small remote temple trapping its occupants in a scene that caused much disquiet among archaeologists brought up in the tradition of peace-loving Minoans.

At Knossos, excavations behind the Stratigraphical Museum, about 1 km to the west of the palace, revealed a building destroyed by fire at the end of the New Palace period, about 1500 BC. The presence of ritual libation vases alerted the team to the possibility that they were entering some sort of shrine, but did not prepare them for the macabre deposits that lay beneath the thick layer of burnt building debris.

In the west room of the building they found the semi-articulated, unburned bones of at least two children, eight and eleven years of age, who seem to have been in good health at the time of death. The bones bore traces of cut marks showing that the children had been butchered in much the same way the Minoans butchered animals. Fine cuts, most likely made with obsidian blades, on the arms, legs and collar bones show that the flesh was deliberately stripped from the bones: the only explanation being that it was meant to be eaten. The skulls had been prised off the necks and the jaws forced open, perhaps to extract their tongues. One of the skulls had been cut open with a circular incision apparently to dig out the brain, again for what other reason than to eat it?

Both excavations have forced archaeologists to take a fresh look at Minoan religious practices and to consider more seriously the primitive aspects of Greek mythology. We know from Minoan iconography that bulls were sacrificed and it is possible that in extreme circumstances a human may have been offered to the gods. It may also have been part of a rite like the later Dionysiac rituals that we suspect had their origins in the cult of Cretan Zeus. Mythology recalls that the young Zeus was captured by the Titans, who lured him away from the Kouretes with toys, and then torn to pieces and devoured. Scholars have long suspected a Cretan origin for the oldest of the Greek myths. The evidence from Anemospilia and Knossos goes a long way to supporting their theories, unsavory as it may seem.

MINOAN ART

The art of the Cretan Bronze Age must be viewed in the wider context of the contemporary eastern Mediterranean. The techniques and even many of the materials of the Minoan craftsman were borrowed and imported from Egypt, the Near East and Mesopotamia, but the result is always distinctively Minoan.

As Early Minoan settlements evolved from family dwellings to villages, and crafts such as metallurgy, stone carving, pottery making and wall-painting came to require technical skills and knowledge beyond the ability of the average agrarian society found a need for specialized craftsmen. These individuals devoted their time to making products for everyday village consumption, but at the same time were responsible for keeping up with the technical advances being made in their craft in the East. When the Old Palaces at Knossos, Phaestos and Malia were established, shortly after 1900 BC, the finest of the craftsmen were called in to work on the first great public monuments in Crete, and the first true Minoan art appeared.

The most important fact the modern viewer must bear in mind is that Minoan art was created for religious purposes; there are no scenes of everyday life. Even the wonderful wall-paintings, with delicate lifelike renderings of flowers and birds, were probably executed to give the viewer a feeling of the season during which a particular festival or rite took place. No works are signed or attributed to an individual artist. The only artist's name that survives in later Greek mythology is that of Daedalus, the architect for the palace at Knossos.

The most distinctive products of the Old Palaces are the fine polychrome ceramics called Kamaresware after the Kamares Cave where they were first found toward the end of the last century. With the introduction of the potter's wheel

around 1900 BC and the establishment of permanent pottery kilns that could reach temperatures of over 1000 degrees Celsius, the vase-makers in Crete where able to take the high quality neogene clays that abound on the lower slopes of Mount Iouhtas, south of Knossos, and create the finest ceramics in the prehistoric Mediterranean. Using designs adapted from nature and white, red, yellow, orange and violet pigments applied on a dark ground, they created master- pieces of uniform design based on the spiral, loop and flower petal, occasionally adding fish and animal motifs and, very rarely, humans. The liveliness and beauty of Kamaresware appealed to the Minoans' contemporaries and examples of the ware are found throughout the Greek islands, the Levant and Egypt where they were no doubt treasured. But Kamaresware makes up only a small percentage of the mass of domestic and utilitarian ceramics of the period, which, along with its fragility, has led specialists to suggest that it was produced for ceremonial purposes.

The finest art of the Aegean Bronze Age was produced during the period of the New Palaces, 1700 to 1500 BC, and is best represented by the wall-paintings that adorned the palace and surrounding houses at Knossos. Not true frescoes, the wall-paintings were applied to a thin layer of very fine white lime plaster. The scenes were organized in advance with indications of undulating landscapes usually painted as seen from above. The main figures and natural elements were then placed within the landscape or an architectural setting. Specialists regard the Knossos frescoes as being part of pictorial programmes in the palaces, perhaps commemorating ceremonies dealing with spring festivals, sacred marriage and initiation rites that took place at different times of the year.

Right: A Minoan pitcher from the Kamares era.

Nelles Maps ...the maps, that get you going.

Nelles Map Series:

- Afghanistan
- Australia
- Burma
- Caribbean Islands 1 / Bermuda, Bahamas, Greater Antilles
- Caribbean Islands 2 / Lesser Antilles
- China 1 / North-Eastern China
- China 2 / Northern China
- Crete
- Hawaiian Islands
- Hawaiian Islands 1 / Kauai
- Hawaiian Islands 2 / Honolulu, Oahu
- Hawaiian Islands 3 / Maui, Molokai, Lanai

- Hawaiian Islands 4 / Hawaii
- Himalaya
- Hong Kong
- Indian Subcontinent
- India 1 / Northern India
- India 2 / Western India
- India 3 / Eastern India
- India 4 / Southern India
- India 5 / North-Eastern India
- Indonesia
- Indonesia 1 / Sumatra
- Indonesia 2 / Java + Nusa Tenggara
- Indonesia 3 / Bali
- Indonesia 4 / Kalimantan
- Indonesia 5 / Java + Bali
- Indonesia 6 / Sulawesi
- Indonesia 7 / Irian Jaya + Maluku

- Jakarta
- Japan
- Kenya
- Korea
- Malaysia
- West Malaysia
- Nepal
- New Zealand
- Pakistan
- Philippines
- Singapore
- South East Asia
- Sri Lanka
- Taiwan
- Thailand
- Vietnam, Laos Kampuchea

CRETE
©Nelles Verlag GmbH, München 45
 All rights reserved
 ISBN 3-88618-371-8

First Edition 1990
Co-publisher for U.K.:
Robertson McCarta, London
ISBN 1-85365-240 -7 (for U.K.)

Publisher:	Günter Nelles	**DTP-Exposure:**	Schimann,
Chief Editor:	Dr. Heinz Vestner		Pfaffenhofen
Project Editor:	Michele Macrakis	**Color**	
Cartography:	Nelles Verlag GmbH,	**Separation:**	Priegnitz, München
	Dipl.Ing. C. Heydeck	**Printed by:**	Gorenjski Tisk, Kranj,
	Dipl.Ing. T. Winter		Yugoslavia

- 01 -

240

TABLE OF CONTENTS

PREPARATION

This section provides general information for the traveler to Crete. For more detailed and up to the date information the traveler should contact the Greek National Tourist Organization in Athens and in Crete (G.N.T.O.), known as E.O.T. in Greece.

Climate

The climate in Crete conforms to the traditional Mediterranean image of sunny and warm weather between mid-April and mid- October. Late spring and fall are the best times to visit – wild flowers in the spring, mellow evenings in the fall. Avoid, if you can, July and August – it is hot and crowded. Winters in Crete can be humid and cold, though, with a temperature ranging from zero to 40 degrees F in the mountains and 30 to 60 degrees F inland. During the summer months temperatures can reach 80 to 100 degrees F, although cool winds often save the day.

Clothing

If you visit Crete in the summer months bring very light clothing, avoiding synthetics and favoring cotton. Sandals are ideal but bring also a pair of hiking shoes – especially if you plan to walk through the Gorge of Samaria. A hat will protect you from the midday sun and a sweater will help you for the night breezes. Shorts are allowed everywhere except visiting churches and monasteries. In fancier restaurants and hotels you will need a somewhat dressier dress and jacket. Take a couple of bathing suits. Nude bathing is allowed only in certain secluded beaches. Topless bathing is allowed in hotel (private) beaches and some public beaches.

Entry Regulations

You need a valid passport only if you are a citizen of Western Europe, the United States, Canada, Australia and New Zealand. No visa is necessary. However, if you want to stay longer than three months you must obtain a permit from the Bureau of Aliens in Athens (9 Halkokondili St.). Citizens of other countries should consult a Greek Embassy or consulate regarding the need for a visa before leaving their country.

Customs

When going through customs, if you don't have anything to declare, take the "no declaration" exit. You are allowed to bring into the country duty-free: your personal belonging, 200 cigarettes (Greeks are heavy smokers), foodstuff and beverages up to 10 kilos, camera and film, portable radios and tape recorders, sports gear, etc. Do not bring: electronic devices, narcotics, medicine – except by prescription –, explosives, weapons, and do not export antiques, plants, furs (unless declared on entrance). For more details contact an embassy, consulate or the Tourist Organization.

Currency and Exchange

You can bring into Crete an unlimited amount of foreign currency and traveler's checks but you can take out only $500 unless you have declared it upon entry into Crete. You can import or export only 3.000 Greek drachmas.

There is an official rate of exchange fixed by the Bank of Greece daily. All banks and most hotels can buy foreign currency. Greek acquaintances are always eager to change drachmas for dollars.

Health Care

Crete is an island with a "fetish" for pharmacies. You can find one on every corner of the big cities. Consult your local newspaper, though, for the 24-hour pharmacies. In case of a medical emergency, call the local tourist police. These are the local numbers:

Agios Nikolaos (E. Crete) 28-156
Hania (W. Crete) 24-477
Iraklion (capital) 283-190

Rethimnon (center) 28-156

Crete does not have any serious diseases, so you do not need any health immunizations to enter the island.

The drinking water is safe but many tourists prefer to buy bottled water.

TRAVELING TO CRETE

By car: If you plan to stay for a longer period on Crete then it is worth coming by car. There are two main roads from central Europe. The first leads from Munich over Belgrade and Saloniki to Athens (ca. 2200 km). Traffic in the summer months is particularly heavy, nevertheless ever since completion of new segments of the highway in Yugoslavia the so-called "foreign worker route" has lost much of its daunting quality.

The second – and more pleasant – possibility is to travel through Italy. Ships leave from Ancona on the Adriatic to Patras (2 days). One can also make the crossing (ca. 20 hours) from Brindisi or Bari, but one should keep in mind that gasoline and highway tolls are both rather high in Italy. A highway leads from Patras to Athens. Ferries to Iraklion or Hania leave from Piraeus.

By air: By charter flights from all major cities in Europe to Iraklion and Hania. Via OLYMPIC AIRWAYS (the national airline of Greece) 4-5 daily flights from Athens to Iraklion and from Athens to Hania. Approximate flying time: 1/2 hour. For summer travel, early reservations recommended.

By ship: From Piraeus, the port of Athens, daily to Iraklion and Hania and vice versa (12 hours, each way). A new line just opened from Piraeus to Rethimnon too. (Tel.: Piraeus: 01/417.2657; Iraklion: 081/226 073; Hania: 1821/ 89.240). You can also choose the longer route, through the Cyclades – Naxos, Paros, Ios, Santorini – etc.

On Arrival

Detailed information about your stay in Greece and your tours through the country is available at:

1. The inland agencies of the G.Z.F.: **Hania** (Crete): a) Pantheon building, Kriari St. 40, Tel.: (0821) 26.426; b) Akti Tombasi 6, Tel.: 43.300. **Iraklion** (Crete): Xanthoudidou St. 1, Tel.: (081) 228.203/225.

2. The information offices of the towns and communities: **Agios Nikolaos** (Crete): Akti I. Koundourou 20, Tel.: (0841) 22.357. **Ierapetra** (Crete): City hall, Tel.: (0842) 28.658. **Rethimno** (Crete): El. Venizelou Allee, Tel.: (0831) 29.148. **Sitia** (Crete): Iroon Politechniou Square, Tel.: (0843) 24.955

TRAVELING IN CRETE

By bus: Regularly scheduled buses serve an extensive network of good roads city-wide, from the capital of each district to the other district capitals, and between the towns and villages in each district.

By rented car: Rent-a-car offices can be found in most towns. The principal companies have branches at the airports.

Speed limits: 100 km per hour on the national network, 70 km per hour on provincial roads, and 50 km per hour in residential areas.

By organized tour: Travel agencies operate organized tours to the sights of the island of 1 or 2 day duration, for example from:

Iraklion to: Knossos, Gortyna, Phaestos, Agia Triada, Matala, Fodhele, Tylissos, Malia.

Hania to: Akrotiri, Agia Triada Monastery, Gonia Monastery, Kastelli, Samaria Gorge, Agia Roumeli, Sphakia, Palaeohora.

Rethimnon to: Arkadi Monastery and Anoghia.

Agios Nikolaos to: Gournia, Lassithi Plain, Kritsa, Sitia, Vai, Zakros.

By yacht: Ports of entry are at Iraklion,

Tel.: 081/226.073 and Hania, Tel.: 0821/ 28 888 These ports have harbor, customs and health officials as well as a passport and foreign exchange control service. Fuel, water and provisions can be obtained here and transit logs must be stamped upon entry and departure. There is a yacht repair and maintenance workshop at Iraklion.

Hitchhiking

On the main stretches one is better off using public transportation instead of hitchhiking. On the byroads one can always give it a try. Locals are aware of the unreliability of the public system and often give hikers a ride. This sometimes means a bumpy ride on the back of a pick-up truck in the company of a dog or a goat. For the sake of politeness one should offer the driver a small obolus which he will either refuse in no uncertain terms or use to invite you to coffee or ouzo.

PRACTICAL TIPS

Accomodation

One can find all kinds of accommodation in Crete from luxury hotels to pensions and rooms. The GNTO has published a list of hotels but for more information inquire at the local police stations. For reservations, write: XENEPEL, 24 Stadiou Street, 10561 Athens, Greece, Telex 214269 XEPE GR, or call: 01/323/7193.

The best known hotels in the big cities are:

The XENIA hotels in Hania (B class) and Iraklion (A class); the DOMA in Hania (B class), a converted neo-classic house with strong Cretan character; the ATLANTIS in Iraklion (lux), and other luxury hotels in Elounda and Agios Nikolaos. For all hotels you need prior booking especially during the tourist season (June/September).

Banks

Banks are open daily except on weekends and official holidays. Monday through Thursday from 8:00 a.m. to 2:00 p.m., Fridays from 8:00 a.m. to 1:30 p.m. Cashing eurochecks is also possible on Saturdays in post offices. Many of the travel agencies also change money at the official rate. The fastest way of transfering money to Crete from abroad is to have it telegraphed to a Cretan bank.

Business Hours

Business and shop hours are very complicated in Crete and vary according to the day of the week and the type of business. In general, though, schedules are more flexible in small towns and villages and more set in the big cities. Generally, businesses are open at 8 a.m. and close on Monday, Wednesday and Saturday at 2:30 p.m. while on Tuesday, Thursday and Friday they close at 1:30 p.m. and reopen from 5 p.m. to 8:30 p.m. All banks are open to the public from 8 a.m. to 2 p.m. Monday through Friday. To avoid disappointment and frustration, inquire beforehand.

Credit Cards

The better hotels, restaurants and shops accept major credit cards; smaller establishments don't, though. Inquire before making purchases.

Eating and Drinking

Eating out in Crete is popular and affordable whether you use a formal restaurant or the more popular tavernas. The best way to choose your meal is by walking into the kitchen and pointing out your choice. You can eat your main meal at midday – between 1:30 and 2:30 p.m. or in the evening between 9:00 p.m. and 11:00 p.m.

Start always with snacks – *mezedes* – an aperitif like *ouzo* – anice flavored – and follow it up with the main dish and fresh fruit. The *meze* = snack in Crete may be *hohlí* = snails fired in oil, *yíyantes* = large beans, *koukiá* = horse beans or fava beans, *melitsanosalata* = eggplant dip, *tzatzíki* = garlicked yogurt/cucumber dip, *dolmadákia* = stuffed grape leaves, *kalamarákia* = fried squid.

For a main meal, besides the Greek specialties of *moussaka* = eggplant and ground lamb with white sauce, and *pastitsio* = maccaroni casserole, Cretans are good in preparing *yemista* = stuffed tomatoes and peppers, *stifado* = stewed meat, *yiouvarlákia* = meat-and-rice balls, *oktapód*i = fried octopus and, if you are lucky and want to go native, *patsá* = tripe stew, offered early in the morning in certain restaurants, instead of breakfast!

As dessert, don't forget to taste the famous *bougatsa*, a sweet or cheesy custard pie, done to perfection at Kir Kor, the Armenian cafe at the Morosini Square of Iraklion, and *skaltsounia* (sweet tarts). If you are in Hania, on the other hand, try their sea urchin salad = *ahinosalata* and their *staka* = a butter dip, a gift from the Gods, offered on top of the Malaxa mountains overlooking Souda Bay.

Crete is known worldwide for its good wines, especially red ones and its throat-scorching *tsikoudia*, a spirit distilled from the lees.

For all the above, try Balahoutis taverna (C category) on the road to Knossos, Iraklion and Birais on the main beach of Rethimnon.

Electricity

A 220 volts AC, 50 cycle system operates. This means that appliances from the United States require converters. You also need an adapter since Greek outlets and plugs are different from American and some European types.

Feasts and Holidays

Official public holidays are: January 1, January 6, March 25, Good Friday, Easter, May 1, Whitsun, August 15, October 28 and Christmas.

The festival calendar

Sylvester/New Year: Greeks spend the turn of the new year playing cards and other games of chance. Shortly before midnight all doors and windows are opened in order to sweep out the old year and let in the new. Afterwards a new year's cake is served into which a coin has been baked. The person who finds the coin is supposed to have good luck in the new year.

January 6: The day of Christ's baptism. After blessing the water the priest throws the cross into the sea. Whoever retrieves it from the waters is acclaimed by the congregation.

Carnival: A week before Ash Wednesday. Some masquerading in Hania, Rethimnon, Iraklion and Ierapetra. On the final day of Carnival offices and stores stay closed. The forty-day fasting period then begins during which time particularly in villages no one eats meat, fish or milk products.

March 25: Festivities with military parades in the cities to commemorate the beginning of the uprising against the Turks in 1821.

Good Friday: Church services.

Easter Saturday: Midnight services after which the priest gives the new light in the form of a candle flame to the congregation which uses it to light its own candles and then passes it on. The standard greeting is "Christos anesti!" (Christ is risen). On town squares large piles of brush are set alight and Judas is burned *in effigio*.

Easter Sunday: The most important holiday in the Orthodox creed. After the church service the Easter lamb is served (often it is the baker who roasts it in a wood-fired oven). Easter in Greece is usually celebrated later.

First Sunday after Easter: Agios Thomas; celebrations in those cities where the churches are consecrated to that saint and in eponymous villages.

April 23: Agios Georgios; festivities in

the villages by that name.

May 1: Mainly a day for excursions. May garlands are hung on doors and on the hoods of cars.

May 8: Celebrations for Saint Ioannis in the Preveli monastery.

May 20-27: Commemoration of the Cretan resistance in Hania during World War II.

May 21: Agios Konstantinos in Pirgos.

Ascension of Christ (Analipsi): Church services, e.g. in the church of Almiros by Agios Nikolaos.

Whitsun: Religious celebrations: they usually take place a little later in accordance with the Greek church calendar.

June 24: Feast day of John the Baptist and midsummer festivities in the villages during which brave young men jump through bonfires.

June 29: Petros and Pavlos. Celebrations in churches and villages to honor these two saints.

July 17: Agia Marina in Voni.

Second half of July: Wine festival in the city park of Rethimnon.

July 26: Agios Paraskevi; people's festival near the Skotino caves in the district of Pedhiadas.

July 27: Agios Pantelimonas: festivities in Fournes near Hania, Kounavi (Iraklion), Pigi (Pedhiadas).

August 6: Metamorfosis tou Sotiros (transfiguration of Christ). Processions on the Iouhtas near Arkhanes, festivities in Skines (Hania), Armeni, Anoghia, Arkalohori.

August 8: Agios Miron in the village of Agios Miron.

August 15: The Ascension of Mary is celebrated all over in particular however in the monastery of Moni Chrysoskalitissa, Gonia near Kolimvari, Alikambos, Apokoronou (Hania), Faneromeni near Gournia. Festivities also in Neapoli, Mochos (Iraklion).

August 25: Agios Titos. Patron saint of Crete and Iraklion. Procession in Iraklion.

August 29: Decapitation of John the Baptist. Pilgrimage to the Rodopou peninsula from August 27 onward, celebrations in Platanias/Kalyves (Hania) and Moni Kapsas (southern shore).

August 31: Festivities in the Lassithi plain.

September 14: Pilgrimages to the chapels on the Psiloritis peaks, the Afendis Stavromenos and on the Kofinas. Festivities in Iraklion and Alikianos (Hania).

September 15: Pilgrimage to the cave church west of the Koudoumas monastery in the Asteroussia mountains.

October 7: John the Hermit. Festivities and processions at the Gouverneto monastery (Akrotiri).

October 28: "Day of the No", to commemorate the day the Greek government refused to submit to Italian fascism.

November 7-9: National holiday on Crete; commemoration of the resistance in the Arkadi monastery, festivities in Rethimnon and Arkadi.

November 11: Agios Minas with processions in Iraklion to the cathedral by the same name.

December 4: Agia Varvara (Saint Barbara). Celebration in Agia Varvara (Iraklion).

December 5: Festivities in the monastery of Savathianon (Iraklion).

December 6: Agios Nikolaos. Celebration in Agios Nikolaos and villages and churches with the same name.

Christmas: The most important celebration in the Orthodox Church after Easter, it is however not profusely celebrated in Greece.

Hiking and Mountain Climbing

The Greek Mountaineering Association operates refuges in the White Mountains (at Kallergi and Volika) and on Psiloritis (Prino and Asites). Tel: Hania (0821) 24647 and Iraklion (081) 267110 – from 16 to 40 persons. Crete is a paradise for hikers and, especially, for mountain climbers, with extensive trails, and mountains untouched by tourists.

Newspapers and Magazines

During the tourist season from May to September newspapers and magazines in German, English, French and Italian are sold in almost all tourist resorts. During the rest of the year foreign publications can be found in Hania, Iraklion, Rethimnon and Agios Nikolaos. Furthermore book stores, souvenir shops and the larger hotels usually carry publications on Crete in English, German and French.

Photographing

It is advisable to bring sufficient film material with you for your stay on Crete, as it is generally much more expensive on the island. Photographing in museums and archeological sites is free of charge as long as you do not use a flash and a tripod. When photographing people it is wise to ask their permission first. It is prohibited to photograph military bases and other installations. Signs indicating this are frequent in the bay of Soudia and on the Akrotiri peninsula. Disobeying these orders, including merely looking into your camera, can result in arrest and interrogation.

Postal Services

Although officially the post office is open Monday to Friday from 7:30 a.m. to 7:30 p.m., and on Saturday until 1:00 p.m., certain services, like registered letters or parcel post, close earlier. So, better do your business in the morning. Avoid sending packages home – too many restrictions involved (inspection before closing the package, your own material to wrap it, etc.). To send a telegram or to make a phone call, use the OTE, the state phone company. For local calls, you can also use the many kiosks on each corner, phone booths, hotels, restaurants. For long distance calls, you will need a metered phone. Inquire.

Shopping

Try to find old hand-woven fabrics and embroideries – rather rare today – woodcarvings, and jewelry (old Minoan replicas). Buy "vouryies", old stones. Shop in Iraklion mainly where there are some antique shops with old maps and rare books.

Sports / Recreation / Beaches

The extend of Crete's coastline make it possible for bathers to enjoy different places to swim, most of them with clean and warm water. The best beaches are:

On the north coast, west of Hania – from the town to Kolimvari. On the west coast of the Hania district, the sandy beach of Phalassarna and, further south, Elaphonissi. At Akrotiri-Stavros, near Souda Bay-Almirida, from Georgioupolis all the way to Rethimnon, the long sandy coast where Panormos, Bali, Agia Pelagia.

On the north coast, east, Agios Nikolaos, the beach at Sitia, and the eastern beaches of Vai, with the famous palm trees, and Kato Zakros where you can combine swimming with sight seeing.

On the south side, the beaches of Palaeohora, Loutro and Frangokastello in the district of Hania, and Preveli, and Agia Galini in the district of Rethimnon. The famous or infamous (discovered by the hippies of the 60s) Matala beach and Kali Limenes in the district of Iraklion, and Ierapetra and Agia Fotia in the district of Lassithi.

For water skiing use the bigger resort areas which have the equipment and instructors.

Tennis

Tennis anyone? Use the tennis clubs of Hania and Iraklion and the facilities of most big hotels.

Time Zone

Greek time is two hours ahead of Greenwich Mean Time. So, when it is 3 p.m. in Greece it is 1 p.m. in London, 8 a.m. in New York, and 5 a.m. in Sidney. The clock is advanced one hour in the summer to give more daylight hours.

Tips

Service charges are included in all bills of hotels and restaurants. Customarily, though, customers leave an additional 5% tip.

Youth Hostels

Greek youth hostels belong to the Greek union of youth hostels and even carry the international insignia, they are nevertheless in private hands. Possession of a youth hostel pass does not necessarily guarantee lodgings. Furnishings and cleanliness often leave much to be desired and do not reflect international standards. The price for a night is about 350 Drs.

Herakleion: 24 Handakos Str.; Rethimnon: 7 Pavlou-Vlastou Str.; Agios Nikolaos: 5 Stratigou-Koraka Str.; Sitia: 4 Therisou Str.; Hania: 33 Drakanianou Str.. Malia, Mirtos, Plakias and Mirthios also have youth hostels.

ADDRESSES
Offices of the GNTO Abroad

Australia and New Zealand: 51-57, Pitt Street, Sydney, N.S.W. 2000, Tel.: 241.1663/4, Telex: 25209.

Belgium: 173, Avenue Louise, 1050, Bruxelles, Tel.: 6475.770, 6475.944, Telex: 24.044.

Federal Republic of Germany: a) Neue Mainzerstr. 22, 6 Frankfurt/Main 1, Tel.: 236.562/3, Telex: 412.034; b) Pacellistr. 2, Promenade Platz, 8000 München 2, Tel.: 222.035/6, Telex: 528.126; c) Abteistr. 33, Hamburg 13, Tel.: 454.498.

France: 3, Avenue de l' Opéra, Paris 75001, Tel.: 4260.6575, Telex: 680.345.

Great Britain and Ireland: a) 195-197, Regent Str., London W1R 8DL, Tel.: 7345.997, Telex: 21.122; b) (Office for planning congresses in Greece) Coworth Park House Askot Berkshire SL 5 UK, Tel.: 990.872.440, Telex: 846.962.

Canada: a) 68, Scollard St., Toronto, Ontario, Lower Level Unit E M5R 1g2, Tel.: 9582.220, Telex: 218604; b) 1233, Rue de la Montagne, Montreal, Quebec H3G, 1Z2, Tel.: 8711.535, Telex: 60.021.

Holland: Leidsestraat 13, NS 1017, Amsterdam, Tel.: 254.212/3/4, Telex: 154.65.

Austria: Opernring 8, 1010 Wien, Tel.: 525.317/8, Telex: 211.816.

Switzerland: Löwen Strasse 25, CH 8001 Zürich, Tel.: 2210.105, Telex: 814.452.

USA: a) 645, Fifth Avenue, Olympic Tower, New York, N.Y. 10022, Tel.: 4215.777, Telex: 66.489; b) 611, West Sixth St. Suite 2198, Los Angeles, California 90017, Tel.: 6266.969, Telex: 686.441; c) 168, North Michigan Ave., National Bank of Greece Building, Chicago Illinois 60601, Tel.: 7921.084, Telex: 283.468.

Embassies & Consulates

United Kingdom - 1 Ploutarhou St, Athens, Tel: 7236211; Vice Consulate, Iraklion, 16 Papalexandrou, Tel: 081/224012. United States of America - 91 Vass. Sophias Ave, Athens, Tel: 7212951. Australia - 37 D. Soutsou St, Athens, Tel: 6447303. Canada - 4 I. Genadiou St, Athens, Tel:7239511. New Zealand - 15-17 Tsoha St, Athens, Tel: 6410311. France - 7 Vass. Sophias Ave, Athens, Tel: 7290151-6. Germany - 10 Vass. Sophias, Maroussi, Tel:36941; Consulate, Iraklion, 7 Grafou St, P.O.Box 1083, Tel: 081/226288. Austria - 26 Alexandras Ave, Athens, Tel: 8211036. Belgium - 3 Sekeri St, Athens, Tel: 3617886. Cyprus - 16 Irodotou St, Athens, Tel:7237883. Denmark - 15 Filikis Eterias Sq, Kolonaki, Tel: 7249315. Finland - 1 Eratosthonous St & Vass. Konstantinou Ave, Athens, Tel: 7515064. Hong Kong - 2

Vass. Alexandrou Ave, Athens, Tel: 7242666. Ireland - 7 Vass. Konstantinou Ave, Athens, Tel: 7232771. Israel - 1 Marathonodromon st, Paleo Psihiko, Tel:6719530. Italy - 2 Sekeri St, Athens, Tel: 3611722. Japan - 2-4 Messogion Ave, Athens, Tel: 7758101. Luxembourg - 11 Stissihorou St, Athens, Tel: 7217948. Malta - 2 Efplias St, Piraeus, Tel: 4181501. Netherlands - 5-7 Vass. Konstantinou Ave, Athens, Tel: 7239701. Norway - 7 Vass. Konstantinou Ave, Athens, Tel: 7246173. Sweden - 7 Vass. Konstantinou Ave, Athens, Tel: 7290421. Switzerland - 2 Iassiou St, Athens, Tel: 7230364-6.

Useful Telephone Numbers

	Hania	Rethimnon
Area Code	0821	0831
Hospital	27231	27491
GNTO/Town Hall	26426	29148
Harbor Master	89240	22276
Olympic Airways	27701/3	22257
Bus terminal/City	23024	22212
Long distance	23052	
Road Assistance	26059	29950
Police	24477	28156

	Iraklion	Ag.Nikol.
Area Code	081	0841
Hospital	231931	22369
GNTO/Town Hall	228203	22357
Harbor Master	226073	22312
Olympic Airways	229191	22034
Bus terminal/City	283925	22234
Long distance	288544	
Road Assistance	289440	22620
Police	283190	22251

GREEK ALPHABET

A	α	alfa	a	
B	β	wita (beta)	w	
Γ	γ	gamma	g	(before a,o,u)
			j	(before e,i)
Δ	δ	delta	th	(engl. the)
E	ε	epsilon	e	
Z	ζ	sita (zeta)	z	
H	η	ita (eta)	i	
Θ	ϑ	thita (theta)	th	(engl. thing)
I	ι	jota	i	
K	κ	kapa	k	
Λ	λ	lambda	l	
M	μ	mi	m	
N	ν	ni	n	
Ξ	ξ	xi	ks	
O	o	omikron	o	
Π	π	pi	p	
P	ρ	ro	r	
Σ	ς	sigma	s, ß	
T	τ	taf (tau)	t	
Y	υ	ipsilon	i	
Φ	φ	phi	f	
X	x	chi	ch	
Ψ	ψ	psi	ps	
Ω	ω	omega	o	

USEFUL GREEK PHRASES

Hello/Goodbye . . . . Hérete
What is your name . . . . Pós se léne
My name is... . . . . Me léne...
My home is in... To spíti mou eínai sto...
Where is the... . . . . Pou eínai...
How far is the... . . . Póso makriá eínai...
How do I get to...? . . . . . . Pos páo sto...?
How much does this cost? . . Poso kánei?
This is expensive. . . . *Aftó einai akrivó.*
I want
something to drink. . Theló káti na pio.
May I have the
bill? . . . . . Boró na ého to logariasmó?
Where do you live? . . . Pou zeis/menis?
What is this? . . . . Ti einai afto?
How are you? . . . . Pos eisai?
What time is it? . . . . Ti ora einai?
We'd like a room . . . . Théloume
for two. . . . . domátio yia dio.

please . . . . parakaló
thank you . . . . efharistó
yes . . . . ne
no . . . . ochi
okay . . . . endáksi
come . . . . éla

249

sorry . . . . signómi
today . . . . símera
tomorrow . . . . ávrio
yesterday . . . . hthes
evening . . . . wrádi
water . . . . neró
good . . . . kalós
milk . . . . gála
yogurt . . . . yaoúrti
sugar . . . . .záhari
raisins . . . . stafîdes
olive . . . . .elia
oil . . . . .ládi
meat . . . . kréas
fish . . . . .psarí
beach . . . . paralía
cave . . . . spiliá
church . . . . ekleesia
ship . . . . plio/vapori
sea . . . . thálassa
village . . . . horio
hot . . . . zestó
cold . . . . krio
food . . . . fai
pharmacy . . . . farmakío
medicine . . . . farmako
hospital . . . . .nosokomío
room . . . . domátio
clean .katharó
dirty .vrómiko
harbor . . . . limáni
shower . . . . .dousch
work . . . . .doulía
left . . . . .aristerá
right . . . . dexiá
straight . . . . .isia
doctor . . . . iatrós
time . . . . ora
city . . . . póli
street . . . . tdhromos
river .potamós
far . . . . makriá
near . . . . kontá
high . . . . .psilá
low . . . . hamilá
down . . . . kato
above . . . . .páno
dog . . . . skílos
help . . . . .woíthia

bus . . . . .leoforío
plate . . . . piato
glass . . . . .potíri
knife . . . . machéri
fork . . . . pirúni
spoon . . . . kutáli
cheap . . . . ftinó
expensive . . . . akriwó
morning . . . . .to proí
noon . . . . .to messiméri
afternoon . . . . .to apójewma
Sunday . . . . Kiriakí
Monday . . . . dheftéra
Tuesday . . . . tríti
Wednesday . . . . tetárti
Thursday . . . . pémpti
Friday . . . . .paraskewí
Saturday . . . . sáwato

1 . . . . éna
2 . . . . dhío
3 . . . . tría
4 . . . . téssera
5 . . . . pénde
6 . . . . .éksi
7 . . . . .éfta
8 . . . . októ
9 . . . . enéa
10 . . . . dhéka
20 . . . . .íkosi
30 . . . . triánda
40 . . . . saránda
50 . . . . .penínda
60 . . . . .eksínda
70 . . . . evdominda
80 . . . . ogdónda
90 . . . . .enenínda
100 . . . . .ekató
1000 . . . . hília
2000 . . . . dio hilliádes
1,000,000 . . . . ena ekatomirio

AUTHORS

Michele Macrakis, a graduate of Rhode Island School of Design and Project Editor of this book was awarded the I.T.T. (Fulbright) fellowship to photograph time in Crete in 1981. Of Cretan ancestry, she now lives in Athens continuing her work on Crete, while working as a professional photographer for many magazines and agencies.

Lily Macrakis, a graduate of the University of Athens, with a PhD from Radcliffe, is a Peloponnesian married to a Cretan residing in Belmont, Mass. She is Chairman of the History Department and Director of The Greek Studies Program at Regis College, Weston. She received the Academy of Athens Prize in 1988.

Nikos Stavroulakis owns a *pirgos* (tower) in Hania and is the director of the Jewish Museum of Greece in Athens.

Tom Stone has lived in various parts of Greece for the past 19 years, three of them in the old quarter of Rethimnon. He has published several books and articles about the country.

Kerin Hope, an erstwhile archaeologist, is the Athens correspondent for the *Financial Times*.

Costas Paris works for *Vis-News* and *REUTERS* in Athens.

Samantha Stenzel was born in Chicago and educated at the University of Illinois and Northeastern University. She became intrigued with Crete after seeing Cacoyannis' *Zorba The Greek*. Since moving to Athens nine years ago, she has explored the island thoroughly, but always discovers something new on each visit. "Sam" is a correspondent for *Variety of New York* and *Hollywood,* the cinema columnist for *The Athenian,* and teaches cinema appreciation at the Hellenic-American Union.

Jean Pierre Altier is the bureau chief of Agence France Presse in Athens.

Sandy MacGillivray is Assistant Professor of Archaeology at Columbia University in New York. He studied Classics at McGill University and received his PhD from the University of Edinburgh. He has served as Knossos Curator and Assistant Director of the British School at Athens, and is currently co-director of the British excavations at Palaikastro.

PHOTOGRAPHERS